New Total English

ADVANCED

Students' Book

JJ Wilson with Antonia Clare

Contents

Contents

Contents

Contents

Do you know ...?

1 Read the text and match the parts of speech (a–j) to each underlined word or phrase.

In 1967, Allen and Beatrice Gardner embarked on an (1) <u>experiment</u> to train a chimpanzee to talk. Realising that chimpanzees don't have the vocal apparatus to be able to speak like humans, but that (2) <u>they</u> can use gestures (3) <u>easily</u>, the Gardners decided to train (4) <u>the</u> animal in ASL, American Sign Language. Their subject was a chimpanzee called Washoe. The Gardners (5) <u>brought up</u> Washoe like a child, giving her regular meals and getting her to brush her teeth before sleep. At first Washoe made meaningless hand gestures, similar to the meaningless 'babbling' of baby children learning a language. But after four years Washoe had learned over 150 signs. She (6) <u>could</u> also combine the signs on some occasions, such as when she made the signs for 'water' and 'bird' on (7) <u>seeing</u> a swan on a lake. Linguists and scientists, (8) <u>however</u>, are (9) <u>sceptical</u> about the Gardners' (10) <u>research</u>, and question whether Washoe can really 'speak'. They say that her 'language use' is simply imitation.

a	present participle	f	phrasal verb
b	link word (contrast)	g	adjective
c	uncountable noun	h	adverb
d	countable noun	i	pronoun
e	article	j	modal verb

2 Find the grammar mistake in each sentence.

1 By this time tomorrow, we will have arrive in Peru.
2 We were hot because we'd run.
3 If I would have seen you, I would have stopped.
4 It's time we go home.
5 It mustn't have been John – John's tall and that man was short.
6 We haven't been knowing her long.
7 The conference will held in the theatre tomorrow.
8 I had my purse stole yesterday.
9 She persuaded me buying the car.
10 He climbed up the Mount Everest.

3 **a** Complete the word maps with words/phrases from the box below.

half-sister   career path   uncharted territory
soulmate   culture shock   spending spree
gamble   be made redundant

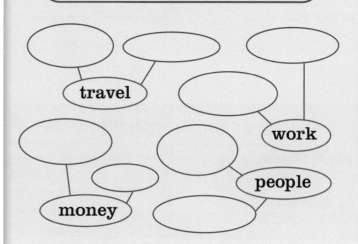

b <u>Underline</u> the main stress in each word/ phrase.

c Add three more words to each word map.

4 **a** Look at the dictionary extract below from the *Longman Dictionary of Contemporary English*. What does it tell you about each of the following: grammar, pronunciation, use and meaning?

dead·line \\'dedlaɪn\\ *n* [C] a date or time by which you have to do or complete something: [+**for**] *The deadline for applications is May 27th.* | [+**of**] *It has to be in before the deadline of July 1st.* | **meet/miss a deadline** (=have or not have something finished on time) *working under pressure to meet a deadline.* | **set/impose a deadline** *They've set a deadline of Nov 5.* | **tight/strict deadline** (=a deadline that is difficult)

b Complete the dictionary extracts below by writing a definition for each one.

1 over·priced /ˌəʊvəˈpraɪst/ *adj*
   _____ :
   The food was overpriced.
2 wan·der¹ /ˈwɒndə/ *v* [+**around**] [I, T]
   _____ :
   We didn't know where to go, so we wandered around.
3 ac·quaint·ance /əˈkweɪntəns/ *n* [C]
   _____ : *I don't know her well – she's just an acquaintance.*
4 i·ni·tia·tive /ɪˈnɪʃətɪv/ *n* [U]
   _____ : *You need to have initiative to do this job.*

Lead-in

1 Look at the photos. Work in pairs and discuss the questions.

1 What types of challenge are shown?
2 Have you ever faced any challenges similar to these? What happened? How did you feel?

2 Look at the sentence beginnings (1–8) and check you understand the <u>underlined</u> phrases. Match them with the endings (a–h).

1 I like to <u>set achievable goals</u>,
2 It's important to <u>face challenges</u>, but
3 She usually <u>rises to the challenge</u>, even if
4 If I succeed, it will <u>make my dream come true</u>, because
5 I <u>couldn't have done it without</u> help, so
6 It was a <u>burning ambition</u>, which
7 It's important to <u>have the right attitude</u>, because
8 It's quite a <u>daunting challenge</u>, but hopefully

a I'd like to thank my family and my sponsors.
b I can achieve it.
c so, before starting, I always think about my objectives.
d if you are a positive person, it will be easier.
e I've wanted to do this since I was a child.
f you mustn't be afraid of them.
g it's something very difficult.
h I finally managed to achieve.

3 What are your goals (on this course, in your career or studies, or in your personal life)? What challenges do you think you will face?

1.1 Polyglots

Grammar	verbs/adjectives/nouns with prepositions
Can do	discuss your language-learning experiences

Reading

1 Work in pairs and discuss the questions.

1 How many languages do you speak? Why and how did you learn them?

2 Why might the people in the photos need to know different languages? What jobs require several languages?

3 Do you think it is easier to learn a new language when you already know other languages? Why/Why not?

4 Do you know any polyglots (people who speak many languages)?

2 **a** Read the article and answer the questions.

1 How did Francis Sommer learn his European languages?

2 What advantage did Stephen Wurm have as a learner of languages?

3 According to Kenneth Hale, what type of talent do polyglots have?

4 How is learning new languages sometimes 'easy', according to David Perlmutter?

5 What do polyglots sometimes worry about?

6 What bonuses and problems has Ziad Fazah experienced because of his linguistic abilities?

b Work in pairs and discuss your answers.

3 Work in pairs and discuss the questions.

1 What are the benefits of being a polyglot? Are there any drawbacks?

2 In your opinion, what personal qualities are necessary to become a polyglot?

Great language learners

According to legend, Cardinal Giuseppe Mezzofanti (1774–1849), who spoke 72 languages, once learned a language
5 overnight in order to hear the confession of two condemned prisoners the following morning. While this story sounds too amazing to be true, there are
10 polyglots who have achieved quite staggering feats of language learning.

Arguably the greatest of all was Francis Sommer. Brought up
15 in Germany, Sommer was still a schoolboy when he succeeded in learning Swedish, Sanskrit and Persian. On a trip to Russia, he mingled with the international
20 community and, so the story goes, learned a dozen European languages. He later moved to the United States, where he worked as a research librarian, and by the
25 1920s, had mastered 94 languages.

Another great linguist is Stephen Wurm, Professor of Linguistics at the Australian National University at Canberra. Wurm benefited
30 from the fact that he came from a multilingual family. His father, also a linguist, asked everyone in the family to speak to the child in their own language. This meant
35 that his mother addressed him in Hungarian, his father in English, his grandfather in Norwegian, and his grandmother in Mongolian. Because of Wurm's father's work, the family
40 also lived for periods in Germany, Russia, China, Argentina and Turkey. As a result, Wurm spoke ten languages by the time he was six.

To most of us, the achievements
45 of polyglots seem superhuman, but the polyglots themselves don't see it that way. Kenneth Hale, a linguistics professor who speaks around 50 languages, believes his
50 talent bears similarity to that of

Vocabulary | learning languages

4 Match the words/expressions (1–8) from the article to the definitions (a–h).

1 master (v) (line 25)
2 let (sth) slide (phrase) (line 58)
3 pick up (phrasal verb) (line 70)
4 garble (v) (line 74)
5 information overload (n) (line 88)
6 babble (v) (line 103)
7 unintelligibly (adv) (line 103)
8 dialect (n) (line 107)

a in a way that is impossible to understand
b to neglect something or allow it to get worse
c a form of a language which is spoken in only one area, with its own words/grammar
d to speak quickly in a way that is difficult to understand
e to learn something so well that you have no difficulty with it
f too much to remember
g to learn without consciously studying
h to mix up or confuse words

5 a Complete the sentences using words/expressions from exercise 4.

1 It's easy to _____ foreign languages _____ if you don't use them regularly.
2 In many countries, people can understand the standard form of their language and also a local _____ .
3 The best way to _____ new vocabulary is by reading a lot.
4 It may be impossible to _____ a foreign language completely.
5 For most students, more than ten new words per lesson equals _____ .
6 Many language learners find that native speakers speak _____ – they use lots of idioms and colloquial expressions.
7 When babies _____ , they are imitating adult language.
8 If you know three or more languages, you're more likely to _____ your words.

b Work in pairs. Discuss which sentences you agree with.

a musician's. And while talent is one factor, a love of languages is essential. Hale recalls the time when he was learning Navajo:
55 "I used to go out every day and sit on a rock and talk Navajo to myself." Languages became an obsession. "I let everything else slide," he says.
60 David Perlmutter, Professor of Linguistics at the University of California, likens the process of language learning to a puzzle. Mastery, he believes, stems from
65 the joy of solving the puzzle. "If you know English and German," he says, "it's easy to learn Dutch." Therefore, once you know Spanish and another Romance language,
70 you can pick up Portuguese quickly.
But is there any chance that these super-polyglots might get confused? Do they ever get nervous about garbling their languages?
75 According to Kenneth Hale, it does happen. Occasionally, he begins speaking in one language and, without knowing it, finds

that he has drifted into another. It
80 happens especially when it's difficult to distinguish between related languages. "Unless I'm attentive ... I can mix up languages like Miskitu and Sumu, both of which
85 are spoken in Central America and are very similar." Francis Sommer felt the same. Fearing information overload, he gave up learning new languages in later life.
90 Of today's polyglots, Ziad Fazah, a Lebanese living in Brazil, is probably number one. A speaker of around 60 languages, Fazah, unlike many great polyglots, was not
95 born into multilingualism. Besides his native Arabic, he learned only French and English at school, and taught himself the other languages. His astonishing abilities have had
100 some interesting consequences. On one occasion, the Brazilian police stopped an undocumented alien who was babbling unintelligibly. They asked Fazah for help. Fazah
105 realised immediately that the man was from Afghanistan and speaking

a dialect called Hazaras. On another occasion, the US Consulate grew suspicious of Fazah's ability
110 to speak Chinese and Russian. Suspecting that he was a terrorist, they brought him in for questioning. After two hours, however, he was released.
115 Fazah is not widely known, though that may change. In recent years, he has appeared on TV programmes in Greece and Spain, where he was quizzed in multiple
120 languages including Hungarian, Korean, Japanese and Chinese. He passed with flying colours. While this earned him a reputation as a phenomenon, he is still a few
125 languages behind the legendary Cardinal Mezzofanti. Unlike Mezzofanti, Fazah cannot claim to learn languages overnight, but he can apparently learn a thousand
130 words a month – a gift that language students around the world would envy and admire!

Listening

6 **a** 🔘 1.02 Listen to Mark Spina talking about language learning. Make notes on the questions.

1 How many languages does he speak?
2 Where/how did he learn them?
3 What special techniques does he use?
4 How does he feel about language?
5 What problems does he have?

b Work in pairs and compare your answers. Then listen again to check.

7 Do you have similar experiences of language learning? Discuss with other students.

Grammar | verbs/adjectives/nouns with prepositions

8 **a** Look at examples 1–5 in the Active grammar box and underline the prepositions. What type of word does each preposition follow?

b Answer the questions for rules A and B in the Active grammar box.

Active grammar

1 *Sommer was still a schoolboy, when he succeeded in learning Swedish, Sanskrit and Persian.*

2 *Mastery, he believes, stems from the joy of solving the puzzle.*

3 *Wurm benefited from the fact that he came from a multilingual family.*

4 *Do they ever get nervous about garbling their various languages?*

5 *This can happen, especially when it is difficult to distinguish between related languages.*

A Prepositions after verbs, nouns and adjectives always have an object. What is the object in each sentence above?

B When the preposition is followed by a verb, the verb is usually in the *-ing* form. Which of the sentences above use this structure?

see Reference page 19

9 **a** Complete the sentences with prepositions from the box. Check any new expressions in your dictionary.

from (x3)   to   in (x2)   about (x2)   for   with

1 Do you think you'll succeed _____ passing your next exam?
2 If you could improve your English by watching DVDs, by living in an English-speaking country or by studying from books, which would you opt _____ ?
3 Do your problems in English stem _____ poor grammar, or are there other problems?
4 Do you feel you are lacking _____ vocabulary?
5 Even at advanced level, some students' spoken English is riddled _____ errors. Does this matter or is fluency more important?
6 What distinguishes your first language _____ English?
7 What types of classroom exercises appeal _____ you?
8 Is pronunciation worth bothering _____ or are you happy to keep your accent?
9 Are you nervous _____ giving presentations in English?
10 How can your vocabulary benefit _____ using the media?

b Match the questions (1–10) in exercise 9a to the possible answers (a–j).

a Some of the vocabulary is similar but the grammar is completely different.
b I always make an effort with the sounds of English, but I know I'll never sound like a native speaker.
c Yes, I think so. I've been studying hard and I really hope I achieve my goal!
d I like class discussions best of all, and also role plays.
e I think accuracy is important, too. It's difficult to listen to someone whose speech is full of mistakes, and it distracts you from the content of what they're saying.
f I'd choose to immerse myself in the language and culture by living in Canada or Australia.
g Listening regularly to the news or looking at websites is good for learning new words.
h Yes. I don't know many idioms, phrasal verbs and informal expressions.
i A lot of the difficulties come from the fact that I can't understand native speakers when they speak fast, but I also need to work on my grammar!
j Speaking in public worries me a little bit, but I think it's a good thing to do in class.

Speaking

10 **a** Work with a partner. Discuss questions 1–10 from exercise 9a. Are the suggested answers from exercise 9b true for you? If not, why not?

b Tell the class what you found out about your partner.

Vocabulary | knowledge

1 Choose the correct words in *italics*.

1 'Who won the first Oscar?'
'I haven't *an idea/a clue*.'

2 'What was the first book ever published?'
'I don't know off the top of my *head/hand*.'

3 'What date did Man first go to the moon?'
'*I don't know/I'm sure* offhand, but I can look it up.'

4 'Where did Elisha Gray come from?'
'Who? I've never *heard/known* of him.'

5 'Do you know Paris?'
'Yes. I lived there for years so I know it like the back of my *head/hand*.'

6 'Which state has the smallest population?'
'I'm pretty *sure/positive* it's the Vatican.'

7 'Do you know Eliot's poem about cats?'
'I know it *by/at* heart. I learned it at school.'

8 'What do you know about company law?'
'I know it inside *in/out*. I have a PhD in it.'

9 'What do you know about Belgian politics?'
'I know *close/next* to nothing about it.'

10 'Which country has the biggest population?'
'I haven't the faintest *idea/clue*.'

11 'Are you sure Russia is the biggest country in the world?'
'I'm fairly *certain/positive* it is, but it might be China.'

12 'Are you sure the Nile is the longest river in the world?'
'Yes. I'm *positive/fairly positive* it is.'

2 **a** Complete the How to... box with the underlined expressions from exercise 1.

b How are the expressions different? Which are strongest? Which mean the same?

How to... say how much you know/don't know

I know	*I'm pretty sure*
I don't know	*I haven't a clue.*

Speaking

3 Work in pairs and do the quiz. Try to use expressions from the How to... box.

WHO DID IT FIRST?

1 Who was the first to fly a plane?
(**a**) Alberto Santos Dumont
(**b**) the Wright brothers
(**c**) Ferdinand von Zeppelin

2 Who invented the telephone?
(**a**) Thomas Edison
(**b**) Alexander Graham Bell
(**c**) Antonio Meucci

3 Who first reached the North Pole?
(**a**) Robert Peary
(**b**) Frederick Cook
(**c**) Roald Amundsen

4 Who invented the light bulb?
(**a**) Thomas Edison (**b**) Alexander Graham Bell
(**c**) Leonardo da Vinci

5 Which country won the first football World Cup (and hosted it)?
(**a**) Brazil (**b**) Uruguay (**c**) Germany

6 Which country first allowed women to vote?
(**a**) Switzerland (**b**) New Zealand (**c**) the United States

7 Who was the first woman to sail solo around the world via Cape Horn?
(**a**) Ellen MacArthur (**b**) Amelia Earhart (**c**) Naomi James

8 Which country first held the Olympic Games?
(**a**) Italy (**b**) France (**c**) Greece

Listening

4 **a** 🔊 1.03 Listen to a radio programme and check your answers to the quiz.

b Work in pairs. Listen again and discuss the questions.

1 Which 'famous firsts' do photos 1–4 refer to? What can you remember about them?

2 Did you find anything surprising in the radio programme? What extra information did you learn?

Grammar | passives: distancing

5 **a** Look at examples 1–6 in the Active grammar box and underline the passives.

b Read rules A–C in the Active grammar box and write true (T) or false (F).

c Why do you think passives are used in these sentences?

Active grammar

1 *Santos Dumont was widely believed to have flown the first plane.*

2 *He's said to be the first person to have owned a flying machine.*

3 *It's commonly assumed that Bell invented the telephone.*

4 *In 2003, files were discovered which suggest that Philipp Reis had invented the phone.*

5 *The cheering of the crowd is said to have been the loudest noise ever heard in Uruguay.*

6 *It is often thought that rugby and sheep are the main claims to fame for New Zealand.*

A We can use the passive to show that a statement is not our own opinion. ☐

B We often use the passive to show that a statement is a personal opinion. ☐

C If we aren't sure that the information is 100% correct, we can use the passive to put 'distance' between ourselves and the statement. ☐

Other verbs for 'distancing' include *It appears/seems that* and *It seems as if/though.*

We can use *appears/seems to have* + past participle to describe a past event.

see Reference page 19

12

6 Write sentences using structures for distancing with the verb in brackets.

People say that Edison invented more machines than anyone else in history. (say)

Edison is said to have invented more machines than anyone else in history.

1 But the evidence suggests that Edison didn't invent as much as we thought. (seems)

But it _____ though Edison invented fewer things than we thought.

2 People believe that da Vinci invented the helicopter. (think)

Da Vinci _____ invented the helicopter.

3 North American historians assert that the Wright brothers flew first. (assert)

It _____ by North American historians that the Wright brothers flew first.

4 At that time, everybody in the US thought that the Wright brothers were the first to fly. (assume)

It _____ that the Wright brothers were the first to fly.

5 A number of journalists in the late 19th century said that William Dickson had 'invented' the movie. (claim)

It _____ that William Dickson had 'invented' the movie.

6 We think Dutchman Joop Sinjou and Japanese Toshi Tada Doi invented the CD player at the same time. (believe)

Sinjou and Tada Doi _____ invented the CD player simultaneously.

7 Newspapers of the time reported that Felix Hoffman had invented aspirin. (report)

It _____ that Felix Hoffman had invented aspirin.

8 We now think that aspirin was first used by Egyptians. (believe)

It _____ that aspirin was first used by Egyptians.

Listening

7 **a** 🔊 1.04 Listen to some news headlines. What achievements do they talk about?

b 🔊 1.05 Listen only to the headlines and write down exactly what you hear.

c Now look at the headlines in **bold** in audioscript 1.04 on page 167. What problems did you have?

Pronunciation | word stress (1)

8 **a** Look at the headlines from exercise 7c. Which are the content words (nouns, verbs, etc.)? Which are the function words (prepositions, auxiliary verbs, etc.)?

b 🔊 1.05 Listen to the headlines again and <u>underline</u> the stressed words.

c Repeat the sentences, stressing the <u>underlined</u> words.

Writing and speaking

9 Work in pairs. Look at the cartoons and answer the questions.

1 Which story is the most interesting?
2 Which is the most likely/unlikely?
3 What preparation or lifestyle would be required to do these things?

FIRST MAN TO LIVE WITH LIONS

FIRST WOMAN TO SKATEBOARD AROUND THE WORLD

FIRST TWINS TO REACH 125 YEARS OLD

10 **a** Write a news bulletin based on one of the cartoons (about 100–150 words). Use at least two passive constructions for distancing.

b Work in pairs. Practise reading your news bulletins. Concentrate on putting stress on the most important words.

c Read your bulletins to the class.

11 Read the Lifelong learning box. Work in pairs and discuss the questions.

Use the news

❗ Listening to radio news or watching English-language news is a great way to improve your listening and vocabulary. Sometimes it helps to hear the news in your own language before listening to the same stories in English.

1 When and how can you access news programmes in English? Are there any programmes you've seen/heard that you particularly like or recommend?

2 What current news stories would you like to listen to in English?

Lifelong learning

1.3 Burning ambitions

Grammar	perfect aspect
Can do	talk about your achievements

Reading

1 Work in pairs. Look at the activities in the box and discuss the questions.

1 Who generally does each activity better: women, men or neither? Why?

2 Are there any other activities which you think men or women do better?

> driving   cooking   gardening
> doing jobs around the house
> expressing emotions
> looking after children   being alone
> teaching   ballet   tolerating pain
> listening to other people

2 Work in pairs. Read about an ambitious person and make notes on questions 1–5 below.

Student A: read about Bia Figueiredo on page 15.

Student B: read about Carlos Acosta on page 147.

1 What is/was their ambition?

2 To what extent have they achieved it?

3 What challenges have they faced?

4 Who has helped them achieve their ambitions? How?

5 Any other information?

3 Tell your partner about the person you read about. As you listen, make notes. What similarities are there between the two stories?

4 Work in pairs and discuss the questions.

1 Do you think that women have limited opportunities in the world of sport? Is this changing?

2 '... there is a prejudice that ballet is not for boys.' Do you agree? Is it the same in all countries?

3 Do you think sport or dance can help reduce levels of delinquency in teenagers and young people?

4 What do you think of the fathers' behaviour in these two cases? Would you have reacted similarly? Do you believe that parents should influence the ambitions of their children?

Vocabulary | achievement

5 a Work in pairs. Find the words/expressions (1–8) in the articles and try to work out the meaning.

1 head (straight for the top)

2 pursue (a dream)

3 deal with (chauvinism)

4 face (barriers)

5 believe in (what you can achieve)

6 have the potential (to do something)

7 persevere (with something)

8 keep pushing someone (to do something)

b Complete the sentences using words/expressions from exercise 5a.

1 It was obvious that Venus Williams had the _____ to become a tennis champion when she was very young.

2 Ralf Schumacher had to _____ with criticism from his colleagues.

3 Ellen MacArthur _____ her dream of sailing solo around the world.

4 McManus is _____ the biggest challenge of his career.

5 If you _____ yourself, you can achieve almost anything.

6 Woods found the course tricky at first, but _____ and came through to the final.

7 If you win this championship, nothing will stop you from _____ straight for the top.

8 Encourage your kids to try new things, but don't _____ them too hard.

Fast female heads for Formula 1

Is Formula 1 ready for its first female star? Matt Rendell travelled to São Paulo to meet Bia, who is tipped to join the ranks of her country's greats – Senna, Piquet, Barrichello. She has already beaten the boys from Brazil at their own game. Now she's ready to take on the world.

As the swarm of go-karts completes its final warm-up lap and hurtles across the starting line, the race is on. Thirty minutes later, when the winner's helmet is removed, a wave of dense dark hair flows freely. For the champion is a girl, Ana Beatriz Figueiredo – Bia, for short – and she is heading straight for the top.

I first met Bia Figueiredo in May 2001. She was 16 and her rivals on São Paulo's kart scene – all male – had been suffering the obvious taunt for eight years: 'Beaten by a girl ... again?'

Now she is in her 20s and still winning. One day soon, the image of her long hair spilling out of her helmet could open motor sport to new audiences, sponsors and perhaps a whole new lease of life. For in Brazil, she is being spoken of as the possible future of Formula 1, the woman to transform an increasingly predictable sport.

The Ayrton Senna Kartodrome in Brazil is a theatre of dreams, and Bia Figueiredo is pursuing hers in the Brazilian Formula Renault Championship. 'The first time I went to the kartodrome,' she tells me, 'I was five or six. I begged my father to take me and fell in love with the noise and the crashes. He told me I had to be seven before I could learn to drive. Somehow, I managed to wait.'

Money pressures are inherent in motor racing, even for a family that is well-off, by most standards. Compared with other drivers at this level, Bia is disadvantaged. Bia's father, Jorge, says that Bia was already dreaming of Formula 1 at the age of six. And having encouraged his daughter's passion, he has accepted the financial burden with good humour. 'I once heard a Formula 1 team boss say it costs $10 million to become a Formula 1 driver. I said to myself, 'OK. I'm only $9,990,000 short!'

Because of the expense, Bia could only do two 50-minute tests before each race, when other drivers did four. She went to one of the best schools in São Paulo, which meant she was doing school work when other drivers were on the track. 'Given these constraints, she has done very well,' her father says. 'She was born with a forceful personality and, today, she's still forceful and has a caustic sense of humour. I feel a little sorry for anyone in her way!'

Motor racing would not be every father's chosen career for his daughter. 'Yes, it can be dangerous,' Jorge concedes. 'But the element of risk can be controlled. I'm much more afraid of Bia not doing what she loves. By pursuing what they enjoy, I think people have more chance of being happy.'

Yet Bia will have to deal with chauvinism. Not the least of the barriers facing her is whether motor sport is prepared to accept a genuine female contender. 'A beautiful woman is always welcome,' Alex Dias Ribeiro says, smiling and then adds: 'But she will have to be quick and mentally tough, because Formula 1 is a pressure cooker'.

One man who believes in Bia's potential is her mechanic and mentor of nine years, Naylor Borigis de Campos. He has worked closely with most of Brazil's best drivers. He compares Bia favourably with the best of his protégés. 'She's as cool, aware and determined as Rubens Barrichello and as any other driver I've ever worked with.'

As for Bia herself, she believes in the future and in what she can achieve: 'I have a lot to learn, but my temperament is right: I've got plenty of animal instinct. I believe I have the potential to reach Formula 1, and perhaps one day be a great driver.'

Listening

6 Work in pairs and discuss the questions.

1 How difficult do you think it is to do the activities below?

2 What do you think is the best way to prepare for each one?
- run a marathon
- work abroad
- start your own business

7 1.06 Listen and answer the questions.

1 Which activity from exercise 6 has each speaker achieved?

2 What did each person say about their experience?

3 What challenges did they face?

Grammar | perfect aspect

8 Read the Active grammar box. Underline the perfect tense in each sentence (1–3) and complete the name of each tense (*Past Perfect*, *Future Perfect* or *Present Perfect*).

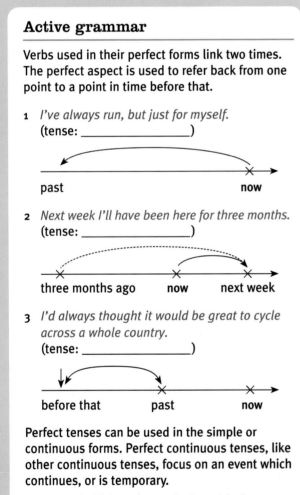

Active grammar

Verbs used in their perfect forms link two times. The perfect aspect is used to refer back from one point to a point in time before that.

1 *I've always run, but just for myself.*
(tense: _____)

past   now

2 *Next week I'll have been here for three months.*
(tense: _____)

three months ago   now   next week

3 *I'd always thought it would be great to cycle across a whole country.*
(tense: _____)

before that   past   now

Perfect tenses can be used in the simple or continuous forms. Perfect continuous tenses, like other continuous tenses, focus on an event which continues, or is temporary.

Next March I'll have been playing with the team for five years.

I've been doing voluntary work all my adult life.

see Reference page 19

9 a Correct the mistakes.

1 Jake, this is my friend Amy, who I've been knowing for absolutely ages.

2 I asked what had been happened, but nobody could tell me.

3 I chose this school because I'd hear it was the best.

4 He should have finish by the time we get back.

5 Before I came to the US, I never been abroad.

6 I'm so exhausted. I'd been working really hard.

7 By the time she retires, she'll have be working there for more than 50 years.

8 I'll phone you as soon as we will have arrived.

b 1.07 Listen and check your answers.

Speaking

10 Complete the How to... box.

expect   decided   expectations   challenge

How to... talk about an achievement

Background information	*I've always ...* *I'd never done ...*
Details	*We set up ...* *We (1) _____ to organise ...*
Problems	*I didn't know what to (2) _____ .* *The whole thing was quite a (3) _____ .* *It was very tough.*
How it felt	*It exceeded my (4) _____ .* *We felt we'd accomplished something.* *It was a fantastic learning experience.*
Results/ follow up	*I've learnt a lot.* *I'm planning to ...*

11 a Prepare to talk about something you have achieved. Make notes using the headings in the How to... box.

b Tell the class about your achievement.

1 **a** Read the story below and <u>underline</u> 12 prefixes.

On Saturday Mick Johnson, the multi-talented Londoner – previously a semi-professional basketball player – rescued a sub-standard performance by the unimpressive league leaders. With a superhuman effort, Johnson scored two goals in two minutes against arch-rivals Blackbridge Rovers. Trailing by one goal until the 68th minute, Johnson's overcautious team had looked tired and under-prepared. Johnson, probably the best footballer ever to play for Sidcup United, single-handedly brought his side back from the brink of disaster. Johnson's manager, Paul Deacon, said, 'They outplayed us. I don't know why we misfired so badly, but it's irrelevant. We got the goals and we took home the points.'

b Read the story again and answer the questions.

1 Which prefixes suggest a large/exceptional degree, or amount?
2 Which suggest 'not enough'?
3 Which prefix means 'not wholly' or 'half'?
4 Which can have a negative meaning?

c Work in pairs. What do the <u>underlined</u> prefixes in sentences 1–4 below mean?

1 Johnson had an early chance to score, but was <u>in</u>decisive with his shot.
2 'Winning the league isn't <u>im</u>possible for us,' said Deacon.
3 'Yeah, we won,' said the <u>mono</u>syllabic Johnson.
4 The team looked <u>de</u>motivated.

2 Complete the sentences with the correct form of the words in brackets. Use prefixes.

A: *He's a little bit rude!*
B: *Pardon?*
A: *He's rather <u>impolite</u>. (polite)*

1 A: Our interpretation of the instructions was completely wrong.
   B: Pardon?
   A: We completely _____ the instructions. (understand)

2 A: I didn't know that you were a vegetarian.
   B: Sorry?
   A: I was _____ that you were a vegetarian. (aware)

3 A: I'm 70 years old. I quit my main job but I still work part-time.
   B: Pardon?
   A: I'm _____. (retire)

4 A: We lost the match because they had more players! There were ten of them, and only six of us.
   B: Really? So the numbers weren't equal?
   A: That's right. We were completely _____. (number)

5 A: I must go on a diet. I weigh too much.
   B: What?
   A: I'm _____. (weight)

6 A: My estimate was wrong. I thought there would be ten people here, not 50.
   B: Really?
   A: Yes, I _____ the numbers. (estimate)

3 **a** Work in pairs. Look at the opposites below. Where do you fit on a scale of 1–5? Tick a box on each line.

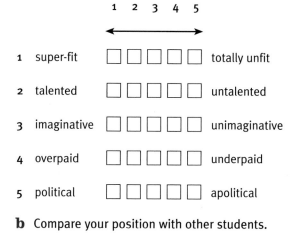

	1	2	3	4	5	
1 super-fit	☐	☐	☐	☐	☐	totally unfit
2 talented	☐	☐	☐	☐	☐	untalented
3 imaginative	☐	☐	☐	☐	☐	unimaginative
4 overpaid	☐	☐	☐	☐	☐	underpaid
5 political	☐	☐	☐	☐	☐	apolitical

b Compare your position with other students.

1 **a** Read the questionnaire and choose a, b or c for each situation.

b 🔵 1.08 Listen to someone describing what the answers say about your personality.

c Work in pairs. Discuss your answers and explain why you chose them. Do you agree with the ideas you heard about? Why/Why not?

2 Work with another pair and discuss the questions.

1 Which would be the most difficult/the easiest challenge for you? Why?
2 What preparation would you need for each challenge?
3 Do you think challenge involves being in extreme situations? Or are there more challenges in day-to-day life?
4 Which do you think are tougher: mental or physical challenges? What examples can you think of?

DO YOU LIKE A CHALLENGE?

1 You are climbing a mountain with some friends. It is cold and wet and you are halfway up. You
   a feel like turning round and going home to a hot bath.
   b keep going. Nothing will stop you once you've started.
   c see what your friends want to do. It doesn't really matter if you reach the top.

2 You get an offer to work abroad for a year. But it means you have to learn a difficult new language and live in an isolated place with no cinemas, cafés or nightlife. You
   a refuse politely. Only a madman would live in the middle of nowhere.
   b accept. Who needs nightclubs and cappuccino? And you may love it.
   c ask all your colleagues, friends and family what they think.

3 You are asked to perform in a local play. You will have to learn some lines and act in front of a large audience. You
   a say no. You aren't going to make a fool of yourself in public.
   b jump up on stage and start singing. This is your chance of fame and fortune.
   c find out exactly what you'll have to do, then say you'll think about it.

4 Your friends decide to do a parachute jump for charity. They want you to join them. You
   a refuse, saying you're too young to die.
   b immediately book lessons. What fun! And what a great view you'll have too!
   c find some statistics on the mortality rate of parachutists before committing yourself.

5 You are asked to cook for 15 people. You
   a immediately find out the name of a good takeaway food restaurant, and make sure they'll be able to take your order on the night.
   b start dreaming of the delicious feast you will prepare. It could be a great night.
   c consult your parents' cookery books and work out how much it'll cost.

6 You are offered a place on a sailing boat that will go around the world. You
   a say no. You can't take the time off work and all that sea gets annoying after a while.
   b buy some large rubber boots and a sailing hat immediately. Nothing will stop you!
   c ask about the exact schedule and if there's Internet access on board and what the food will be like.

7 You are asked to be the babysitter for six young children for one evening. You
   a quickly think of a brilliant excuse – for example, you have tickets for a game or you need to wash your hair that evening, so you won't be available.
   b buy a large bag of balloons, chocolate cake and lots of children's games – it's going to be the party of the century!
   c ask for details of the children's behaviour, exact ages, and dietary requirements, then think about it.

8 A magazine wants you to write a piece about your hobby. You
   a explain that you're far too busy doing it, so you don't have time to write about it.
   b jump up and down with excitement, write three different drafts and offer them all to the editor the next day.
   c read previous issues of the magazine to see if you like it, then arrange a meeting with the editor to discuss the piece.

Verbs/adjectives/nouns with prepositions

There are many fixed phrases which use prepositions.

Verb + preposition:

opt **for**, distinguish **from**, succeed **in**, stem **from**, appeal **to**, bother **about**, rely **on**, benefit **from**

Adjective + preposition:

short **of**, riddled **with**, lacking **in**, nervous **about**

Noun + preposition:

to the delight **of**, a new form **of**

Passives: distancing

Passives can be used for 'distancing'. This means that the speaker/writer doesn't want the whole responsibility for the ideas they express. The passive is often used to make a statement less personal and slightly more polite:

We don't allow that. → That **isn't allowed**.

(It isn't the speaker's decision; it is an impersonal rule.)
You must hand in the essay by Friday.
→ The essay **must be handed** in by Friday.

in formal writing, when the focus is on achievements and events rather than the people responsible:

The vaccine **was discovered** by chance.

Here are some common passive expressions to show that we are not certain of a statement:

It is believed that the thief was an ex-employee.
It is said that he was able to speak more than 20 languages, but there is no proof.
It was claimed that the president had not seen the documents before the scandal broke out.
She was thought to have come from Germany originally, but there was little evidence.
He was reported to have been living in Brazil, but there was only one sighting of him.

Perfect aspect

We use the perfect aspect to refer from one point in time to another point in time before that. It shows that the speaker sees one event as: (1) linked to a later event; (2) finished by a certain time.

She**'d lost** her ticket so she missed the show.
By 6.00 I **will have finished** work.

We use the Present Perfect to describe something that happened during a period that includes past and present:

We**'ve been** here since Friday.

in the past but when the exact time isn't relevant to this discussion or isn't known:

She**'s lived** in over 20 countries.

in the past, but has a result or effect in the present:

Oh no! I**'ve lost** my passport.

in the very recent past (especially with *just*):

I**'ve just heard** the news.

We use the Past Perfect to talk about completed actions that happened before another in the past:

He wanted to go to Rome, but I**'d already been** there.

We use the Future Perfect with time phrases with *by* (*by this time next week*, *by the end of the day*, etc.):

By June we **will have finished** the project.

We often use the perfect aspect with *for*, *since* and *just*:

By January, I **will have been** here **for** a year.
I**'ve just been speaking** to Mickey.

Perfect continuous tenses focus on an event which continues or is temporary:

She**'s been working** as a nurse since 2001.
We**'d been playing** football when it started to rain.

Key vocabulary

Challenges

set achievable goals   face challenges
rise to the challenge   make my dream come true
couldn't have done it without   burning ambition
have the right attitude   daunting challenge

Learning languages

pick up   let (something) slide   master   garble
information overload   babble   unintelligibly   dialect

Knowledge

I haven't a clue   I don't know off the top of my head
I'm pretty sure   I've never heard of him
I know it by heart   I know it like the back of my hand
I know it inside out   I don't know offhand
I know next to nothing about   I'm fairly positive
I haven't the faintest idea

Achievement

head (straight for the top)   pursue (a dream)
deal with (chauvinism)   face (barriers)
believe in (what you can achieve)
have the potential (to do something)
persevere (with something)
keep pushing someone (to do something)

Prefixes

super-fit   unfit   multi-talented   impossible
unimpressive   underpaid   overpaid   apolitical
monosyllabic   demotivated   arch-rival   indecisive
single-handedly   outplayed   semi-professional
sub-standard   misfired   irrelevant   superhuman
overcautious   underprepared

 Listen to the explanations and vocabulary.

ACTIVEBOOK

see Writing bank page 155

1 Complete the text with the correct words/expressions (a, b or c).

The language Hawaiian Creole was invented through necessity. In 1880, thousands of immigrants from Europe and Asia went to work for the English-speaking owners of sugar plantations in Hawaii. Among all the other challenges these immigrants (1) _____ , the most (2) _____ was to understand each other, their bosses, and to understand the Hawaiian people. To these immigrants, other ethnic groups must have sounded as if they were (3) _____ . After a short time, they were able to (4) _____ some English, but barely enough to communicate. Instead, they (5) _____ body language and a simple code of sounds.

However, things changed fast, and by 1910 a new language had emerged: Hawaiian Creole. This included words and sounds from other languages, but could be (6) _____ all of them by its different grammar. Hawaiian Creole, a simple dialect, is (7) _____ complex structures. With this new easily understood language, everybody (8) _____ increased communication.

Many years later, Derek Bickerton studied the origins of Hawaiian Creole. He was amazed that within a generation, the immigrants had (9) _____ creating a language that was (10) _____ to all. In fact, in his book *Roots of Language*, he says that the children invented the language while playing together.

1	a made	b knew	c faced
2	a daunting	b definite	c harsh
3	a babbling	b garbling	c cramming
4	a discuss	b pick up	c pick out
5	a persisted in	b appealed to	c relied on
6	a riddled with	b distinguished from	c defined by
7	a reminds you of	b stemming from	c lacking in
8	a benefited from	b benefited	c mastered
9	a opted for	b succeeded to	c succeeded in
10	a intelligible	b unintelligible	c intelligibly

2 Find the mistake in each sentence and correct it.

1 Giant multinational research centre Sci-Corps seems to abandoned its research into cloning after pressure from the government.

2 Ex-President Michael Nkrumah is said be recovering well from the stroke he suffered last Thursday.

3 Michaela Kritzkoff, the explorer who disappeared for a month while canoeing along the Amazon, has been found in a village in Brazil. It believed that she had drowned during a storm.

4 British Commonwealth boxing champion Roderick Bland appears to finally retired, at the age of 46.

5 And finally, it seems if summer really is coming. Sarah Smith reports on tomorrow's weather.

3 Find the mistakes in nine of the sentences and correct them.

I've never seen the man before yesterday, when he knocked on my door.

I'd never seen the man before yesterday, when he knocked on my door.

1 By the time she finishes her degree, she will be at the university ten years.

2 He was delighted when they told him he had got the job.

3 I feel healthier now that I took up kickboxing.

4 Where were you? I've been waited here for at least an hour!

5 It was a shock when I saw him. I would expected to see a big man, but he was tiny.

6 When she got to work, she found out she was fired. Her desk was empty, everything gone.

7 Hi, John! We've just talked about you!

8 It's 9 o'clock. Mandy will land at the airport by now.

9 I've been running for years before I entered my first competition.

10 We'll have use up all the world's oil long before 2100.

4 Write B's replies in the correct order.

A: What is Pelé's real first name?

B: pretty / I'm / Edison / it's / sure / .

I'm pretty sure it's Edison.

1 A: Have you ever been to Prague?
B: Yes, / I / of / the / hand / like / my / back / it / know / .

2 A: How many women have succeeded in Formula 1 racing?
B: I / many / know / not / but / don't / offhand / .

3 A: Can you help me? I need some information about space travel.
B: know / nothing / it / to / next / about / I / .

4 A: When's the best time to go there?
B: far / as / concerned / As / never / I'm / .

5 A: Who's Michael Vaughan?
B: never / him / heard / I've / of / .

6 A: Who's the President of Colombia?
B: head / I / top / tell / off / the / can't / of / my / you / .

Lead-in

2

1 Work in pairs and look at the photos. Discuss the questions.

1 What types of community are shown?
2 What are the positive/negative aspects of each?

2 **a** Check you understand the <u>underlined</u> words/phrases. Write positive (+) or negative (−) next to each feature (1–16).

1 reasonable <u>cost of living</u> ☐
2 <u>cosmopolitan</u> ☐
3 good transport <u>infrastructure</u> ☐
4 <u>mild</u> climate ☐
5 personal <u>freedom</u> ☐
6 efficient <u>healthcare</u> system ☐
7 high <u>standard of living</u> ☐
8 interesting historical <u>monuments</u> ☐
9 high <u>crime rate</u> ☐
10 high level of <u>unemployment</u> ☐
11 traffic <u>congestion</u> ☐
12 a lot of <u>pollution</u> ☐
13 racial <u>tension</u> ☐
14 <u>no-go areas</u> ☐
15 no <u>cultural</u> life ☐
16 <u>vibrant</u> nightlife ☐

b Work in pairs. Which four features from exercise 2a are the most important to you? Why?

Reading

1 Look at the photos. Work in pairs and discuss the questions.

1 Where do you think each community is?
2 What do you think life is like there?

2 Read the comments (A–D). Who thinks their community is changing for the worse? Who has positive things to say?

B

There's a very strong sense of community where I live. People don't mind helping others. You see it all the time. Youngsters visit the elderly. People look after each other's children. Everybody knows everybody else. I can't imagine living in a big, soulless city, where you're anonymous and don't know your neighbours, where you avoid going out at night because you're worried about the high crime rate. I know the world is evolving, but we've held onto old values here and I think that's a good thing.

Devin, Cork, Ireland

D

Here in Melbourne there is a big, very visible Greek community and I don't think that will change any time soon. You can buy Greek food like tzatziki and baklava everywhere you go, and you still hear Greek spoken in the bars and restaurants. And of course we have the Antipodes Festival, which showcases Greek culture. Community is so important to us. Maybe it's because Greece is made up of lots of little islands, so people live cheek-by-jowl and rely on each other. That has carried over to our communities in Australia.

Kouros Calombaris, Melbourne, Australia

A

My family emigrated from Italy to the US 50 years ago. When they arrived, they were penniless and spoke no English. It was the community that helped them get on their feet. Other Italian-Americans got them jobs, lent them money when they couldn't afford to buy groceries, even found the apartment where my grandmother still lives. When my father was thinking of going to college, the elders in the community not only advised him to do it, they also paid some of his fees. It was a real community. The area was full of bakeries and *trattorias* where people from the old country still spoke the dialect and served Italian food. That's all gone now.

Vincenzo, New York, USA

C

I think our communities are changing fast. For example, the big supermarket chains have driven out local shopkeepers. Personally, I can't stand shopping in those places. I think they damage the local economy, and people don't want to go to five different shops when they can stock up on everything in a supermarket. The schools are closing one by one. Lots of families object to sending their kids to a school six miles away, but what choice do we have? Our hands are tied. The local shop that has been there for a hundred years is going to close. It's a shame, but I guess that's the way the world is going.

Paula, Cornwall, UK

3 Answer the questions. Read the comments again to check.

1 What does Vincenzo say about language and food as part of the Italian-American community?

2 What three examples of a 'strong sense of community' does Devin give?

3 How have things changed for shoppers and families in Paula's community?

4 Why is community important to Greeks, according to Kouros?

4 Work in groups and discuss the questions.

1 Do you agree with Vincenzo that communities are not as strong as they used to be? If so, why?

2 How much contact do you have with your local community? Do you know your neighbours? Do you use local shops and services?

Grammar | verb patterns (1)

5 **a** Look at the extract below and underline three verb patterns (verb + verb). The first has been done for you.

> Other Italian-Americans ... lent them money when they couldn't afford to buy groceries ...
>
> When my father was thinking of going to college, the elders in the community not only advised him to do it, they also paid some of his fees.

b Find six more examples of verb patterns used by Devin and Paula on page 22.

6 Find the mistakes in the sentences (1–15) and correct them.

A

1 I'm thinking to visit the community where I used to live.

2 If you can't afford eating in expensive restaurants, there are lots of cheaper *trattorias*.

3 I can't imagine live in a different community.

4 We look forward to see you.

5 You can avoid to offending people by learning the host country's customs.

B

6 I don't mind to look after my niece and nephew.

7 I don't fancy eat Greek food tonight.

8 She doesn't want that she lives far away from her family.

9 I can't stand to shop in big supermarkets.

10 If you object to pay lots of money for clothes, don't go shopping in Ginza, Tokyo.

C

11 I advise you going to the Antipodes festival.

12 I'd encourage all foreigners try some *baklava*.

13 I'd urge you visiting the different communities in New York.

14 I'd recommend to go to the local restaurant.

15 She persuaded us visit Cork in the spring.

7 Work in pairs and answer the questions.

1 Which group of sentences from exercise 6 (A–C) is connected with recommendations? Which is connected with likes/dislikes?

2 Which underlined verbs in group B have a very similar meaning? Which is/are the strongest?

3 Which underlined verbs in group C have a very similar meaning? Which is/are the strongest?

8 Complete the table in the Active grammar box with the underlined verbs from exercise 6.

Active grammar

verb + *-ing*	verb + infinitive
verb + object + infinitive with *to*	**verb + preposition + *-ing***

see Reference page 33

9 Rewrite the sentences (1–8) with the verbs in brackets. Begin each sentence with *I*, *I'd* or *I'm*.

You really must go to the National Gallery. (urge)

I'd urge you to go to the National Gallery.

1 I don't have the money to go to the theatre. (afford)

2 You should go to Brixton Market on Sunday. (advise)

3 I think people ought to use the parks more. (encourage)

4 It will be good to see you next weekend. (look forward)

5 You should buy tickets early for Buckingham Palace. (recommend)

6 It's better not to take Intercity trains because they're more expensive. (avoid)

7 I'd like to take a short trip to Paris. (fancy)

8 I may go to Thailand in February. (think)

Speaking

10 Complete the How to... box with the words from the box.

> wary   were   out   found   value   sure   all

How to... give advice/make recommendations about places

Saying it's good	*It's a must/a must-see.*
	It's good (1) _____ for money.
Saying it's not so good	*It's a bit overrated/overpriced.*
	It's not (2) _____ it's cracked up to be.
	I (3) _____ it a bit dull/touristy.
Recommending	*If I (4) _____ you, I'd go to ...*
	Make (5) _____ you go to ...
	Don't miss .../You should try ...
	I suggest going .../that you go there.
Warning	*Watch (6) _____ for ...*
	One thing to be (7) _____ of is ...

11 **a** Think of a place with a strong sense of community (customs, food, things to see, etc.). Make notes about what you would/wouldn't recommend about the place.

b Work in groups. Take turns to describe the places you chose. Try to use language from the How to... box.

Listening

12 Work in pairs and discuss the questions.

1 Have you (or do you know anyone who has) lived abroad?

2 What were your/their impressions of the place?

3 What problems might there be living in a foreign country?

13 **a** ⊕ 1.09 Listen to three people and make notes in the table.

	speaker 1	speaker 2	speaker 3
Where did he/she live?			
What was he/she doing there?			
What did he/she like about the host country?			
Was there anything he/she didn't like, or that was difficult?			
What are his/her favourite memories of the country?			

b Match the speakers (1, 2 or 3) to the things they did (a–j).

a pretended something ☐

b got a few surprises ☐

c was there at the wrong time ☐

d is from a small town ☐

e would like to return ☐

f learned about the culture by talking to the local people ☐

g says the place was multicultural ☐

h has lived in many countries ☐

i doesn't mention the scenery ☐

j describes a special type of cooking ☐

c Listen again and check.

14 Work in pairs. Discuss the questions.

1 In which of the places from exercise 13a would you most like to live?

2 Would you like to live abroad?

3 Why do you think the speakers talk mainly about food, scenery and people? Which is the most important?

Listening

1 Work in pairs and discuss the questions.

1 How often do you use the Internet? What do you use it for?

2 Are there any websites that you use frequently? What do you like about them?

3 Do you trust what you read on the Internet? Why/Why not?

4 Has the increased use of computers and the Internet been a good thing for you, and in general?

2 🔊 1.10 Listen to two people discussing some of the questions from exercise 1. Which do they discuss? Are their views similar to yours?

3 Listen again and tick (✓) the phrases you hear.

1 (*it's*) *miles easier*

2 (*it's*) *far easier*

3 (*it's*) *nowhere near as ... as*

4 (*it's*) *nothing like as good as*

5 *the less we ..., the less we ...*

6 *the more we ..., the more we ...*

7 (*it's*) *not quite as ... as ...*

8 (*it's*) *definitely not as ... as*

9 (*it's*) *considerably* + comparative (formal)

10 (*it's*) *marginally* + comparative (formal)

11 (*it's*) *much the same*

12 (*it's*) *much* + superlative

Grammar | comparatives (review)

4 **a** Read the rules and examples in the Active grammar box. Then write the phrases from exercise 3 in the table.

b Write the phrases below in the table in the Active grammar box.

> sightly   a tiny bit   far   decidedly

Active grammar

When using comparatives, if we want to be specific about the degree of difference between two people/things, we use modifiers, e.g. *far*, *nowhere near*, *slightly*.

*I'm **slightly** taller than my brother.*

*The green house is **nowhere near** as beautiful as the red one.*

We can use combined comparisons to describe how a change in one thing causes a change in another.

***The longer** you wait, **the worse** it will be.*

1 A big difference	
2 A little difference	
3 *the* + comparative + *the* + comparative	

see Reference page 33

5 Cross out the incorrect words in *italics*.

1 Buying things in shops is *not like/nowhere near/nothing like* as cheap as shopping online.

2 *It's decidedly easier/It's best/It's considerably easier* to write on a computer than doing it by hand.

3 The more you know about computers, *the easier/easier/the simpler* they become.

4 Buying things online is *marginally/extremely/slightly* more risky than face-to-face transactions.

5 It's *a mile/considerably/far* quicker to find information on the Internet than in books.

6 *The more we rely on/The more we use/As much as we use* computers, the more vulnerable we are to hackers and computer viruses.

Speaking

6 **a** Look again at the sentences from exercise 5. How far do you agree with each sentence?

b Work in groups and discuss your views.

Reading

7 Work in pairs. Do you use Wikipedia? If not, what do you think it is?

8 Read the article and match the paragraphs (1–7) to the headings (a–g).

a Why you can't trust Wikipedia
b Jimmy Wales
c The future of Wikipedia
d Editors who care
e The wiki
f Locking out the vandals
g First stop for fact-seekers

9 Answer the questions.

1 What expression in the article is used to describe groups combining their knowledge?
2 Why, according to the article, is Wikipedia generally reliable?
3 Who is Jimmy Wales and what is he like?
4 What technological innovation led to the popularity of Wikipedia?

10 **a** Read the article again quickly. Is it formal or informal in style?

b Complete the How to... box with headings from the box below.

> Humour   Informal vocabulary   Style (spoken English)
> Ellipsis (omitting words)

How to... recognise features of informal language

(1) _____	savvy (paragraph 4) guy (paragraph 5)
(2) _____	Join the gang. (paragraph 1) Short forms: It's a gang (paragraph 1), It'll surely need more (paragraph 7)
(3) _____	Want to know the capital of Turkmenistan? (paragraph 1). The full question = Do you want to know the capital of Turkmenistan? 'And the future?' (paragraph 7)
(4) _____	One famously compared the site to a public toilet seat: you never know who's used it before you. (paragraph 2)

c Work in pairs and answer the questions.

1 What are the formal words for 'savvy' and 'guy'?
2 Are there other examples in the text of informal vocabulary, spoken English, or humour?
3 What is the full version of: 'And the future?'

The Internet's largest encyclopaedia

1

Want to know the capital of Turkmenistan? Or how to make chicken fricassee? Or what goes in a Cuban cigar? The first place you probably turn to is Wikipedia. Join the gang. It's a gang that now has access to over 18 million entries in 279 languages. And the striking thing about Wikipedia is that it isn't high-flying professors who are providing the answers. It's amateurs. Wikipedia is a perfect example of 'crowd sourcing'. Anyone can add an entry. Anyone can edit it. No qualifications are necessary. In short, the site uses the masses to pool their information, and the result is the world's biggest encyclopedia.

2

But is it the most reliable? Ask one of its founders, Larry Sanger – who went on to lecture at Ohio State University – and the answer is an unequivocal 'no'. Sanger doesn't let his students use Wikipedia for their research; he knows they can simply invent information, put it anonymously on Wikipedia, and claim it's accurate. Other academics also have their doubts. One famously compared the site to a public toilet seat: you never know who's used it before you. But they are now probably in the minority.

3

If it's so easy to edit, how come, in several recent research studies, Wikipedia has been found to be as accurate as other encyclopedias including the *Encyclopedia Britannica*, which has existed for 250 years? How come, with all the potential 'vandals' keen to rewrite history according to their own ideologies, Wikipedia, it turns out, is generally trustworthy? The answer is that the editors of Wikipedia care more than the vandals. The Massachusetts Institute of Technology (MIT) did a study and found that obscene comments added on Wikipedia were, on average, removed within a hundred seconds. For the vandals, it's about as worthwhile as a graffiti artist using invisible ink.

4

Those who run Wikipedia are also savvy enough to know when a bout of vandalism is going to occur. During the 2004 Bush–Kerry US election, realising that the supporters of each candidate would attempt to smear the opponent on Wikipedia, the company

locked the entries on George Bush and John Kerry.

5 _____

So, in this utopia of crowd sourcing, who exactly is making the decisions? The boss is founder Jimmy Wales. In 2000, Wales was a regular guy looking to combine his two hobbies: nosing through the _Encyclopedia Britannica_ and surfing the Internet. Online he found himself discussing all sorts of topics and meeting all sorts of people on obscure mailing lists. He decided he wanted to set up something longer-lasting and fun. 'Fun' is a big word for Jimmy Wales. One of the world's great optimists, Wales has breezed through life enjoying pretty much everything he's turned his hand to, including trading options and futures and founding nupedia, Wikipedia's forerunner.

6 _____

Nupedia didn't have a massive impact. It used 'the old model' of experts writing entries, but then Wales and his co-founder, Larry Sanger, decided to experiment with a relatively new technology: a wiki. The wiki got its name because the inventor had his honeymoon in Hawaii, where you catch the 'wiki wiki' (quick) bus from the airport. The idea of a wiki is that anyone can contribute to a website; it's a pooling of knowledge. With this technology in place, Wikipedia exploded in popularity. Within its first year contributors wrote 20,000 entries in 18 languages.

7 _____

And the future? For most of its short history, Wikipedia has been staffed by a group of volunteers, with only a handful actually getting paid. By 2011 the company's paid employees had grown to over 50. It'll surely need more in the future, as the company tries to expand its popularity in Asia, South America and the Middle East. It's also trying to improve the quality of entries by teaming up with universities to get some expert input and working with museums to supply better images. As the world shrinks and people's thirst for information grows, it's likely that Wikipedia will keep growing, too. As for the capital of Turkmenistan, it's Ashgabat. And if you need proof, you know where to look.

11 Look at techniques 1–4. Are they generally used in formal or informal texts?

1 full verb forms
2 lots of phrasal verbs
3 sentences beginning with _and_ or _but_
4 repeated use of the passive

12 Read the two formal emails below. Some language is too informal. Replace it with more appropriate language from the box.

> Regards   attend   don't hesitate to   concerning   following
> requested   will be very happy to attend   will be unable to attend
> a previous arrangement   we would be grateful if you could
> queries   could you please confirm your attendance

1

Dear Mr Fry,

After our telephone conversation, I would like to invite you to the meeting of the Online Encyclopaedia Anglia Group on 15 November at 7.00 p.m. at 24 Bland Street. We will be discussing how to take forward the proposals for a new interactive website. I have attached a preliminary agenda for the meeting, and also a map showing how to get to Bland Street. There will also be a dinner in the evening, to which you are invited.

Let us know if you're coming by 4 November. Bring copies of the sample contract. Feel free to get in touch if you have any questions.

Best wishes,

Mary Johnson

2

Dear Ms Johnson,

Thank you very much for the invitation to come to the meeting on 15 November, about the plan to start a new website. Thanks for the agenda. I can come to the meeting.

As asked, I will bring copies of the sample contract. Unfortunately, I won't be able to come to the dinner because of something I've already organised.

I look forward to seeing you there.

Yours sincerely,

Peter Fry

13 Work in pairs and read the Lifelong learning box. Compare the emails and article on this page and discuss questions 1–6.

Keeping your reader in mind

! When you are planning a piece of writing, think about who your readers are and consider the following points.

1 Why are they reading your piece?
2 How much information do they already know?
3 How much do they need to know?
4 What are their expectations?
5 How formal and what length do they expect the piece to be?
6 What is the relationship between writer and reader?

This information will help you to choose the best tone for your piece (formal, informal, academic, etc.), to organise your ideas, and to think about what to include or omit.

Lifelong learning

2.3 Destination paradise

Grammar introductory *it*

Can do describe a place

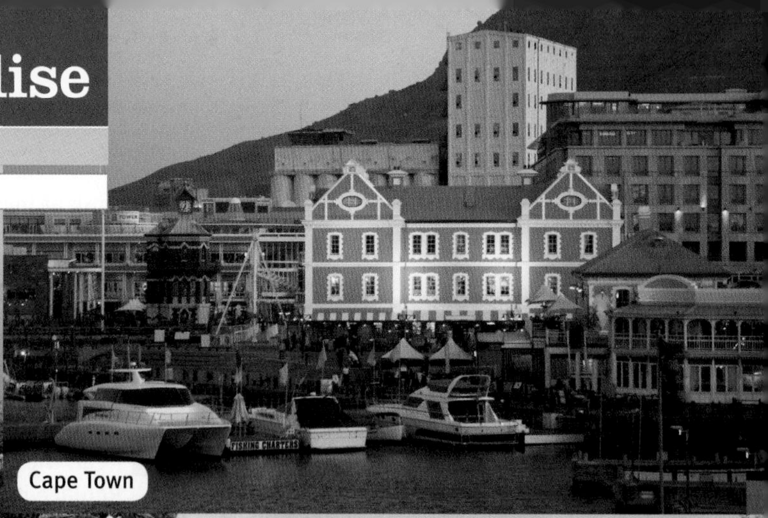

Cape Town

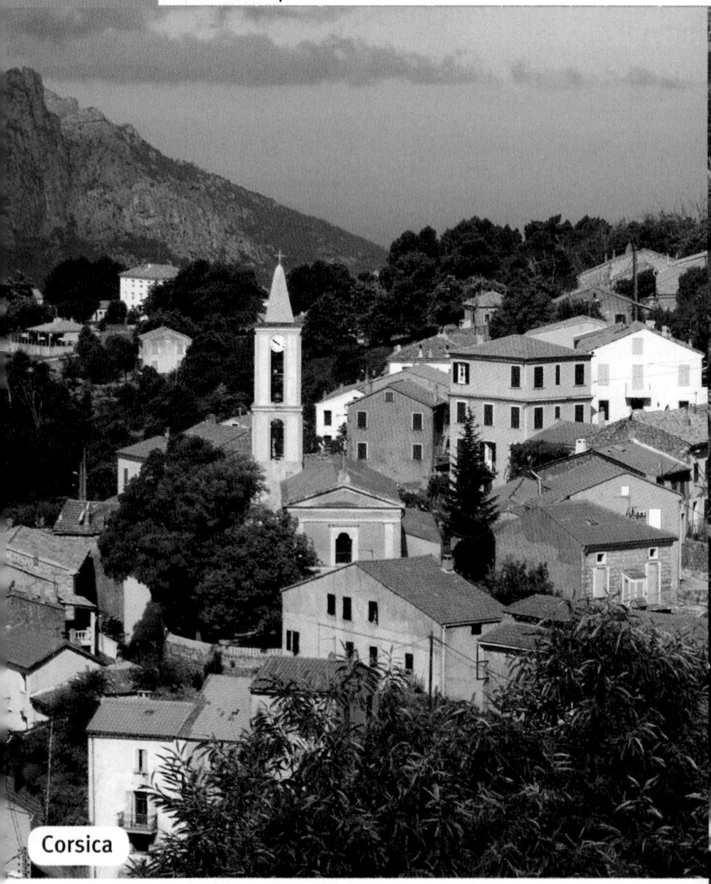

Corsica

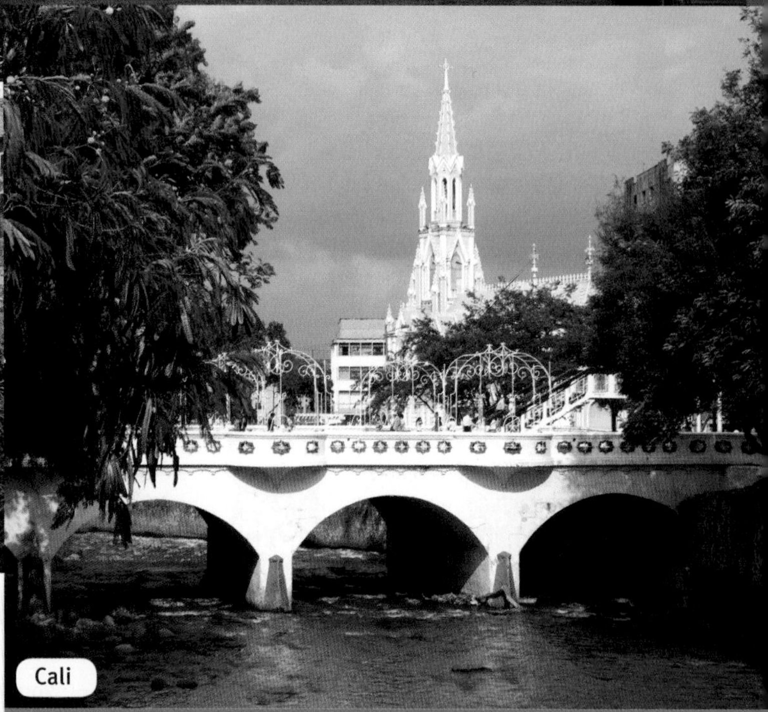

Cali

Speaking and reading

1 Work in pairs and discuss the questions.

1. What do you know about the places in the photos?
2. What do you think they are like?
3. Would you like to visit them? Why/Why not?

2 **a** Work in small groups. Read about a place and make notes on the topics below.

Student A: read about Cali.

Student B: read about Cape Town on page 149.

Student C: read about Corsica on page 153.

- atmosphere
- things to do
- things to see
- food
- the local community

b Use your notes to describe the place to your group.

3 Work in pairs and discuss the questions.

1. Each place is described as a type of 'paradise'. Which aspects sound good to you? What makes them unique?
2. Which place would you prefer to go to? Why?
3. Do you think tourism is good for these three places? What problems might it bring?

Cali

In Cali, they say, even the ghosts dance salsa. Its rhythms, born in Cuba, nurtured in New York and carried on the winds all the way to hot Cali, can be heard in bars, on buses, along the avenues of Juanchito and Plaza Caicedo. And here too, in a taxi moving at the speed of light, taking me to the heart of the bustling city. The driver slows down at a traffic light, turns to me and says '*las calenas*,' (the women from Cali) 'are the most beautiful women in the world!' And we're off again, driving past gangs of *mulato* men laughing in the street. It's no wonder this city is adored by everyone who visits.

My hotel is a run-down old building whose blue skin is peeling in the heat. It has a stunning view from the balcony and I gaze down on the square. The guidebooks tell you to visit the Gold Museum and the Museum of Colonial Art, the churches of San Antonio and La Merced, but there's only one thing on my mind as I leave the key at reception: salsa.

The *salsotecas* don't get busy until midnight so instead I stop at a restaurant serving typical Colombian food:

Vocabulary | adjectives to describe places

4 Work in groups. Match the definitions (1–10) to words/phrases from the articles.

1 energetic and noisy, full of life (Cali, line 6; Cape Town, line 25; Corsica, line 29)

2 in poor condition, uncared for (Cali, line 13; Cape Town, line 18; Corsica, line 31)

3 amazingly beautiful (Cali, line 14; Cape Town, line 14; Corsica, line 16)

4 having variety (Cali, line 26; Cape Town, line 43; Corsica, line 19)

5 not damaged in character or atmosphere (Cali, line 30; Cape Town, line 39; Corsica, line 44)

6 next to each other (Cali, line 31; Cape Town, line 21; Corsica, line 22)

7 extremely large (Cali, line 32; Cape Town, line 20; Corsica, line 36)

8 peaceful (Cali, line 34; Cape Town, line 38; Corsica, line 45)

9 in areas people don't normally go to (usually outside the city) (Cali, line 35; Cape Town, line 17; Corsica, line 48)

10 very busy, crowded (Cali, line 44; Cape Town, line 32; Corsica, line 47)

5 **a** Complete the sentences (1–8) with words/phrases from exercise 4.

1 The roof is falling off and the windows are broken. The old house looks very _____.

2 It's hard to find the little villa in the countryside because it's _____.

3 You can hardly move during carnival time because the streets are absolutely _____.

4 There are many different nationalities living there, so the culture is very _____.

5 Huge skyscrapers stand _____ with tiny wooden houses.

6 The Sahara Desert is 9,100,000 square kilometres. It's absolutely _____.

7 We're going to spend a _____ few days camping, far from the noisy city.

8 The town remains _____, even though there are lots of tourists now. It hasn't changed at all.

b Describe the places in photos A–C with the words/phrases from exercise 4.

sancocho – a stew made with chunks of beef, vegetables, cassava (a tropical plant with edible roots) and plantain (a type of banana, but not
25 so sweet) served with rice. Then I must choose from the amazingly diverse selection of Colombian fruit. I settle for guanabana and maracuya and I'm not disappointed. I stroll for a while, tempted by dark smoky cafés, the fans spinning weakly on the
30 ceilings. This is the old, unspoilt Cali, which lives side by side with a newer version, the Cali of junk food, Internet cafés and vast touristy discos. I walk past the trees and sculptures that line the river, and into San Antonio park, a tranquil spot
35 off the beaten track.

Later, on Avenida Sexta – Sixth Avenue – I find what I'm really looking for: a *salsoteca*. Some charming young Colombians teach me a few dance steps and we chat about Cali. They say
40 that when times are tough, they dance away their worries. And I must never forget '*las calenas* are the most beautiful women in the world!' By 2.00 a.m. the salsa is swinging, the drinks are flowing, the place is packed and I know one thing
45 for sure: I've found the Cali that I was looking for – the salsa dancer's paradise.

Speaking

6 **a** Think of places you have been to that match the topics below.

- it has stunning views
- it is off the beaten track
- it is unspoilt despite tourism
- it has modern parts side by side with the old parts
- it is tranquil
- it is bustling at the weekends
- it has some run-down parts

b Work in pairs. Describe the places you thought of to your partner.

Grammar | introductory *it*

7 **a** Read the paragraph below. Is it about Corsica, Cape Town or Cali?

> With its wonderful food, semi-tropical climate, and great nightlife, it appears that the city has everything going for it. Local bartender Juan Hernandez tells me, 'It's no coincidence that the city is growing. We've worked hard to improve everything: the infrastructure, the standard of living, the nightlife. When I think back to 20 years ago, it's surprising how fast things are changing here. We love it when tourists come to stay.' It cannot be denied that the city is on the way up and it's a pity I only have a few days here, but I'll be back!

b Look at the underlined phrases above. What do they have in common? Find another example in the first paragraph of the article about Cali from exercise 2.

c Read rule A in the Active grammar box. Complete examples 2–4 with underlined phrases from the paragraph in exercise 7a.

d Read rule B in the Active grammar box. Complete example 8 with an underlined phrase from the paragraph in exercise 7a.

Active grammar

A We often use introductory *it* when we describe our feelings and opinions. This sounds less direct than using *I think*, *I believe*, etc.

1 *I thought there would be more tourists.*
    → ***It's surprising that*** *there aren't more tourists.*

2 *I'm sorry to say ...* → _____

3 *I have the impression ...* → _____

4 *There's no doubt, in my opinion, ...* → _____

B We also use *it* in the middle of a sentence (after certain verbs) to introduce a clause.

5 *I could hardly believe **it** when I saw how much the city had changed.*

6 *I'd appreciate **it** if you could send me information about the city.*

7 *I hate **it** when I go to see a tourist attraction and it's closed.*

8 _____

---

8 Match the sentence beginnings (1–8) to the sentence endings (a–h).

1 It's no coincidence that the
2 It's a shame that
3 It shocked me to
4 It cannot be denied that
5 It's no use
6 It's no wonder people
7 It seems strange,
8 It's essential that

a you have to leave this wonderful town.
b the food here is the best in the country.
c see so much poverty in the city centre.
d love this place. It's absolutely perfect!
e you learn the basics of the language before you travel.
f but I actually prefer cold, rainy climates to hot weather.
g complaining about the transport infrastructure. You should walk!
h crime rate is lower. They've doubled the number of police.

9 **a** Complete six of the sentences so they are true for you.

1 It's really wonderful to think that ...
2 It always surprises me when ...
3 It's a pity that ...
4 It's no use ...
5 It cannot be denied that ...
6 It appears to me that ...
7 I always appreciate it when ...
8 I hate it when ...

b Work in pairs and compare your sentences.

see Reference page 33

1 Read the texts below. Would you like to join any of these communities? Why/Why not? Would you like to join them temporarily or permanently?

1
They said it was a passing trend that would never catch on. They were wrong. When I turned up at the Chrysalis Hippy Commune 40 years after I'd left it, nothing had changed. Living here, you can still get by on $50 a week and you'll have no problems fitting in. Everyone is welcome.

2
We decided to do up a small barn in a tiny rural village. No water, no electricity, no Internet! We filled in some forms to get planning permission, and this took months. Then the terrible weather held us up so we couldn't start renovating. Finally, a year later, the house was finished. We knew nobody in the community except John, who had carried out most of the work.

3
I first came across Claudio and the surfing community in São Paulo. I'd never surfed before, but I took to it immediately. Claudio told me they were expecting giant waves at the end of the summer, so I practised every day and saw to it that I was ready. When the big waves came, I got through it OK.

4
I came up with the idea of starting an online book community. It seemed like a good way to keep up with the latest books. Anyone is welcome to write reviews and post them on the site. It really comes down to democratising the process, because we wanted to get away from the idea that you need a degree in order to write and read reviews.

2 Find four phrasal verbs in each text and match them to the correct meanings (a–p).

Text 1
a arrive
b feel comfortable in a social group
c survive financially
d become fashionable

Text 2
e complete paperwork
f restore/redecorate
g delay someone
h put ideas/instructions into practice

Text 3
i finish successfully
j meet/find by chance
k organise/manage
l like something/someone

Text 4
m escape/avoid
n be essentially
o invent/think of
p know about recent developments

3 There are four types of phrasal verb. Match the types (a–d) to the examples (1–4).
a transitive (1)
b transitive (2)
c intransitive
d three-part phrasal verbs

1 The plane <u>took off</u>.
  (verb + particle, no direct object)
2 I <u>paid back</u> the money. / I <u>paid</u> the money <u>back</u>.
  (verb + particle, with a direct object. If the object is a noun, it can come between the verb and the particle or after the particle.)
3 She <u>looked after</u> me. *NOT:* She looked me after.
  (verb + particle, with a direct object that always goes after the particle)
4 I went on a spa break to <u>get away from</u> it all.
  (verb + particle + preposition, with a direct object that usually goes after the preposition)

4 **a** Work in pairs and discuss the questions.
1 Did you take to your partner or best friend immediately? Why/Why not?
2 Do you have to come up with ideas at work/school?
3 Have you come across any interesting people/books/places in the last few months?
4 Do you usually turn up early, on time or late for appointments? What does it depend on?
5 Do you do anything special to get away from your daily routine? What?
6 Do you keep up with new developments in your work/hobby? How?
7 When was the last time you filled in a form? What was it for?

b Tell the class one thing about your partner.

5 Read the Lifelong learning box and do the exercise.

Note it down

! When you read/hear phrasal verbs that you think are useful, write them down in context. Note what type of phrasal verb they are (see the four types from exercise 3) and look for patterns in the use of particles.

Circle four phrasal verbs in the paragraph below and add them to your notes. What types of phrasal verb are they?

I visited Sydney, Australia, for a few days so I could catch up with my long-lost cousin. He put me up in his spare room. In the end, he looked after me so brilliantly and we became such good friends that I stayed on an extra month and did all his cooking and cleaning!

1 **a** Read about a club. Do you think the club is silly, funny or a good idea?

THE NOT TERRIBLY GOOD CLUB

In 1976, Stephen Pile formed 'The Not Terribly Good Club'. To qualify for membership, you had to be not terribly good at something and then attend meetings. During these meetings, people gave public demonstrations of things they couldn't do, such as painting and singing, and gave awful presentations on things they knew nothing about. Stephen Pile kept a record of these unsuccessful events and then published them as *The Book of Heroic Failures* in 1979. The stories included epic examples of incompetence, such as the World's Worst Tourist, who spent two days in New York, believing he was in Rome; 'the slowest solution of a crossword' (34 years); and the burglar who wore metal armour to protect himself from dogs – the armour made so much noise that he got caught and it was too heavy for him to run away. Included in *The Book of Heroic Failures* was an application form for membership to 'The Not Terribly Good Club'. Amazingly, within two months of the book's publication, the group had received 20,000 applications to join, and the book appeared on various bestseller lists. As a result of his sudden fame, Pile was kicked out of his own club and the club itself soon disbanded. It had become too successful.

CAN YOU TELL ME THE WAY TO THE COLISEUM?

2 **a** 🔊 1.11 Listen to two people describing clubs they belong to. Make notes on the topics below.

Old boys' club

- the main idea of the club
- other things that it does
- type of meeting
- who can be a member
- problems

Ballroom-dancing club

- number and type of people in the club
- how long she has been a member
- when and where it meets
- problems
- things they have learned

b Work in pairs and compare your notes.

3 Work in groups. You are going to form a club. Think about the following questions.

1 What type of club is it?
2 What events will you organise?
3 How will you know if the club is successful? (What are your goals?)
4 What is the name of the club?
5 Where will you meet?
6 How often?
7 How many people can join the club?
8 What do people have to do to join?
9 What rules will the club have?
10 What will the club's symbol, logo, motto or song be?

b If you were joining The Not Terribly Good Club, what would your presentation be about?

4 Present your ideas to the rest of the class. Which clubs would you like to join?

Verb patterns (1)

When one verb follows another, the second is either an *-ing* verb or the infinitive.

Some verbs which use an *-ing* form are related in meaning. The following verbs all show personal tastes: *adore, fancy, don't mind, detest, can't stand.*

*I **adore living** here.*

Other verbs take an object + the infinitive:

*I **told her to come** here.*

Some of these verbs are related in meaning. The following verbs show one person (or thing) influencing the actions of another: *warn, tell, advise, urge, order, persuade, encourage, force, forbid, allow.*

*I **persuaded her to visit** me.*

Verbs which are followed by a preposition use the *-ing* form:

*I **look forward to meeting** her.*

Some verbs can only be followed by the infinitive or the *-ing* form. See page 23.

Comparatives (review)

There are many expressions we can use to show if the difference between two things is big or small. For a small difference we can use: *slightly, a little bit, a tiny bit, marginally* (formal), etc.

*I'm **slightly taller** than Peter.*

*The population is **marginally larger** than that of Ghana.*

For a large difference we can use: *much, far, miles* (informal), *considerably* (formal), etc.

*They're **miles** better than us at football.*

*The government was **considerably more** corrupt 100 years ago.*

as + adjective + *as* means the two things are equal:

*It took me **as long** to drive to Cardiff **as** it did to travel there by train.*

If we want to say two things aren't equal, we can say:

*She's **not as big as** me. (= she's smaller)*

*The new menu **isn't as nice as** the one they had during the summer.*

There are many expressions with *as* + adjective + *as* which show whether the difference is big or small. For a small difference we can use *not quite as*:

*This bed **isn't quite as comfortable as** the other one. (= It's nearly as comfortable)*

For a big difference we can use *nowhere near, nothing like*:

*He is **nowhere near as good as** me at tennis.*

Introductory *it*

There are a number of set phrases that begin with *it*. These are often used for describing personal opinions. In these expressions, *it* is the subject of the verb.

***It's a shame** you won't be here tonight.*

***It's no use** complaining all the time.*

***It amazes me** to hear you say that.*

There are several set phrases with *it* that refer to general impressions.

***It strikes me** that he's not as good as he was.*

***It appears** as if they aren't coming.*

***It seems** like a hopeless case.*

After certain verbs, *it* can also be used to introduce a clause. In this case, *it* is the object of the verb.

*I **hate it** when she does that.*

*We'd **appreciate it** if you turned down the music.*

*I'd **love it** if we won the league this year.*

Key vocabulary

Communities

cost of living   cosmopolitan   infrastructure
mild climate   freedom   healthcare system
standard of living   monuments   crime rate
unemployment   traffic congestion   pollution
racial tension   no-go areas   cultural life
vibrant nightlife

Adjectives to describe places

off the beaten track   unspoilt   diverse   tranquil
side by side   vast   run-down   stunning   packed
bustling

Phrasal verbs

catch on   turn up   get by   fit in   do up   fill in
hold up   carry out   come across   take to   see to
get through   come up with   keep up with
come down to   get away from   take off   pay back
look after   catch up with   put (someone) up
stay on

Listen to the explanations and vocabulary.

ACTIVEBOOK

see Writing bank page 156

2 Review and practice

1 Complete the sentences with the correct form of verbs from the box (infinitive or -ing form). You may need to add a preposition.

> take   pay   spend   apply   consult   hear
> make   wear   buy   live

1 I encouraged the architects _____ the community about their new project.
2 We didn't mind _____ a few days in the town, but we didn't want to live there.
3 I look forward _____ from you soon.
4 We urged them not _____ a house in that area because it's very expensive and noisy.
5 She's thinking of _____ for a job as a tour guide.
6 I object _____ such a high rent in such a horrible part of town.
7 They persuaded us _____ an effort and actually see some of the city.
8 I can imagine _____ here for the rest of my life. I love it.
9 Members of the ski club are advised _____ helmets while skiing, for their own protection.
10 To relieve stress, I recommend _____ a long holiday in the countryside.

2 Complete each sentence with one word.

Chile is _____ pretty as Argentina.
Chile is <u>as</u> pretty as Argentina.

1 You'd be _____ off going to Texas in the spring than in the summer.
2 Paraguay is nowhere _____ as big as Brazil.
3 I _____ sooner go to Cartagena than Bogotá for a holiday.
4 Fiji is nothing _____ as rich as New Zealand.
5 Switzerland is much the _____ as it always has been: safe, clean and expensive.
6 The more cars we use, the _____ polluted our environment becomes.
7 Poland _____ quite as cold as Norway, but its climate is similar in the north-east.
8 Honduras is a tiny _____ bigger than Guatemala.
9 China is by far _____ most populated nation in the world.
10 Rather _____ getting a job in Madrid, why don't you travel around Spain?

3 Complete the text with words/phrases from the box.

> stunning   came up with   come across
> keep up with   side by side   get away from
> turn up   held up   run-down   carried out
> bustling   vast

In 1883, Italian priest Don Bosco dreamed of a futuristic city in the heart of Brazil. Seventy-seven years later, his dream came true. Brasilia was completed in 1960, the construction of this specially designed city (1) _____ in just three and a half years. Brasilia has never forgotten Don Bosco: a cathedral in the city bears his name.

The city was commissioned by President Kubitschek to house the government and its buildings. Brasilia's supporters say the city promotes growth in the whole of Brazil, which is a (2) _____ country (easily South America's biggest), not just on the famous east coast. Its detractors say it was built so that politicians could (3) _____ the high crime rates of Rio and São Paulo and so they wouldn't have to live (4) _____ with the population in (5) _____ areas.

Instead of a (6) _____ city centre full of people, Brasilia seems quite empty and almost like a machine. Its architects (7) _____ a rigidly organised design, with designated areas for government buildings, housing, etc. In the original design, there were no traffic lights; cars would go through tunnels and bridges in the sky, never getting (8) _____ by excess traffic. In order to (9) _____ a growing population, however, Brasilia eventually had to install traffic lights.

It isn't a charming city, compared to other parts of Brazil, as it is very regimented and lacks pretty little streets. But if you (10) _____ in the centre of Brasilia you will (11) _____ some excellent restaurants. You should also pay a visit to the futuristic cathedral built by Niemeyer, the television tower with its (12) _____ views, and the zoo near the airport.

Tales

Lead-in

1 Look at the pictures. Work in pairs and discuss the questions.

1 How are the pictures connected?
2 What types of story do they illustrate?
3 Are you good at storytelling?
4 What makes a good storyteller?

2 **a** Work in pairs. Discuss the difference between the pairs of phrases (1–5).

1 a plot/a biographical sketch
2 a fake/a myth
3 a tall story/a fairy tale
4 a legend/an anecdote
5 a punch line/a joke

b Can you think of any examples of the words/phrases above?

3 **a** Check you know the meaning of the underlined phrases.

1 Do you think it's OK to tell a white lie if it makes life easier?
2 What would you do if you heard that someone had been spreading rumours about you?
3 Are you sometimes a bit of a gossip?
4 Have you ever taken part in (or heard about) an elaborate hoax?
5 When you describe things, are you prone to exaggeration?
6 Do you know anyone who is good at making up stories?
7 Did you listen to bedtime stories when you were a child? Which were your favourites?

b Work in pairs. Discuss the sentences from exercise 3a.

Reading

1 a Work in pairs. Look at the photos and discuss the questions.

1 Where are the people in the main photo?

2 What do you think they are doing?

3 What do you think their relationship is with Manuel Elizalde?

4 What is a hoax?

b Read the article and check your ideas.

2 Write true (T) or false (F).

1 The Philippines government encouraged thousands of visitors to see the tribe. ☐

2 After losing power, Manuel Elizalde gave some money to the tribe. ☐

3 There have been many hoaxes connected with anthropology. ☐

4 Piotr Zak, Sidd Finch and Nat Tate were all invented characters. ☐

5 The public loved Piotr Zak's and Nat Tate's work, but the critics knew it was a hoax. ☐

3 Work in pairs and discuss the questions.

1 Why do you think people were so excited about the discovery of the Stone Age tribe?

2 Why do you think the people created these hoaxes? Did Elizalde, Shinichi, Plimpton and Boyd have different reasons?

3 What type of person would you need to be in order to create a successful hoax?

4 Why do intelligent people such as journalists and academics fall for hoaxes, (i.e. believe them)?

HOAXES THAT FOOLED THE WORLD

In 1971, while he was working as a government minister in the Philippines, Manuel Elizalde announced a great discovery. He had found a Stone Age tribe living in a remote part of the country. They lived in caves, used stone tools, and ate any food they could find. This isolated tribe, just 27 people, had been living this way for many generations, and in fact they didn't even speak the same language as other people in the area. Journalists arrived from all over the world, a documentary about the tribe was filmed for TV, and thousands of dollars were spent on research trips. The Philippines government, however, not wanting to destroy a way of life that had existed for thousands of years, allowed only a few people to visit them.

It was only years later, when the government (and Elizalde) lost power, that the truth came out. Researchers found the tribe living in villages, wearing Levi's jeans and communicating happily with other people. They explained that they had been pretending all along – Elizalde had paid them to act like a Stone Age tribe. What's more, Elizalde had left the country with all the money.

Elizalde's hoax was just one in a long line. Anthropology has been a particularly rich field for hoaxers, with stories ranging from the famous Piltdown Man hoax – a supposedly ancient skull that was actually made of the bones of a medieval human and an orangutan, and chimpanzee teeth – to Fujimura Shinichi, the Japanese archaeologist who faked vital discoveries for years before being found out in 2000.

But perhaps the most interesting hoaxes are those that involve fictitious people. Piotr Zak was a Polish composer. An avant-garde modernist, he was not well-known among the public. At least not until 1961, when the BBC broadcast his piece *Mobile for Tape and Percussion*. Some music critics hailed it as a great work. Unfortunately for them, the piece had consisted of BBC staff making silly noises edited by BBC technicians. It was a classic hoax.

Nearly a quarter of a century later, another great hoax was to shake the world of American sports. It was 1 April, April Fools' Day, which is a day for playing practical jokes. *Sports Illustrated* ran an article about Sidd Finch, a truly extraordinary baseball player. The subheading of the article read: 'He's a pitcher, part yogi and part recluse. Impressively liberated from our opulent lifestyle, Sidd's deciding about yoga – and his future in baseball.' Read the first letters of these words again, carefully. They spell out 'Happy April Fools' Day'. On 15 April, the magazine came clean: Finch was an invention. The writer of the article, George Plimpton, then extended his article into a novel, published in 1987.

Just a year later, British writer William Boyd published *Nat Tate: American Artist, 1928–1960*, the tragic biography of a New York painter. A number of prominent critics claimed to remember Tate's work, claiming that he had been one of the greatest artists of the century. He'd never existed. The name Nat Tate is derived from two of Britain's most famous art galleries: The National Gallery (Nat) and the Tate Gallery.

Grammar | narrative tenses review

4 a Read the first paragraph of the article again. <u>Underline</u> examples of the Past Simple, Past Continuous, Past Perfect Simple and Past Perfect Continuous.

b Work in pairs and explain the difference in meaning (if any) between the pairs of sentences (1–3) in the Active grammar box. Why might one verb form be more appropriate than the other in this context?

c Complete the rules (A–D) in the Active grammar box with the words from the box below.

> progress   length   chronological   before

Active grammar

1 a) *When the truth came out, Elizalde had already left the country.*
   b) *When the truth came out, Elizalde left the country.*

2 a) *People believed the tribe had been living the same way for centuries.*
   b) *People believed the tribe had lived the same way for centuries.*

3 a) *When researchers arrived, the people from the tribe weren't living in caves any more.*
   b) *When researchers arrived, the people from the tribe didn't live in caves any more.*

A Use the Past Simple for finished actions in the past. Use it to describe a sequence of events in _____ order.

B Use the Past Continuous for actions in _____ when something else happened.

C Use the Past Perfect Simple for actions completed _____ other events in the past. Use it when you are already talking about the past.

D Use the Past Perfect Continuous for progressive actions that started before the main events happened. Use it to emphasise the _____ of the action.

see Reference page 47

5 a Read about some famous hoaxes. Complete the paragraphs with the correct form of the verbs in brackets.

> In 1957, a news programme called *Panorama* broadcast a story about spaghetti trees in Switzerland. While the reporter told the story, Swiss farmers in the background (1) _____ (pick) spaghetti from trees. Following this, thousands of people (2) _____ (call) the show, asking how to grow spaghetti trees.

> In 1998, large numbers of Americans went to Burger King asking for a new type of burger. The food company (3) _____ (publish) an ad in *USA Today* announcing the new 'left-handed Whopper', a burger designed for left-handed people. The following day, Burger King (4) _____ (admit) that they (5) _____ (joke) all along.

> Swedish technician Kjell Stensson (6) _____ (work) on the development of colour TV for many years when he (7) _____ (announce) in 1962 that everyone could now convert their black-and-white TV sets into colour. The procedure was simple: you (8) _____ (have) to put a nylon stocking over the TV screen. Stensson demonstrated, and fooled thousands.

> Pretending that it (9) _____ (develop) the product for some time, a British supermarket announced in 2002 that it (10) _____ (invent) a whistling carrot. Using genetic engineering, the carrot grew with holes in it, and, when cooked, it would start whistling.

b 🔊 1.12 Listen and check.

Pronunciation | contractions (1)

6 a 🔊 1.13 Listen and write the sentences you hear. Which words are being contracted?

b Work in pairs. Look at audioscript 1.13 on page 169 and practise reading the sentences aloud. Can you hear the contractions?

Speaking

7 a Prepare to tell a story about something that happened in your life (e.g. a time you did something funny or learned an important lesson). Think about the topics below.

1 What were you doing when it happened?
2 How long had you been doing it?
3 Where were you? Who were you with?
4 What had happened before this? Why?
5 What happened next? How did you feel?

b Invent some minor details to add to your story.

c Work in pairs and take turns to tell your story. As you listen, think of questions to ask. Guess which details your partner invented.

Vocabulary | synonyms

8 Find synonyms for the words/phrases (1–10) from the article on page 36.

1 tricked (v) (title)
2 alone (adj) (line 9)
3 ruin (v) (line 19)
4 faking (v) (line 30)
5 a big, elaborate trick (n) (line 35)
6 extremely old (adj) (line 40)
7 extremely important (adj) (line 45)
8 freed (adj) (line 70)
9 expanded (v) (line 79)
10 extremely sad (adj) (line 83)

9 **a** Read about four hoaxes. Try to think of possible synonyms for the underlined words/phrases.

1 Footage was supposedly filmed in 1947 of doctors performing an autopsy on an extra-terrestrial. The story goes that the alien crash-landed in Roswell, New Mexico, US. The 17-minute clip since spread around the world on the Internet and even spawned a film, but it turned out that two English businessmen had staged the scene in 1995.

2 In 2009, a large weather balloon floated into the sky. The owners, Richard and Mayumi Heene, panicking, claimed their six-year-old son was in it. After a one-hour journey 2,000 feet into the air, and pursued by US National Guard helicopters, the balloon landed, but there was no sign of the boy. Had he fallen out? No. He was hiding in the family garage, as his parents had ordered him to.

3 In 2008, a film poster appeared heralding the arrival of a new superhero film. Titled *Gundala*, its hero was based on an Indonesian comic book. The film had its own Facebook page and website, with photos of the film in production and even a Wikipedia entry. However, it was a hoax perpetrated by Indonesian digital artist Iskandar Salim.

4 Actor/director Orson Welles's 1938 radio production *The War of the Worlds* conned thousands of Americans into thinking they were in the middle of a full-scale Martian invasion. The fake 'news bulletins' about the invasion sounded so genuine that many listeners thought they were real.

b Match the words from the box below to the underlined synonyms from exercise 9a.

> announcing   allegedly   appearance   attack
> authentic   carried out   chased   deceived
> doing   instructed   led to   rose

10 **a** Read the Lifelong learning box. Then rewrite the underlined words in sentences 1–5.

> ### In your own words
>
> ❗ When learning new words it can be useful to keep a note of synonyms.
>
> Using synonyms can help us to:
>
> 1 avoid repeating a word we have just used.
> 2 make what we say and write more interesting and memorable.
> 3 be more specific about the things we are describing.

Lifelong learning

1 Advertisers use a lot of tricks to trick people into believing that a product is exactly what they need.
2 Many so-called authentic products look authentic but when you examine them closely you can see they are counterfeits.
3 Instead of being extremely old artefacts, discoveries that are said to be extremely old often turn out to be modern fakes.
4 Destroying the environment will destroy our children's future, but some people insist that global warming is a hoax.
5 Hoaxes perpetrated on the public are very serious – the perpetrators should be punishable by imprisonment.

b Work in pairs. Do you agree with the sentences from exercise 10a? Give reasons and examples.

3.2 A good read

Vocabulary compound words

Can do describe a person in detail

Vocabulary | books

1 Work in pairs and discuss the questions.

1 What sort of books do you like reading?

2 What three books would you take to a desert island?

3 Would you like to be a writer? Why/ Why not?

2 **a** Match the sentence beginnings (1–8) with the sentence endings (a–h).

1 I was

2 It's very

3 The story

4 I found the

5 The characters

6 It's based on

7 I'm a real

8 It's a

a is gripping.

b best-seller.

c story quite moving.

d readable.

e bookworm.

f a true story.

g are one-dimensional.

h hooked.

b Match the sentences from exercise 2a to the sentences below.

1 I'm an avid reader.

2 I couldn't put the book down.

3 The story really holds your attention.

4 It depicts real events.

5 It has a nice, easy style.

6 It has sold a lot of copies.

7 I was emotionally involved in it.

8 They didn't really come alive for me.

3 Complete this book review with the correct words (a, b or c).

I love Stieg Larsson's trilogy *The Girl With the Dragon Tattoo*, *The Girl Who Played with Fire* and *The Girl Who Kicked the Hornet's Nest*. The series is absolutely (1) _____ and I was (2) _____ after just a few pages. Although a lot of the characters are quite (3)_____ dimensional, the heroine, Lisbeth Salander, is fascinating. To see her journey from sulky cyber-geek to superwoman avenger is the main reason I couldn't (4) _____ the book down. Although not exactly a (5) _____, I've always been an (6) _____ reader of crime fiction, and Larsson's work is among the best in the genre. The style is very (7) _____, which is one reason why teenagers like the books. The heroine's story, although full of violence, is actually very (8)_____ because she has to overcome so many personal problems just to function successfully in the world.

1	a interesting	b moving	c gripping
2	a hooked	b gripping	c hooking
3	a one-	b single-	c mono-
4	a leave	b put	c drop
5	a book worm	b bookworm	c well-read
6	a appreciated	b interesting	c avid
7	a readable	b understanding	c alive
8	a emotionally involved	b moving	c movable

4 **a** Work in small groups. Make a list of books which could be described by the words from the box.

> gripping   based on a true story   moving
> a best-seller   readable

b Discuss the books on your list.

The Da Vinci Code is a best-seller. It's very readable and quite gripping.

Listening

5 **a** 🔘 1.14 Listen to three people answering some of the questions below. Which questions do they answer? Make notes on what they say.

1 Who is your favourite fictional character?
2 How do you visualise them (what do they look like)?
3 What personal traits (characteristics) do they possess?
4 What memorable things do they do?
5 What problems do they overcome?
6 Do you know anyone like them in real life?

b Listen again and check.

6 **a** Make notes on your own answers to the questions in exercise 5a.

b Work in small groups and discuss your favourite fictional characters.

Reading

7 Read the book extracts (1–6). Decide which extract describes the types of character below (a–f). There may be more than one possible answer.

a a dangerous character
b a middle-aged and not very handsome character
c a character who is probably very bossy and talkative
d a very active child
e a character who probably has a tough job outdoors
f a character who is old but has a youthful mind

8 Work in small groups. Read the extracts again and discuss the questions.

1 What type of person is being described in each extract?
2 What physical details are included? Do they show the people's character?
3 What actions are described? How do these reveal the people's character?
4 Do any of the people sound attractive? Why/Why not?
5 What type of book do you think it is from (funny, serious, etc.)?
6 Which person do you think is the most/least attractive? Why?
7 Would you like to read any of the books?

1

For one thing he was unlike any other man we'd ever seen – or heard of, if it came to that. With his weather-beaten face, wide teeth-crammed mouth, and far-seeing blue eyes, he looked like some wigwam warrior stained with suns and heroic slaughter. (*The Edge of Day* – Laurie Lee)

2

My father is still living, but less and less. Judge James Charles Endicott Jackson … that tall, lean, hollow-cheeked man who had made such a religion of the law, preached from the head of our dining-room table each evening of my young life. (*The Best Revenge* – Sol Stein)

3

Nola is a tomboy, a hell-raiser, a maverick, and she's captured my heart like no other. She's got the broad choppy legs of an athletic boy and the scowl of an old maid. No matter how many baths she takes, she manages to smell unwashed. She stands in the sunlight, an amber specimen in a glass jar, still as an Indian or a stone. Then quick as an insect, she sparks into action, running down the hill where the wasps won't follow, stepping on the dried brown grass. (*The Stuntman's Daughter* – Alice Blanchard)

4

He was 55, but he could have been ten years either side of that. Thin sandy hair, a big awkward mouth. Bad teeth, crooked and dark when he smiled, jug-handle ears. As a self-conscious boy he'd tried different things with those ears. He'd made an elasticised band with elaborate leather flaps to flatten his ears while he slept. He'd tried his hair short. He'd tried it long. He'd tried all kinds of hats. Eventually he'd grown the moustache as a kind of diversionary tactic, and he'd kept it. (*The Idea of Perfection* – Kate Grenville)

5

Her grandmother was small and thin, with tiny hands and feet – fast-moving feet the size of a child's – and washed-out red frizzy hair that she dyed the colour of Red Delicious apples. She had disappearing lips, painted large, twice their size, the colour of plums. All her life, she'd been a dancer, every kind of dancer. Even now, at 75, she'd put on tights and a leotard and tutu, and do her ballet exercises in front of the long mirror on Alyssa's bedroom door. (*Blister* – Susan Shreve)

6

He was just a hot-headed, 20-year-old kid at the time, but he was greasy-fast with a gun. The problem was that he was spoiling for a fight and got it. At over six feet and 190 pounds, he was a big boy and he had set out to prove to everyone that he was a man to reckon with. (*Slade* – Robert Dyer)

Vocabulary | compound words

9 Work in pairs. Look at the <u>underlined</u> compound words in the extracts and answer the questions.

1 All of the extracts on page 40 except one contain compound adjectives. Which one contains only a compound noun?

2 Which compound adjectives describe someone's character? Which describe something physical?

3 Sometimes we can guess the meaning of compound adjectives. Which compound adjectives in the extracts are easy to guess because they have a literal (non-idiomatic) meaning?

4 What compound adjectives do you think would describe people with the characteristics below?

> work hard   keep an open mind
> look good   think freely   love fun

10 a Read sentences 1–8 below. Work in pairs and explain in your own words what the <u>underlined</u> compound adjectives mean.

1 He's <u>single-minded</u>. It took him ten years to learn the violin and he never gave up!

2 She's very <u>self-sufficient</u> for a child. She makes her own food and entertains herself for hours.

3 Writers have to be <u>thick-skinned</u>. Lots of people criticise their work, but they try not to get upset.

4 He's so <u>kind-hearted</u>. He always helps everybody even if he's busy.

5 They can be rather <u>stand-offish</u>. At the party they refused to talk to anybody.

6 He's very <u>career-orientated</u>. He even reads about law when he's on holiday.

7 They're really <u>level-headed</u>. Even when they won all that money they didn't get too excited.

8 I'm a bit <u>absent-minded</u>. I keep forgetting where I put my glasses.

b Are the compound adjectives positive, negative or neutral?

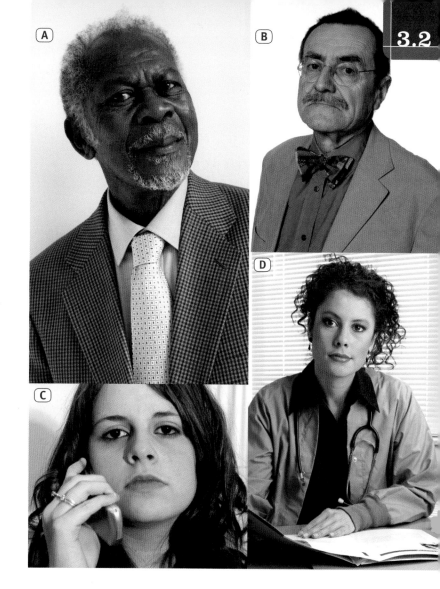

Speaking

11 a Look at the photos and write down compound adjectives to describe each person.

b Work in pairs and compare your opinions of each person.

12 Read the How to... box and prepare to write a short description of someone you know well. Make notes about first impressions, physical details, character, etc. Use compound words.

How to... describe people	
First impressions	*She comes across as ... (adjective) ... but once you get to know her, she's ... (adjective)*
	The thing that strikes you about ... is that ...
Character – good things and bad things	*The thing I (don't) like about ... is ...*
	What I (don't) really like about ... is ...
	He's so + (adjective)
	He's such a (+ adjective) + person/man, etc.
	He can be a bit ... (negative adjective)

13 Describe your person to the rest of the class. Did any of the descriptions sound similar?

Grammar	participle clauses
Can do	tell a humorous story

Reading

1 Work in pairs and discuss the questions.

1 Do you have any favourite comedians?
2 Which comedians are famous in your country?
3 Have they made any films?

2 Read about Groucho Marx. Guess the answer to the question at the end of each section.

1 Julius Henry Marx was born in New York into a poor but loving family on 2 October 1890. His father worked at home as a tailor and his mother, Minnie, worked as a promoter for her brother, comedian Al Shean. Growing up with a comedian in the family would have important consequences later. But, as a child, Groucho's first love was reading. He was also an extremely good singer.

What happened next?
a He became a singer.
b He wrote a book.
c He started performing with his uncle.

Go to 4 to find out.

2 Groucho became host of a radio show called *You Bet Your Life*. It was so popular that they moved it to TV. Groucho would interview the contestants and ad-lib jokes. Some of the more memorable questions included: 'What colour is the White House?' and 'Who is buried in Grant's Tomb?' Returned now to national prominence, Groucho embarked on his solo film career, with a string of films throughout the 50s and 60s. But by now he was entering his 70s.

What happened next?
a Groucho went to live in the Bahamas, for health reasons.
b Groucho started writing fiction.
c Groucho returned to fame in the Seventies.

Go to 8 to find out.

3 Desperately attempting to win some money, Groucho met Irving Thalberg, a big name in Hollywood, during a card game. Thalberg, impressed with his new friend's act, helped the Marx Brothers to get established in the movie business. In the 30s and early 40s, the brothers made their most famous films: *A Night at the Opera* (1935) and *A Day at the Races* (1937).

What happened next?
a Groucho got sick and then retired.
b The Marx Brothers disbanded.
c The brothers set up their own production company, which made them rich.

Go to 5 to find out.

4 At the age of 14, he began singing with the LeRoy Trio. His first tour wasn't a great experience. Having been left behind in Colorado, Groucho had to work his way back home. At this stage he wanted to become a doctor, but his mother had other plans for him.

What happened next?
a He ran away to study medicine.
b Groucho and his brothers formed a musical act.
c Groucho won a TV competition.

Go to 7 to find out.

King of the Jokers

5 Following a film called *The Big Store* (1941), the Marx Brothers disbanded. It seemed as though Groucho was going to fade into obscurity, when suddenly another opportunity arose.

What happened?
a He started a radio show.
b He became a politician.
c He was invited to perform in front of the British royal family.

Go to 2 to find out.

6 After suffering a severe stroke, Minnie died. Then the stock market crashed, signalling the beginning of the Great Depression. After hitting the heights of fame and fortune, suddenly Groucho and his brothers had lost everything. Depressed by the situation, Groucho began to suffer from insomnia, a condition that would plague him for the rest of his life.

How did the Marx Brothers recover in the 1930s?
a They invested in property.
b They toured the world, playing in small theatres.
c They started making films.

Go to 3 to find out.

7 Groucho and his brothers, encouraged by their ambitious mother, formed a group called The Six Mascots. Having been no more than a moderate success, one day they suddenly started cracking jokes on stage. The audience loved it. Being funny came naturally to them. Soon the Marx Brothers were performing in the best venues all over the country. Groucho, with his fast-talking characters, chicken-walk, painted-on moustache, big glasses, and a cigar that he never smoked, was the star. Then everything changed in 1929.

What happened in 1929?
a The brothers' mother died and Groucho lost all his money.
b Groucho went to live on a Pacific island.
c The brothers argued about money and split up their act.

Go to 6 to find out.

8 Groucho made a comeback in the 1970s, with a live one-man show. But with his health failing, he retired. He died of pneumonia in 1977 at the age of 86, three days after Elvis Presley. Voted the fifth greatest comedy act ever by his fellow comedians in a 2005 poll, Groucho lives on, at least in memory. His films may not be watched much these days, but everyone recognises those famous glasses with the fake nose and moustache.

THE END

3 **a** Do you think the following statements about Groucho Marx are true? Write D (definitely), P (probably), PN (probably not) or DN (definitely not).

1 He had a hard life. ☐
2 He had a great relationship with his mother. ☐
3 He had a great relationship with his brothers. ☐
4 He had a long career. ☐
5 He was a lucky man. ☐
6 His type of humour is still funny today. ☐

b Work in pairs and compare your answers. Give reasons.

4 **a** ⬤ 1.15 Listen to someone describing Groucho Marx's life. What mistakes does she make?

b Work in pairs and compare your answers.

Grammar | participle clauses

5 **a** Read rule A in the Active grammar box and find an example of a past participle and a present participle in section 3 of the article on page 42.

b Read rule B and find an example of *Having* + past participle in section 7 of the article.

c Read rule C and find an example in section 6 of the article.

d Read rule D and find an example in section 1 of the article.

Active grammar

The article on page 42 contains several examples of participles and gerunds. There are two types of participle: past participles (-*ed* forms) (for regular verbs) and present participles (-*ing* forms).

A We often use participles to add extra information to the idea in the sentence. The past participle sometimes acts as an adjective. The present participle sometimes gives background information.

Returned now to national prominence, Groucho embarked on his solo film career ...

B *Having* + past participle shows the cause of a second action (or a sequence of actions).

Having been left behind in Colorado, Groucho had to work his way back home.

C We often use the -*ing* form after conjunctions (*after*, *before*, *when*) and prepositions.

After suffering a severe stroke, Minnie died.

D We can use the -*ing* form as the subject of the sentence.

Being funny came naturally to them.

---

see Reference page 47

6 **a** Find the mistake in each sentence and correct them with participles.

1 When tell a joke, timing is very important.
2 Work as a comedian must be a great job because you make people laugh.
3 Have become famous, comedians usually get depressed.
4 Making to look out of date by modern comics, old comedians like Chaplin and Groucho Marx are not funny these days.
5 Tell jokes in a foreign language is extremely difficult.
6 On been told a joke, you should laugh even if you don't think it's funny.
7 After to watch Mr Bean and Chaplin, etc., I think physical humour can be as funny as verbal.

b Work in pairs. Do you agree with the statements in exercise 6a?

Vocabulary | humour

7 **a** Match the types of humour from the box to the people or ideas in sentences 1–8. Use your dictionary to check any words you don't understand.

> farce   puns   cartoons
> black humour   surreal
> irony   exaggeration
> satire

1 bizarre (very strange) humour
2 a series of things go wrong, and the situation gets funnier and funnier
3 Tom and Jerry
4 jokes about death and other serious issues
5 word play
6 not saying exactly what you mean, or saying the opposite of what you mean
7 saying something is much more than it is (sometimes for comic effect)
8 laughing at politicians and 'important' people

b Work in pairs and discuss the questions.

1 Do you know any famous actors/comics/writers/films associated with these types of humour?
2 Which types of humour do you like?
3 Do you ever tell jokes in your own language or in English?
4 In your country, are there any special days when people play jokes on each other? What happens?

Pronunciation | speech units

8 **a** ● 1.16 Cover the text below and listen to someone telling a joke. Do you find it funny?

b Why do you think the speaker pauses at certain moments? Listen again and read the joke. Mark the pauses with / /.

Three colleagues, a photographer, a journalist and an editor are covering a political convention. // One day, during their lunch break, they walk along a beach and one of them sees a lamp. He picks it up and rubs it and a magic genie suddenly appears. The genie says 'You can each have one wish.' So the photographer says, 'I want to spend the rest of my life in a big house in the mountains with a beautiful view, where I can take photographs.' Bazoom! Suddenly the photographer is gone to his home in the mountains. Then it's the journalist's turn. 'I want to live in a big house in the countryside with an enormous garden where I can sit and write for the rest of my life.' Bazoom! The journalist is gone. Finally, the genie says to the editor, 'And what about you? What's your wish?' So the editor says, 'I want those two back before lunch. We've got a deadline at 6.00 tonight.'

Speaking

9 **a** Work in groups of three. You are going to tell a joke. Read your joke and try to memorise it. Think about where you will pause.

Student A: turn to page 149.
Student B: turn to page 151.
Student C: turn to page 153.

b Tell the joke to the other students in your group. Whose joke was the funniest? Who told it best?

3 Vocabulary | Metaphors

1 a Look at the picture. Work in pairs and discuss the questions.

1 What kind of relationship do the people have?
2 What do you think is happening?

b Read the story and answer the questions.

1 Who is the narrator describing?
2 What made them the way they were?

Top chefs aren't known for their <u>warm personalities</u>. Assistants who overcook the pasta by ten seconds usually <u>struggle</u> to get out of the kitchen alive. My father was a top chef. We'd had a <u>stormy relationship</u>, but I decided to <u>follow in his footsteps</u> anyway, and train as a chef. It was better than the <u>dead end</u> I'd reached with the job I'd been doing.

After three years I became head chef in a restaurant called The Tortoise. As the boss, I <u>called the shots</u>, but if anything went wrong, I was the one <u>in the firing line</u>. Experiencing the sweaty kitchens, the egos, the closeness, I learned why my father was the way he was. When I began, I didn't <u>have my sights set on</u> anything much – I just wanted a regular job – but soon I realised my career <u>was taking off</u>. The rich and famous started to visit the restaurant and eventually I <u>reached a crossroads</u>: I could either open my own restaurant or go and work for one of the big ones. Then destiny intervened. My father retired and I got his job.

On my first day, I received a <u>frosty reception</u>. No one would talk to me. What was worse, I was <u>feeling under the weather</u> – I had a cold, and my hands were shaking as I went into the kitchen. I held my breath, stood up in front of everyone and said, 'My name is Leah Kleist. You all know my father. Whether you loved him or hated him, I don't care. He is the past. Now let's get to work.' And we did.

2 Match the <u>underlined</u> metaphors from the story with the definitions below.

Describing life as a journey

1 do the same things someone did before you
2 with no progress possible
3 start to become successful
4 a time when you have to decide about your future

Describing character/feelings as weather

5 friendly character
6 with arguments and strong feelings
7 unfriendly welcome
8 ill

Describing business as war

9 fight
10 make the important decisions
11 responsible if something goes wrong
12 have a goal/an objective

3 Complete sentences 1–8 with the metaphors from the story.

1 I went to the doctor because I was feeling a bit _____ the _____ .
2 We tried to develop the project, but soon we'd reached a _____ _____ .
3 They're always shouting and screaming at each other. They definitely have a _____ _____ !
4 I'm the chief executive and major decision-maker, so I have to _____ _____ shots.
5 My career began to _____ _____ when I landed a role in a TV series.
6 As the manager, you are _____ the _____ line when things go wrong.
7 She had her sights _____ _____ fame and fortune so she went to Hollywood.
8 Will you follow _____ your mother's _____ or work in a different field?

4 Work in pairs. Talk about the topics below.

• something you struggled to do
• a dead-end job you'd hate
• something you have your sights set on
• someone whose footsteps you'd like to follow in
• someone who'd get a frosty reception in your home

5 a Write metaphors for the things below. They can be metaphors you know, or you can make up your own.

a good/bad person
a good looking man/woman
a problem   a boss   life
an easy task
a husband/wife   a city

a good person – an angel

b Work in pairs. Take turns to read your metaphors. Your partner guesses what it describes.

1 Work in small groups. Read the openings to some pieces of fiction (1–8) and discuss the questions below.

1 What can you guess about each story? What type of story might it be?

2 Which extracts make you want to read more? Why?

3 Look at the ideas below for how to write a great opening line for a story. Which story openings (1–8) match the ideas in the notes?

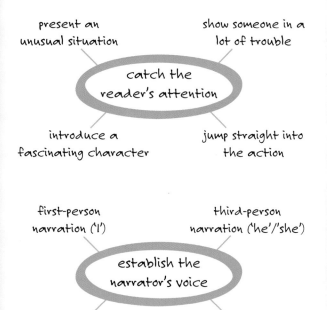

present an unusual situation

show someone in a lot of trouble

catch the reader's attention

introduce a fascinating character

jump straight into the action

first-person narration ('I')

third-person narration ('he'/'she')

establish the narrator's voice

humorous/ informal/'spoken' style

serious/formal/ literary style

2 **a** You are going to write a story called 'Truth and Lies'. Think of an opening sentence for your story and write it down.

b Pass your sentence to another student. Write a continuation of the story.

c Check your story. Does it continue logically from the opening line? Does it have a beginning, middle and end?

d Work in small groups. Take turns to read out your stories. Which was the best opening line? Which was the best story? Why?

1 All happy families are alike; each unhappy family is unhappy in its own way. (*Anna Karenina* – Leo Tolstoy)

2 I'm often asked what it's like to be married to a genius. The question used to please me … (*The Mind-Body Problem* – Rebecca Goldstein)

3 In my younger and more vulnerable years, my father gave me some advice I've been turning over in my mind ever since. (*The Great Gatsby* – F. Scott Fitzgerald)

4 It is a truth universally acknowledged, that a single man in possession of a good fortune must be in want of a wife. (*Pride and Prejudice* – Jane Austen)

5 As Gregor Samsa awoke one morning from uneasy dreams, he found himself transformed in his bed into a gigantic insect. (*Metamorphosis* – Franz Kafka)

6 All children, except one, grow up. (*Peter Pan* – J.M. Barrie)

7 Someone must have been telling lies about Joseph K, for without having done anything wrong he was arrested one fine morning. (*The Trial* – Franz Kafka)

8 He was an inch, perhaps two, under six feet, powerfully built, and he advanced straight at you with a slight stoop of the shoulders, head forward, and a fixed from-under stare which made you think of a charging bull. (*Lord Jim* – Joseph Conrad)

Narrative tenses (review)

We often use narrative tenses together in order to make the order of events in a story clear.

Use the Past Simple to talk about completed actions in the past:

*We **went** to Paraguay last year.*

The Past Simple can be used for short actions, long actions or repeated actions.

Use the Past Continuous to talk about actions in progress at a particular time in the past:

*We **were talking** about her when she walked in.*

We often use the Past Continuous to set the scene in a narrative:

*The sun **was shining** and the children **were playing** in the garden. Suddenly ...*

Use the Past Perfect Simple to talk about completed actions that happened before another action in the past. The Past Perfect Simple is only used when we refer to two actions/moments in the past:

*She took out a DVD, but I**'d already seen** it.*

We <u>don't</u> need the Past Perfect when we are describing past events in chronological order:

*We **ordered** the food, **ate** and **paid**.*

Use the Past Perfect Continuous to talk about actions or situations which continued up to the moment in the past that we are talking about:

*Before he gave up, he**'d been smoking** for years.*

The Past Perfect Continuous is often used to show the reasons for a situation:

*He was angry because he**'d been waiting** for ages.*

Participle clauses

We can use participle clauses in many ways.

As reduced relative clauses. Instead of complete verbs, we use a participle clause:

*I recognise the man **who is sitting** over there.*
*→ I recognise the man **sitting** over there.*

We can use participle clauses like full adverbial clauses, expressing cause, result, conditions, etc. Adverbial participle clauses sound formal and are more common in writing than speech.

***Feeling hungry**, he bought a cake.*
*= **Because he was feeling hungry**, he bought a cake. (cause)*

Having + past participle is a special form that shows the cause of a second action/a sequence of actions.

***Having run the marathon**, he was exhausted.*
*= **After running the marathon**, he was exhausted.*

We can use participle clauses after many conjunctions and prepositions, e.g. *as, after, before, since, when, once, without, in spite of*.

***Before leaving**, he gave me a present.*

*He swam **in spite of having** a sore arm.*

We can also use participle clauses as the subject of the sentence.

***Talking** is the best therapy.*

The subject of the participle clause is usually the same as the subject in the main clause.

***Running** around till they were tired, the kids had fun. (= the kids ran and the kids had fun)*

NOT: ~~*Waiting for hours, the day seemed to Tom as if it would never end.*~~ *(Tom was waiting; the day wasn't.)*

Key vocabulary

Tales

plot   biographical sketch   fake   myth   tall story
fairy tale   legend   anecdote   punch line   joke
tell a white lie   spread rumours   a bit of a gossip
elaborate hoax   prone to exaggeration

Books

it's very readable   I was hooked
it was quite moving/gripping   bookworm
the characters are one-dimensional   a best-seller
based on a true story   avid reader   depict
emotionally involved   come alive
I couldn't put (it) down

Compound words

single-minded   self-sufficient   thick-skinned
kind-hearted   stand-offish   career-orientated
level-headed   absent-minded

Humour

farce   puns   cartoons   black humour   surreal
irony   exaggeration   satire

Metaphors

follow in his footsteps   reach a crossroads
a career takes off   a dead-end job   frosty reception
feel under the weather   stormy relationship
warm personality   a struggle   have your sights set on
call the shots   in the firing line

Listen to the explanations and vocabulary.

ACTIVEBOOK

   see Writing bank page 157

1 Find seven mistakes with narrative tenses in the article and correct them.

In April 2000 journalists at *Esquire* were deciding that life at the magazine was getting a bit boring. So they published an article about FreeWheelz, an Internet company that gave customers free cars which were covered in advertising. The article had claimed that FreeWheelz 'will transform the auto industry more than Henry Ford did'. The company didn't yet become famous but it would 'on 1 April, when FreeWheelz launches on the web for real'. Readers who were seeing the website, which had been created by the author of the article, were impressed. Within days, the site had been receiving over a thousand hits and messages from other entrepreneurs who claimed they had been planning similar businesses. The website contained a questionnaire for potential clients which was including a number of bizarre questions such as 'Does hair loss concern you?' In the following edition, the magazine owned up, explaining that the article had been an April Fools' hoax. The magazine prepared to forget all about it when suddenly an offer for the domain name FreeWheelz came in. The author of the article sold the name for $25,000, splitting the profits with the owners of the magazine. The conclusion? Never trust a strange story which contains the date 1 April.

2 Rewrite the sentences so that they have the same meaning. Use participle clauses with the correct form of the verb in brackets.

Because we couldn't find our way, we had to turn back. (lose)

Lost, we had to turn back.

Robbie ate all the cherries and then he was sick. (have/eat)

Having eaten all the cherries, Robbie was sick.

1 Life's biggest pleasure is when you do things for other people. (do)

2 Anyone who wishes to take the exam must register in June. (wish)

3 Most of the dead animals that were found after the earthquake were domestic pets. (find)

4 Because she felt sleepy, Luisa went to bed. (feel)

5 When you swim, it is compulsory that you wear a bathing cap. (swim)

6 He had been famous for years, and he finally wanted some peace and quiet. (have/be)

7 As they were banned from exhibiting their paintings in the national exhibition, they decided to set up their own. (ban)

8 David woke up early as usual and looked out of the window. (wake up)

3 Put the underlined letters in order.

Posted by Nico
I am a complete bookworm and I'm a particularly (1) ivda reader of Spike Davies's fiction. I found his latest book, *Charms*, a real (2) eapg-eutnrr. It's full of (3) albkc uhroum, which made me laugh aloud. I was absolutely (4) odehko.

[posted 16:41, viewed 10 times]

Posted by Nina J
Whilst I'd say that *Charms* is very (5) rbadlaee, I thought that the characters were a bit (6) oen-idsilanomne compared to normal. His previous book, which was (7) edbsa on a true story, was very (8) ggniprpi – in fact I (9) ulcdno't tup ti dnow. I wasn't surprised it became a (10) sebt-lelres. But *Charms* seems a bit self-conscious. There are too many weak (11) sunp and it lacks the clever (12) ynior of his best work.

[posted 17:22, viewed 8 times]

Posted by Olivier
His first novels were very (13) ogmniv – I cried about five times when reading *Brain Food* – but those were (14) siildecafntoi accounts of things that really happened to him. His recent novels don't (15) etdipc the same type of characters or situations. They all have (16) rlsuare plots that don't make sense and aren't funny. I've lost interest in his work.

[posted 20:05, viewed 3 times]

4 Complete the dialogues by adding one word.
A: He's the new boss, isn't he?
B: Yes, he _____ the shots.
Yes, he calls the shots.

1 A: How are you?
  B: I'm feeling a bit under _____ weather, actually.

2 A: How are Julia and Antonio?
  B: Well, they seem to have a very stormy _____ .

3 A: In 1988 you became Head of Exports. Is that right?
  B: Yes, that's when my career really took _____ .

4 A: So are you going to become a carpenter too?
  B: No. I really don't want to follow in my father's _____ .

5 A: I don't know whether to get a job or continue with my education.
  B: It seems you've _____ a crossroads in your life.

6 A: So she takes responsibility for all the decisions?
  B: Yes, she's the one in the _____ line.

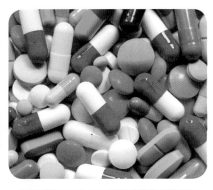

Lead-in

1 Look at the photos, which all show types of progress. Work in pairs and discuss the questions.

1 What types of progress are shown in the photos?
2 What developments have there been recently?
3 What developments might there be in the future?

2 **a** Match the news headlines (1–4) to a photo.

1 Resistance to antibiotics on the increase
2 New virus destroys global computer systems
3 Human cloning to make spare parts for children
4 Space mission in danger as budget crisis grows

b Match the words/phrases from the box to the news headlines in exercise 2a.

> network   cell   crash a system   organ   hacker   skin tissue   gene
> test tube   software   strain   microchip   mission   firewall   orbit
> scan   shuttle   genetic engineering   superbug   launch   analysis

c ⬤ 1.17 Listen to the four news stories and check.

3 Check the meaning of the <u>underlined</u> words/phrases. Then work in pairs and answer the questions.

1 Would you describe yourself as a '<u>computer nerd</u>' or a '<u>technophobe</u>'?
2 Are you <u>up-to-date</u> with the <u>latest technology</u>? Are there any new <u>gadgets</u> you would like to buy/own?
3 Do you enjoy reading scientific <u>journals</u> or watching <u>documentaries</u>? Which scientific areas interest you most? Why?

HOW TO BE A

Speaking

1 Work in pairs. Read the facts and then answer the questions (1–3).

Bigger. In the developed world in the 17th and 18th centuries, men were 165 cm tall, on average. Today the average is around 173 cm.

Faster. In 1896, the world's fastest sprinter ran 100 metres in 11.8 seconds. In 2009, Usain Bolt ran it in 9.58 seconds. The 'impossible' feat of running a mile in four minutes was first achieved by Roger Bannister in 1954. Since then, dozens of runners have done the same, and the record is three minutes 43 seconds.

Longer. In the developed world, life expectancy has doubled in 150 years. In 1850, people were expected to live until their late 30s. The age is now the late 70s.

1 Do you think these changes represent progress? If so, what type of progress is it?

2 In the future, do you think people will get bigger, stronger and faster? Will we live longer?

3 What powers do the superheroes in the pictures have? Will normal men and women ever have these powers? What role might science play and why might governments work with scientists to develop 'supermen' and 'superwomen'?

Got what it takes to become a superhero? For most of us, the answer is a resounding 'no' – things that are part of the day-job for world-savers are beyond the reach of mere mortals. But that hasn't stopped scientists from trying to recreate super powers artificially. And you might be surprised at how successful they have been.

Wall climbing
Gecko lizards are so good at this that they can hang upside down from a glass surface by a single toe. The secret lies in the millions of tiny hairs which are on the gecko's skin. Scientists at Manchester University are developing a material covered with similar hairs that would enable a person to walk on a ceiling or up a wall. One square centimetre of the tape holds a million artificial hairs and could support a kilogram of weight. There is every chance that this system could allow people to walk up walls.

Teleportation
Just as superhero Nightcrawler can teleport, scientists in Australia have discovered how to teleport matter for real – even though it is only on a tiny scale. The researchers have succeeded in transmitting information about small particles across space and using this information to reassemble copies of the original particles. It is unlikely that this method could be used for larger objects because of the vast amounts of information involved.

Regeneration
Both Superman and the X-men's Wolverine can regenerate tissue instantly. * Doctors at a children's hospital in Boston have pioneered a similar way of helping terminally ill patients to re-grow healthy organs. There is every likelihood that the procedure could eventually be used to grow organs for transplants.

Super-strength
No matter how many steroids you take, you don't stand a chance of achieving the strength of the Incredible Hulk. However, there is a distinct possibility that genetics could help those seeking a Hulk-like physique. Scientists at Johns Hopkins University have created Mighty Mouse – a genetically modified mouse. They are normal in every respect, except their muscles are two to three times

SUPERHERO

larger than normal,' says molecular biologist Se Jin-Lee. *
Presumably, it'll also help scientists to better understand
muscle-wasting diseases.

Force field

Superman's hideaway, the Fortress of Solitude, is protected
by a force field. The Defence Science and Technology
Laboratory run by the UK Ministry of Defence has developed
a similar force field to protect tanks from grenades. *

Web-shooter

The US army has developed a device for the New York
police which acts like Spider-Man's web shooter. The nets
are designed to restrain people without causing serious
injury and are shot from a type of gun. The victim caught
in the net stands no chance of escape as the nets come in
three varieties: a regular net, one that can give an electric
shock, and, most fittingly of all, one that becomes sticky on
contact with air. *

X-ray vision

Everyone would love to have Superman's ability to see
through walls. * This works just like an X-ray but without the
harmful effects. While the odds are against the general use
of X-rays because they are dangerous, and repeated exposure
to them is bad for your health, researchers are developing
terahertz imaging for defence and medical purposes.

Flying

* Researchers are looking into the possibility of using
spinning discs to cheat gravity. The original research was
carried out by a Russian working in Finland in 1996 but
so far, no other researchers have managed to reproduce his
results. It is doubtful that we will be able to achieve this in
the foreseeable future.

Invisibility

The Invisible Woman is part of the Fantastic Four. Now a
virtual-reality expert in Japan has created a 'see-through'
coat, which appears to make the wearer's body disappear. It
is done by coating the material with microscopic reflectors
that work like a cinema screen. A tiny video camera is then
attached to the back of the coat. The image from the back
of the coat is projected onto the front of the coat, which
makes observers think that they can see through it.

Reading

2 Read the article and check your answers
to question 3 in exercise 1.

3 The article has sentences missing where
there is a * symbol. Complete the article
with sentences 1–6 below.

1 The solution could be 'terahertz
imaging'.

2 Once shielded by the force field there is
very little chance that the tanks can be
destroyed.

3 Superman, who first appeared in 1932,
has the ability to fly without the aid of
wings or rockets.

4 These crime-stopping devices are bound
to cause some sticky problems for New
York criminals!

5 They can be hit by a bullet and recover
in seconds.

6 'They look like Schwarzenegger mice.'

4 **a** Read the article again quickly. Tick
(✓) the research which you think is
important. Write (✗) next to research
which is less important and write (!) next
to any information which worries you.

b Work in small groups. Compare your
views.

Grammar | future probability

5 Look again at the article on page 50 and the sentences from exercise 3. Underline phrases used to talk about future probability and write them in the Active grammar box.

Active grammar

To talk about future probability we can use special phrases, as well as modal verbs like *will, could, may* and *might*.

Sure to happen	*It definitely will …* *will presumably …*
Very likely to happen	*It almost definitely will …* *There is a strong possibility …* *The chances are that …*
Likely to happen	*It may/might well …*
Unlikely to happen	*There's a slight/remote possibility that …* *I doubt whether …* *It probably won't …*
Impossible	*You haven't a hope of …* *It is inconceivable that …*

---

see Reference page 61

6 **a** Choose the words in *italics* which are not possible.

1 There is no *chance/option/doubt* that we'll make it to the laboratory on time.
2 It's *hopeless/doubtful/possible* that I'll see you again before I go into hospital.
3 They haven't a *hope/doubt/chance* of finding life on Mars.
4 There is a *remote/chance/slim* possibility that the virus will spread.
5 The experts are *bound/sure/hope* to agree with what you have said.
6 There is every *doubt/likelihood/chance* that Superman will kiss the girl at the end.
7 There is *every likelihood/a distinct possibility/any chance* that the antibiotics will work.
8 Is there any *chance/hope/doubt* of you getting the results back earlier?

b What is the difference in meaning (if any) between the two correct options?

7 Rewrite the sentences with the words in brackets so that the meaning is the same.

There is no chance that I'm lending her my laptop. (stand)

She doesn't stand a chance of me lending her my laptop.

1 It's highly unlikely that they will make a breakthrough in the near future. (doubtful)
2 It is vaguely possible that we'll be able to travel to Mars by 2050. (inconceivable)
3 I'm sure they'll notice it's missing. (bound)
4 We can't be entirely confident that the family haven't already been informed. (chance)
5 We're being met at the airport so we don't need train tickets. (presumably)
6 Unfortunately, he doesn't stand a chance of getting the job. (hope)
7 China has a good chance of winning the space race. (distinct)
8 There doesn't seem to be much hope that the relationship will improve. (doubt)

Speaking

8 Work in pairs. Discuss the chances of events 1–5 happening in the next 20 years.

1 We will be able to have holidays in space.
2 There will be a cure for cancer/AIDS.
3 Nuclear energy will have been abolished.
4 Parents will routinely be able to choose the sex, hair, eye and skin colour of their babies.
5 All foods will be genetically modified.

Listening

9 **a** ● 1.18 Listen to an interview with Stan Lee, the creator of Spider-Man. Put the questions (a–d) in the order he answers them.

a Will there ever be real superheroes? ☐
b Why make him a scientist? ☐
c How did you think of Spider-Man? ☐
d Are you at all scientific? ☐

b Listen again. What does he say about the topics from the box below?

> Fantastic Four   a fly   a scientist
> science-fiction   a 'dummy'   diseases   wars
> Mars   genetics

10 Work in pairs and discuss the questions.

1 Do you agree with what Stan Lee says about diseases, going to Mars and genetics?
2 Do you think that 'anything will be possible'?

Vocabulary | arrangements

1 Work in pairs and discuss the questions.

1 How do you keep in touch with your family/ friends?

2 Do you agree with the quotation below? Do you think communications technology has made our lives better or worse?

> 'Modern communications technology is designed to keep us too busy to actually see anyone.'
> (*Paul Mendez, psychologist*)

2 Read the emails below. What is Tom trying to do? What happens in the end?

Hi Maz and Bobby,
I don't know what <u>you're up to</u> this Sunday, but if you're <u>at a loose end</u>, come over to my place. We're going to have a barbecue.
Tom

Hi Tom,
Thanks mate, but I'm completely <u>snowed under</u> at the moment. I have to write an essay by Monday afternoon, so I'll be working all weekend. I've got nothing <u>lined up</u> for the following weekend though, so maybe we can meet then? I'll call you later.
Bobby

Dear Tom,
Like Bobby, I'm a bit <u>tied up</u> tomorrow. Unfortunately, I have to go to my great uncle's house for a family lunch. He was ill so we thought it might <u>fall through</u>, but it looks as if it will <u>go ahead</u>. I really can't <u>get out of</u> it because it's his 60th birthday and most of the family will probably be there.
Maz

OK guys,
I think I should <u>call off</u> the barbecue. Judging from the grey sky, it's going to rain all weekend anyway. Maybe you'll have done your various duties by the end of the evening and we can go for a drink instead! If you want to <u>wind down</u>, I'll be in The Hart, a pub on King Street. Gloria and I are meeting there at about 8.30, as long as nothing else <u>crops up</u>! Don't forget it closes at 10.30 on Sundays.
OK, time to <u>put my feet up</u> and take it easy!
Later,
Tom

3 Read the emails again and match the <u>underlined</u> words/phrases to the definitions (1–12).

1 you're doing
2 happens unexpectedly (a duty or problem)
3 busy
4 planned/arranged
5 relax (usually at home)
6 avoid
7 cancel
8 extremely busy
9 not happen/take place (a plan)
10 proceed as expected (a plan)
11 bored because you have nothing to do
12 become relaxed

4 Complete the sentences below with one word.

1 The match was ruined by rain and eventually we had to call it _____ .

2 _____ your feet up – you deserve a break.

3 If you aren't _____ to anything this afternoon, why don't you come over here?

4 She's finished it so now she's _____ a loose end.

5 A problem has cropped _____ : the printer is broken.

6 I'm tied _____ all of January, but I'll have some free time in February.

7 We've got a good band lined _____ for tonight.

8 I went to the beach in order to wind _____ .

9 Despite the rain, the festival _____ ahead.

10 She can't come tomorrow because she's absolutely _____ under with work.

11 My mum says I have to clean my room now and I can't get out _____ it.

12 Their wedding plans fell _____ when she realised she didn't love him.

5 **a** Work in pairs. Answer the questions below.

1 What are you up to this evening?

2 When do you usually put your feet up?

3 What do you have lined up for next weekend?

4 What do you do when you're at a loose end?

5 Are there responsibilities you'd like to get out of?

6 Have any problems cropped up at work/school?

b Predict what the answers might be for two other students in the class. Ask them and see if you were correct.

Grammar | future forms (review)

6 **a** Look again at the emails on page 53. Which different verb forms are used for talking about the future?

b Match the beginning of explanations 1–8 with the correct endings a–h in the Active grammar box.

Active grammar

1 Use the Present Simple: _e)_
*Don't forget it **closes** at 10.30 on Sundays.*

2 Use *will*: _____
*I'll **call** you later.*

3 Use *will*: _____
*Most of the family **will probably be** there.*

4 Use *be going to*: _____
*We're **going to have** a barbecue.*

5 Use *be going to*: _____
*Judging from the grey sky, it's **going to rain** anyway.*

6 Use the Present Continuous: _____
*Gloria and I **are meeting** there at about 8.30.*

7 Use the Future Continuous: _____
*I'll **be working** all weekend.*

8 Use the Future Perfect: _____
*Maybe you'll **have done** your various duties by the end of the evening.*

a) for predictions you make because of present evidence.

b) for something that will be finished before a time in the future.

c) for immediate decisions made at the same time as you speak/write.

d) for something you think, guess or calculate about the future.

e) for fixed timetables, schedules and arrangements.

f) for something that will be in progress during a period of time in the future.

g) for fixed plans or arrangements.

h) for a personal intention or arrangement.

---

see Reference page 61

7 **a** Complete sentences 1–12 with future forms of the verbs in brackets.

1 She looks terrible. I think she _____ (faint).

2 You've dropped your pen. It's OK, I _____ (pick (it) up).

3 We _____ (get) married in July.

4 Oh no! The train is delayed. We _____ (be) late.

5 Do you think you _____ (retire) by 2030?

6 Sorry, you can't borrow the car tonight. I _____ (use) it.

7 This time next month, we _____ (lie) on a beach in Thailand!

8 What do you think you _____ (do) in ten years' time?

9 She offered to help us at 9 o'clock! That's useless. We _____ (finish) by then!

10 The play is at the Olivier Theatre and it _____ (start) at 7.30.

11 I _____ (write) to you as soon as I can.

12 We can't get there until late. By the time we arrive they _____ (eat) all the food.

b Work in pairs and compare your answers. Which sentences can use more than one future form? Why?

8 Complete the questions using *will* (*do*), *will be* (*doing*) or *will have* (*done*).

In a year's time …

1 Do you think you _____ (still study) English?

2 Do you think you _____ (have) the same lifestyle?

3 Do you think you _____ (live) in the same place?

4 Do you think your country _____ (have) a different government?

In ten years' time …

5 Do you think you _____ (change) much?

6 Do you think you _____ (have) the same hobbies?

7 Do you think you _____ (have) the same close friends?

8 Do you think you _____ (see) more of the world?

Pronunciation | auxiliary verb *have*

9 **a** Read the sentences below. In which sentence is *have* an auxiliary verb? In which sentence is *have* the main verb? How are these pronounced?

1 Do you think you'll have changed your job?

2 Do you think you'll have the same standard of living?

b 🔊 1.19 Listen and check. Repeat the sentences.

c 🔊 1.20 Listen to the questions from exercise 8. Apart from the auxiliary verb *have*, which other words are contracted?

d Listen again and repeat the questions, paying attention to contractions.

10 **a** Work in pairs. Discuss the questions from exercise 8.

b Tell the class two things you learned about your partner.

Listening and speaking

11 🔘 1.21 Listen to two telephone conversations. What is the speakers' relationship? What plans are they trying to make?

12 We use vague or imprecise language when we don't want to (or can't) give details. Listen to the conversations again and complete the phrases in the How to... box.

How to... be vague/imprecise

Give imprecise information about how often something happens	(1) *once in a blue* _____ (2) *from time to* _____
Give imprecise information about quantity, time and/ or numbers	(3) *more or* _____ (4) _____ *of mistakes* (5) *about* _____ *-ish* (6) *in an hour* _____
Give imprecise information about things you do/have been doing	(7) *bits and* _____ (8) *that kind of* _____
Give imprecise answers to direct questions	(9) *sort of/*_____ *of* (10) *in a* _____

13 Put the words in order.

1 We / go / time / to / to / that / still / time / from / café / .

2 We / to / before / bits / various / leave / pieces / going / do / and / we / are / .

3 I'm / pushed / weekend / time / sort / this / for / of / .

4 Her / job / solving / thing / that / kind / whenever / crop / involves / problems / up, / of / .

5 They'll / less / or / here / more / a / for / month / stay / .

6 Because / I'm / a / in / busy, / I / moon / see / my / sister / once / only / blue / .

7 By / time / loads / next / new / I'll / have / this / of / met / year, / people / .

8 We're / ish / at / about / hoping / meet / four- / to / .

9 I'll / at / or / arriving / so / ten / be / .

10 In / home / a / at / I / prefer / on / staying / nights / way, / Saturday / .

14 **a** 🔘 1.22 Listen to six questions. Write short answers. Try to make your answers imprecise or vague.

b Work in pairs and compare your answers.

15 Work in pairs and play 'Twenty questions'. Follow the instructions below.

Think of a famous person. Don't tell your partner who it is.

Try to find out who your partner is thinking of. Take turns to ask questions.

You have 20 questions each and you can only ask yes/no questions. However, you can add imprecise or vague information to your answers, if you like (provided it doesn't make it too easy for your partner to guess who you are thinking of). The first to guess the identity of the famous person wins.

A: Does your person appear on TV?

B: Yes, I suppose so, from time to time. Is your person middle-aged?

A: Yes, sort of ... he/she is 50-ish, I think.

Vocabulary | special abilities

1 Work in pairs. What can children usually do by the time they reach the ages below?

- two years old
- five years old
- ten years old

2 Match words/phrases 1–7 to synonyms a–g.

1	gifted	a	for the future
2	in the making	b	difficult
3	prodigy	c	abnormal
4	adulation	d	talented
5	peers	e	admiration
6	demanding	f	genius
7	freak	g	contemporaries

Reading

3 Look at the photo and words/phrases 1–7 from exercise 2. What do you think the article is about?

4 Read the article quickly. Were any of your predictions correct?

5 Read the article again and answer the questions.

1 Why were Son's parents surprised?

2 What does Son think of his gift?

3 According to the article, what problems do child prodigies face?

4 What is the 'big question' about child prodigies?

5 What answer does the article suggest?

6 Work in pairs and discuss the questions.

1 Have you heard any stories about other child geniuses?

2 How do you think society treats them?

3 What might be the benefits and drawbacks of having a child prodigy in the family?

4 Do you know any children who have a special gift for something?

5 Do you think child prodigies are 'born' or 'made'?

HOW TO MAKE YOUR CHILD A GENIUS

They compose operas aged six, become chess grandmasters when barely out of nappies, and paint masterpieces when their peers can't even hold a pencil. According to educator Maria McCann, 'They are our beautiful freaks'. They are child prodigies, and increasingly they are coming out of Asia, a hotbed of mathematical and musical excellence.

Take Nguyen Ngoc Truong Son. Living in a run-down home in the Mekong Delta, Vietnam, the toddler would watch his parents play chess for hours on end. Before he was three years old, he asked them if he could join in. Fully expecting the pieces to end up on the floor, they let him play. Not for one minute had they imagined what would happen next. Not only did the boy set up the pieces correctly, but he also began playing according to the rules. Within weeks he was beating his parents. Within months he was playing in national tournaments against opponents who were twice his age and twice his size. He became world under-10 champion in 2000 and was a grandmaster at 14.

For Nguyen Ngoc Truong Son's parents, it was nothing short of a miracle. They were teachers who took home less than $100 a month combined. They had not trained their boy to be a chess prodigy. In fact, they hadn't even taught him the rules of the game. For Nguyen, it just came naturally. No sooner had he started playing than he was able to adopt complex strategies. 'I just see things on the board and know what to do,' he said.

How do child prodigies become what they are? The subject has been a constant source of mystery to both the public and scientists. These gifted children have been showered with adulation, labelled as overly demanding, treated as money-making machines, and scrutinised like lab rats. Rarely have they been understood.

Perhaps the key question is whether they are born or made. Numerous studies have looked at the inheritability of intelligence. Overall, they confirm that it can be handed down through the generations of a family, but the studies do not confirm the link between intelligence and the particular traits of prodigies. Prodigies are not smart in any general kind of way; they are able to master highly specific activities and skills. Their reasoning may be no better than average, but they can think like computers, grasp complex mathematical structures, or develop fully realised worlds.

There is one thing that the experts are beginning to agree on, however: the importance of upbringing. Taiwanese educator Wu Wutien says, 'Prodigies are half born, half made.' Only if they are in a stimulating home environment will their natural talents flourish. When parents have a house full of books and interesting objects, read to their child from an early age, take them on outings to museums and places of natural beauty, these all stimulate the child. Parents of prodigies also, typically, allow their kids to be independent. This lets prodigies in the making discover things for themselves such as the way music works or the way the parts of a car engine fit together or even, in the case of Nguyen Ngoc Truong Son, the rules of chess.

Grammar | inversion

7 **a** Look at the examples of inversion (1–3) in the Active grammar box. Find two other examples of inversion from the article on page 56.

b Match rules C–F with examples 4–7 in the Active grammar box.

Active grammar

We use inversion to emphasise the adverbial phrase in a sentence and to add variety to a text. Inversion is often used in more formal texts.

1 ***Not for one minute had they imagined*** *what would happen next.*

2 ***Not only did*** *the boy* ***set up*** *the pieces correctly, but he also began playing according to the rules.*

3 ***Rarely have they been understood.***

A We put a negative or adverbial expression at the start of a sentence (*never, nowhere, not only,* etc.) followed by an auxiliary verb + subject.
  He plays *football and tennis.* → ***Not only does he play*** *football, but he also plays tennis.*
  He arrived *and we left immediately.* → ***No sooner did he arrive*** *than we left.*

B We do not use auxiliary verbs when the main verb is *to be* or a modal verb.
  He is *a great singer and can also dance.* → ***Not only is he*** *a great singer, but he can also dance.*

C We use inversion after phrases with *not*.

D We use inversion after negative adverbs which emphasise a time relationship.

E We use inversion for general emphasis with phrases that use *only*.

F We can use inversion with *no way* in informal speech.

4 *No way am I going to sing in public!*

5 *Only if we start to play more intelligently will we win this game.*

6 *Not since I was a child have I enjoyed myself so much.*

7 *No sooner had I arrived than I had to go out again.*

---

8 Read the pairs of sentences (1–6) and tick (✓) the correct option (a or b).

1 a Not since Mozart there has been a greater genius.
  b Not since Mozart has there been a greater genius.

2 a Only after three did she begin to show her gift.
  b Only after three she did begin to show her gift.

3 a Nowhere do the rules say you can't teach advanced subjects to children.
  b Nowhere the rules say you can't teach advanced subjects to children.

4 a Only later did we understand the truth about our gifted child.
  b Only later we understand the truth about our gifted child.

5 a Not only did he able to write poetry when he was five years old, he also played the violin well.
  b Not only was he able to write poetry when he was five years old, he also played the violin well.

6 a No sooner had we given her a paintbrush than she produced a masterpiece.
  b No sooner had we given her a paintbrush, she produced a masterpiece.

Pronunciation | word stress (2)

9 🔊 1.23 Listen to the answers to exercise 8. Which words are stressed? Check in audioscript 1.23 on page 170.

10 **a** Complete the sentences.

1 No way would I want to ...

2 Rarely do I go ...

3 Not only can I ..., but I can also ...

b Work in pairs. Practise saying the sentences. Pay attention to word stress.

see Reference page 61

Listening

11 **a** You are going to listen to an expert on gifted children describing an unusual case. Before listening, read the notes. What kind of information is missing?

People involved
The case involved twins called (1)_____ .
Physically they were (2)_____ & wore thick glasses. At school, people (3)_____ at them.

Their gifts
They could tell you (4)_____ in the past & future 40,000 yrs.
They could remember long sequences of (5)_____ .
If you asked them about a day in their lives, they could remember (6)_____ .

Conclusions
Their ability = mathematical & (7)_____ .
Asked how they do it, they reply, '(8)_____ .'

b 🔘 1.24 Listen and complete the notes.

c Work in pairs and discuss the questions.

1 In which jobs would the twins' abilities be useful?
2 How else could they use these abilities?

12 **a** Look at the notes from exercise 11a again. Are they easy to understand? Why/Why not?

b Read the Lifelong learning box and follow the instructions.

Taking notes – get organised!

Lifelong learning

! We take notes for different reasons (recording what was said in a meeting, summarising academic lectures, or writing down instructions so we don't forget them). The purpose of notes is to have a written record which we can review and understand later.

Match techniques 1–6 with explanations a–f.

1 Use underlined sub-headings.
2 Use symbols and abbreviations.
3 Make use of space.
4 Summarise the information.
5 Personalise the information.
6 Use more than just words.

a Don't write everything. Only write the most important points, so your notes are concise.
b Draw diagrams, graphs or pictures if this will help you remember the information more easily.
c Don't write whole words if it isn't necessary. This will help you write your notes quickly.
d Start a separate line for new ideas. Grouping ideas makes your notes easy to understand.
e Divide the information into smaller sections. This makes the notes easier to follow.
f Transform the information by interpreting it and using your own words. This makes it more memorable.

---

c Look at the notes from exercise 11a again. Which of the techniques from the Lifelong learning box are followed?

Speaking

13 **a** Work in pairs. You are going to tell your partner about a child prodigy. Read about the child and take notes following the advice in the Lifelong learning box.

Student A: look on page 150.
Student B: look on page 154.

b Use your notes to tell your partner about the person you read about. Discuss the questions below.

1 What do the two boys have in common?
2 Which story do you think is the more interesting? Why?
3 Which type of ability do you think is more commonly associated with child prodigies: musical or artistic?
4 If you could have one special ability (e.g. memorising numbers or words, being able to learn many foreign languages quickly), what would it be? Why?

Kieron Williamson

Nathan Chan

1 a Work in pairs. Read the sentences below. Do you agree? Can you give examples?

1 Now and again, an amazing invention, for example the Internet, accelerates the world's progress.

2 By and large, life is probably better now than it was 100 years ago.

b Underline the two-part expressions in each sentence from exercise 1a. What do you think they mean?

c Match the underlined two-part expressions in sentences 1–10 to definitions a–j.

1 A country cannot make progress if it doesn't have law and order.

2 The city is developing rapidly according to the facts and figures.

3 I learned most of what I know about computers through trial and error.

4 I'm sick of all their petty rules and regulations.

5 Apart from the usual aches and pains she felt all right.

6 These are tried and tested security procedures.

7 Most teenagers would rather be out and about with their friends.

8 When the doorbell rang he was ready and waiting.

9 Let's settle this once and for all.

10 I'm sick and tired of your excuses.

a testing different methods in order to find which one is the most successful

b slight feelings of pain that are not considered serious

c a situation in which people respect the law and crime is controlled by the police

d a method which has been used successfully many times

e official instructions saying how things should be done/what is allowed

f prepared for what he was going to do

g angry or bored with something that has been happening for a long time

h deal with something completely and finally

i in places where you can meet people

j the basic details and numbers concerning a situation or subject

2 Work in small groups. Close your books and test your partners on the expressions from exercise 1c.

A: *Trial?*

B: *and error. Law?*

C: *and order.*

3 Cover exercise 1 and complete the sentences.

1 The police have a tough job keeping _____ in the run-down parts of the city.

2 The documentary confused me with all those _____ .

3 We eventually found the answer by means of _____ .

4 I hated being in the army because of all the _____ .

5 I must be coming down with flu. I am all _____ .

6 If you like the cake, I'll give you my _____ recipe.

7 He won't be at home now. He's always _____ .

8 We really need to make a decision about this _____ .

9 Has Martina arrived yet? Yes, she's _____ .

10 I am _____ of always having to do his work for him.

4 Work in pairs. Discuss the questions.

1 What do you think of the current state of law and order in your country? Do you think anything should be done about it? If so, what?

2 Is there anything that you are sick and tired of? If so, what could be done to make the situation better?

3 Are there any rules and regulations you have to abide by (at home/school/work)? Do you think they are good/reasonable rules and regulations?

4 Can you think of anything that you learned by trial and error? How long did it take you to learn?

5 What sort of things do you do only now and again?

6 Can you think of a decision you would like to make (or would like someone to make) once and for all?

7 Are there any facts or figures you have read recently which you find interesting or surprising?

5 a Write three questions using expressions from exercise 1.

b Work in pairs and ask and answer your questions.

1 ● 1.25 Listen to four speakers talking about important discoveries/inventions. Make notes on what they say.

2 Listen again and tick the expressions from the How to... box that you hear.

> ### How to... present a case for something
>
> *It changed ... completely*
> *It paved the way for ...*
> *It's made a massive difference to ...*
> *It's revolutionised ...*
> *We shouldn't underestimate ...*
> *It has had a huge impact on ...*

3 Work in small groups and discuss the questions.
1 Can you think of any other important discoveries/inventions?
2 How have they changed our lives and/ or made the world a better place?

4 Read about three areas of research (A–C) and answer the questions.
1 Is each area of research valid/likely to succeed/likely to affect your life?
2 Would you contribute money to further research in this area?
3 How could you raise funds to support it?

5 **a** Work in groups. You are going to present a case for research funding. Discuss questions 1–4 in relation to your area.

Group A: present a case for research into space travel.

Group B: present a case for research into how robots can help mankind.

Group C: present a case for research into genetic engineering.

1 What important discoveries do you think might be made in this area in the future?
2 What do you think is needed to make this research possible?
3 How do you think the research should be funded?
4 How will the research affect people's lives?

b Decide how you are going to present your case for research, and rehearse your arguments. Use language from the How to... box.

c Present your group's ideas to the rest of the class. Which group makes the strongest/most convincing case?

A Space travel/exploration

NASA spend billions of dollars every year to send professional astronauts to the moon, Mars and beyond. Now Virgin Galactic is offering to take private citizens into space. They have already collected $6 million in deposits. For $200,000, the paying public will fly 70 miles above the Earth, see the planet's curvature, and experience weightlessness for at least six minutes.

B Robots

Various domestic robots are available which can do your ironing or mow the lawn, etc. Now, some hospitals in the UK are experimenting with 'robo-docs' so that doctors can 'visit' their patients from a distance (another ward, or even another country). Also, scientists are improving robots for space exploration.

C Genetic engineering

Using DNA, scientists can now manipulate the development of life. In 2001, a cloned cat called 'Little Nicky' was sold to a Texan woman for $50,000. Now scientists are researching the use of DNA to predict hereditary illnesses in unborn babies. The scientists could then potentially alter the babies' genes to prevent the illnesses. Many people worry that the techniques will be used commercially, for example, to manufacture 'superchildren' with unnatural physical advantages.

Future probability

Use *will* to talk about something that is definite or a very strong probability.

Use *could*, *may* or *might* to talk about something that is possible but not certain.

There are many other phrases for describing possibility.

Adverbs/adverbial phrases:

it will almost definitely, it almost definitely won't, presumably it will

Verb phrases:

it may well, it might well, I doubt

Adjectives/adjectival phrases:

bound to, certain to, sure to, unlikely to

Noun phrases:

the chances are that, there's a strong/slight possibility, you haven't a hope of -ing

Future forms (review)

Use the Present Simple to talk about timetables.

*The plane **departs** at 14.30 from Warsaw.*

Use *will* to talk about a decision made at the time of speaking (including offers and promises):

*I **don't think I'll have** a coffee, thanks.*

Use *going to* to talk about a plan or intention (maybe details haven't been decided yet):

*I'm **going to work** in finance.*

Use the Present Continuous to talk about a future arrangement (details such as time and place have been decided):

*I'm **playing** tennis at 4.30 with Zara.*

Use *will* to make predictions based on what you know/believe. We often use *think*, *hope*, *believe*, etc. with *will* in this case:

*I think Mike **will be** a good manager.*

Use *going to* to make predictions based on what you can see/hear/think/feel now:

*I think I'm **going to** be sick.*

Use the Future Continuous to talk about something in progress at a definite time in the future:

*This time next year I**'ll be living** in France.*

We can use the Future Continuous to ask about someone's plans, especially if we want something or want them to do something:

***Will you be working** late tonight?*

Use the Future Perfect with time phrases with *by* (*by that time, by this time next week, by the end of February, by the end of the day*, etc.):

*By June we **will have finished** the project.*

Inversion

We use inversion to emphasise the adverbial phrase in a sentence. Inversion is usually used in more formal or literary texts.

The form is negative adverb + auxiliary verb + subject. Note: the word order is the same as the question form.

*Not once **did she** look up from her book.*

We do not use auxiliary verbs when the main verb is the verb *to be* or a modal verb.

*Not only **is he** a great musician, but he can also teach.*

Inversion can be used after restrictive words like *never*, *rarely*, *little*, *hardly*, etc.

*Never before **had he seen** such a beautiful vase.*

We also use inversion with phrases beginning with *only*. These emphasise the first clause.

*Only when I heard her speak **did I** remember her.*

We use *no way* + inversion to show that something is impossible or that the speaker doesn't want to do something. This is informal.

*No way **would I** do a bungee jump!*

Key vocabulary

Progress

antibiotics   virus   human cloning   space mission   network   cell   crash a system   organ   hacker   skin tissue   gene   test tube   software   strain   microchip   mission   firewall   orbit   scan   shuttle   genetic engineering   superbug   launch   analysis

Arrangements

be up to   at a loose end   snowed under   lined up   tied up   fall through   go ahead   get out of   call off   wind down   crop up   put my feet up

Special abilities

gifted   in the making   prodigy   adulation   peers   demanding   freak   abnormal   talented   admiration   genius

Two-part expressions

law and order   facts and figures   trial and error   rules and regulations   out and about   by and large   tried and tested   once and for all   now and again   ready and waiting   sick and tired   aches and pains

---

Listen to the explanations and vocabulary.

ACTIVEBOOK

see Writing bank page 158

1 Rewrite the sentences in three different ways with the words in brackets. There may be more than one answer.

1 We expect the weather to improve in the coming months. (chance/distinct/well)

2 I doubt if they will succeed in contacting us. (remote/probably/slim)

3 We will almost certainly move house in the spring. (likelihood/chance/bound)

4 I don't believe they will offer him the job. (hope/chance/distinct)

5 The organisers are confident that attendance will be high this year. (presumably/bound/strong)

6 There is a slight chance that Thompson could score a goal. (inconceivable/odds/possibly)

2 Choose the most appropriate words in *italics*.

1 Max *retires/is retired/will retiring* soon, so *we'll be looking/look/will be look* for a new manager.

2 Wait a moment. I'm *just coming/will come/will be coming*.

3 By this time next year, he's *going to be/'ll be/is* at school.

4 Will you *going to see/have seen/be seeing* Jade this week?

5 Don't worry if you haven't finished. *I'm working/I'm going to work/work* on it later.

6 I'm sure he'll *make/makes/will be making* a great recovery, whatever the doctors *say/will say/will be saying*.

3 Choose the correct option (a, b or c).

1 No sooner _____ left the airport than I realised I had picked up the wrong suitcase.
a did I   b had I   c would I

2 No _____ should you be made to pay the difference.
a means   b cases   c way

3 Not _____ did they think it would be possible.
a for once   b for one moment   c for ever

4 On no _____ should I be disturbed during the meeting.
a way   b time   c account

5 _____ that I am asked such a difficult question.
a Not often it is   b Not is it often
c It is not often

4 Complete the text with suitable words.

A new problem has arisen in the school. No (1) _____ can teachers afford to lose their temper with pupils at any time. It has been noted recently that some pupils are using their mobile phones to film angry teachers. (2) _____ now (3) _____ we discovered what these videos are being used for. (4) _____ only are the videos sent to friends for amusement, but in some cases teachers' heads have been superimposed on another body to make them look stupid. Little (5) _____ we know that the resulting images had also been posted on Internet sites. (6) _____ no (7) _____ can this behaviour be allowed to continue. In order to curb the problem, all teachers are to ensure that mobile phones carried into the classroom are switched off. (8) _____ before has it (9) _____ so important to exercise patience and maintain high standards at all times.

5 Complete the sentences with the prompts in brackets and phrases from the box.

> put my feet up   more or less   in a blue moon
> time to time   cropped up   fell through   up to
> snowed under   bits and pieces   at a loose end

1 I see her once _____ . (very occasionally)
2 I have to do a few _____ . (things)
3 I'm _____ . (have nothing to do)
4 What are you _____ tomorrow? (doing)
5 I've _____ finished. (nearly)
6 A few problems _____ yesterday. (appeared)
7 I still go to that café from _____ . (not regularly)
8 I just want to _____ . (relax)
9 I am absolutely _____ at the moment. (very busy)
10 The dinner _____ . (was cancelled)

6 Complete the text with suitable words.

In the future, there will be a number of new developments in healthcare to add to tried and *tested* procedures. The development of (1) _____ engineering will be important, not only for curing our everyday aches and (2) _____ , but for repairing skin (3) _____ damaged in accidents. Another development will be the insertion of (4) _____ into the human body. These tiny devices will carry medical information about the person. Machines will simply (5) _____ the individual to find out his or her genetic history instantly.

Scientists will continue looking for ways to cure common illnesses (6) _____ and for all. New (7) _____ will be discovered, to add to penicillin and others, but unfortunately new (8) _____ will also evolve to attack the body. New rules and (9) _____ will be necessary to stop the increasing use of human (10) _____ .

Lead-in

1 **a** Work in pairs and discuss the questions.

1 How many ways can you think of to earn a fortune?
2 Which are the easiest/most risky/quickest?

b Check you understand the meaning of the <u>underlined</u> words/phrases in sentences 1–8.

1 She <u>came into a fortune</u> when her mother died.
2 He <u>haggled</u> to get a good deal.
3 The <u>stock market</u> is a little unpredictable at the moment.
4 The employees have asked for a <u>rise</u>.
5 The taxes will affect <u>high-income</u> families.
6 Warhol's paintings are <u>priceless</u>.
7 The sales team is <u>paid on commission</u>.
8 He's been in a bad way since his business <u>went bankrupt</u>.

c Discuss which ones could be used to describe the photos.

2 Work in small groups and discuss the statements.

1 Art belongs to everyone. Priceless paintings should be available for all to see.
2 It's rude to haggle when you buy something. You should pay the asking price.
3 Paying people on a commission basis makes them work hard.
4 High-income families should pay higher taxes.
5 Gambling on the stock market is a sure way to go bankrupt.
6 The best way to get a rise is to be nice to your boss.

Vocabulary | business

1 **a** Read the proposal below. Is it a good idea or not? Why?

Your task is to help a group of six people <u>launch a company</u> from which they hope to <u>make a living</u>. Here's the catch: the group members are all ex-criminals and a TV crew will film your every move. The employees will <u>be recruited</u> on a voluntary basis and they will need to be team players because the business will be a <u>profit-share</u>. You must provide <u>hands-on work experience</u> to prepare them for the business world. The TV company will provide <u>start-up funds</u>, and one of the <u>fringe benefits</u> for workers is that they will have some TV exposure to help with <u>publicity</u>. However, the business has to <u>make a profit</u> or at least <u>break even</u>, as the TV company will not <u>bail them out</u> if the business fails.

b What do you think the <u>underlined</u> expressions mean?

c Complete sentences 1–8 with <u>underlined</u> expressions from exercise 1a. You may need to change the verb form.

1 We were going to go bankrupt, so I had to ask my father to _____ us _____ .

2 The new company needs _____ - _____ _____ to buy equipment.

3 It's not easy to _____ a _____ as an actor. Many actors have other jobs.

4 The biggest _____ _____ of my job is the free food.

5 After a year, if the company still hasn't _____ _____ , we'll stop subsidising you.

6 We're going to _____ a new _____ in June. It'll sell web apps.

7 Our company is a _____ - _____ . We only get paid if the whole organisation is doing well.

8 The spy was _____ from our embassy in Iceland.

Reading

2 Read the article about what really happened when the programme was filmed and answer the questions.

1 What type of business was it?

2 What problems were there?

Starting up and starting over

One of the world's most innovative florists, Paula Pryke had written numerous books about flowers, founded a school dedicated to floral design, and taught floristry for the best part of two decades. She was the leader in her field (or garden!) and her life was – excuse the pun – a bed of roses. Then she was given a challenge too big to refuse.

A group of ex-convicts arrived at her door. They'd been recruited through advertisements in cafes, snooker halls and launderettes and Paula's task was to train them to become florists. The whole process was to be filmed for a new television show called One Last Job.

Paula was not in the least bit alarmed by working with criminals. The reason she could be so calm was that she'd deliberately avoided finding out what crimes they'd committed. Happily oblivious, she gave them eight days' training. All six of the ex-convicts were hardened criminals, but what they reminded her of was the children she used to teach in a British comprehensive school. The ex-cons fidgeted in their seats, talked at the wrong times, and couldn't concentrate, but according to Paula, "they did know an awful lot about credit card fraud". At least, unlike the schoolchildren in her care, they didn't set fire to the school.

After their training, they were given some hands-on work experience, and then they launched a company called 'A New Leaf' in Islington, London. It was, naturally, a flower shop. In the spirit of teamwork, A New Leaf was a profit-share, owned and run by its staff. Its initial financial goal was to break even. Although Channel 4 had provided start-up funds, the TV company stipulated that it would not bail out the company if it went bankrupt.

All six of the ex-convicts wanted to turn over a new leaf – start their lives again, free from crime – but the project was by no means easy. During the training, Paula noted their unreliability. The thing that amazed her was that they all wanted to be on TV but didn't always appear for the filming. Once the shop opened, even with the advantage of TV publicity, it proved very difficult indeed to make a profit. Two of the owners dropped out and two were bought out of the business by the remaining two, Judith and Cliff, who became sole owners. Paula was not surprised. Six people trying to make a living from one shop was never likely to work. "It was obvious," she says, "that we would end up with only those who really wanted their own shop."

While Judith and Cliff are becoming more independent, Paula says that when an emergency strikes – for example, they have to make a fancy bouquet for the first time at 5.30 p.m. on a Friday – "it's me they call". But the company has survived and, just like flowers, keeps growing and growing.

3 Write true (T) or false (F).

1 The ex-convicts volunteered to be retrained as florists for the TV programme. ☐

2 Paula used to be a schoolteacher. ☐

3 The group started immediately with hands-on work experience. ☐

4 The group always came to work because they wanted to be on TV. ☐

5 There are only two employees left out of the original six. ☐

6 The group phones her every day at 5.30 p.m. ☐

Grammar | emphasis

4 **a** Read rule A in the Active grammar box and find an example of each type of emphasis in the article on page 64.

b Read rules B and C in the Active grammar box and find examples of cleft sentences and a *what* clause in the article.

Active grammar

A We can add emphasis by including certain words.
  1 *own* – to intensify possessive adjectives.
  2 *very/indeed*
  3 emphasising negatives: *in the least bit/at all*
  4 adjectives/adverbs to add emphasis: *actually/by no means/even*
  5 Auxiliary verbs: *do/did*

B We can use cleft sentences (sentences split into two clauses) for emphasis.
  The reason why *we left the party early* ***is*** *...*
  The thing that *most annoys me about it* ***is*** *...*
  The person who *I most admire* ***is*** *...*
  It was *Simon* ***who*** *asked ...*

C We can also use *what* clauses for emphasis.
  What you need is *a cup of coffee ...*

see Reference page 75

5 **a** Rewrite the sentences to add emphasis, with the words in brackets.
  1 He can't complain. It's his fault he lost the money. (own)
  2 We're not certain that it isn't the same man committing the crimes. (by)
  3 I really miss having enough time to spend with friends. (what)
  4 They didn't understand what we wanted. (all)
  5 He didn't stop at the red light. He just drove straight through. (even)
  6 The costs were very high. (indeed)
  7 Sammy always got into trouble. (it)
  8 Keith wasn't annoyed when we cancelled the meeting. (least)
  9 We came home early because it started raining. (reason)
  10 I find those pop-up ads annoying. (thing)

b 🔊 1.26 Listen and check.

Pronunciation | emphasis (1)

6 🔊 1.26 Listen to the sentences in exercise 5a again. Which words are stressed? Practise saying the sentences.

7 Work in pairs and discuss the questions. Use emphasis where possible.
  1 What are the three most important elements of a successful business?
  2 Would you consider starting your own business. Why/Why not?
  3 Who would/wouldn't you choose for a business partner? Why/Why not?

Listening and speaking

8 **a** You are going to listen to five extracts from a radio programme about choosing a business partner. Before you listen, look at the notes below. What information do you think is missing?

The speaker warns against doing business with
(1) _____ .

The only way to get rid of a bad business partner legally is to (2) _____ .

Successful partnerships will combine two types of people: (3) _____ and (4) _____ .

It's a good idea if partners have complementary
(5) _____ .

One may be good in the area of product design, the other in marketing. If your business is lacking in a particular area, you may need to (6) _____ .

Good (7) _____ is essential to ensure that arguments do not interfere with the business.

Ideally, your business partner will be committed to the
(8) _____ success of the business.

b 🔘 1.27 Listen and complete the notes.

9 **a** Listen again. Notice how the speaker uses the phrases below and check you understand the meaning.

Section 1	50-50 partners/family-owned business/make someone a partner/buy someone out of the business/an expensive proposition
Section 2	a strategic 'big picture' thinker/business model/plan/roll up their sleeves/execute the strategy/strike the right balance/strategy and tactics
Section 3	make the business work/product design/marketing background/crunch the numbers/contract negotiation/bookkeeping/hire a consultant
Section 4	communicate directly and honestly/business may suffer/hold back information/jeopardise the friendship
Section 5	start-up phase/an attractive job offer/a life-changing event/the going gets tough

b Work in pairs. Take it in turns to reconstruct what the speaker says in each section using the notes from exercise 9a.

10 Work in pairs and discuss the questions.

1 Do you agree with what the speaker says? Do you know people in successful/unsuccessful partnerships? Why do you think the relationship does/doesn't work?

2 Are you a 'visionary' or an 'operations' person? What skills, experience and qualities would you bring to a business partnership? In which areas are you lacking? Would you work well with the other students in your group?

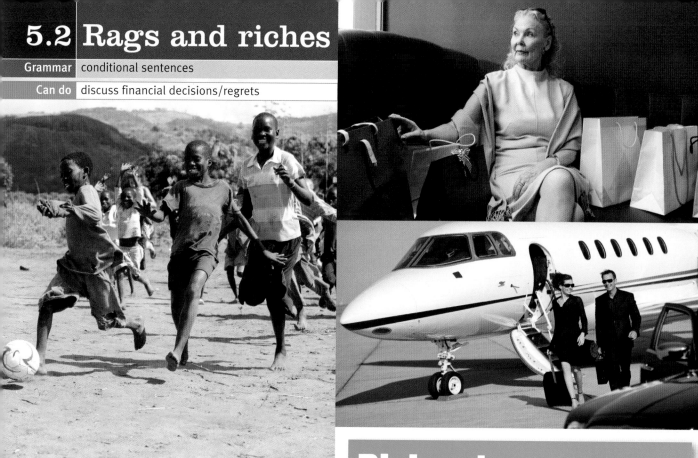

Reading

1 Work in pairs. Look at the photos above and read the statements (1–3). Which do you agree/disagree with?

1 The most contented people are often those with the least amount of money.

2 Whoever said money can't buy happiness simply didn't know where to go shopping.

3 Money is only a tool. It will take you wherever you wish, but it will not replace you as the driver.

2 Work in pairs. Read an article and make notes on the topics below.

Student A: read the article on this page.

Student B: read the article on page 154.

• What type of childhood did the person have?

• How did they make their money?

• Did they invest the money? In what?

• How is their family connected to their story?

• What do they do today?

3 Tell your partner about the person in your article using your notes.

4 Work in pairs and discuss the questions.

1 Do you know any similar stories involving either rich people who became poor or poor people who became rich?

2 What personal qualities do you think are necessary for successful businesspeople like Zhou Xiaoguang?

Riches to rags

Leon Spinks had it all – money, fame and the physique of a Greek god. Then he lost it. The former heavyweight boxing champion had the world at his feet when he took the title from Muhammad Ali in 1978, but his life began spiralling out of control soon afterwards. A combination of bad deals and 'friends' who stole his money meant that within a few years his fortune was gone.

Today, Spinks has some balance in his life. The boxing gloves he wore in his glory days have been replaced by cleaning gloves: he works as a janitor at a YMCA. Spinks earns just a few dollars an hour, supplemented by his other work – unloading trucks at McDonald's. "I get 50% off Big Macs," he says.

The public perception of Spinks is that he partied away $5 million in the time it takes to pop a champagne cork. But that doesn't tell the whole story. If his lawyers hadn't tricked him, things might have been different. "I gave [them] power of attorney," he says. He went into the ring for a rematch with Ali, expecting to earn $3.75 million. He never saw a penny.

Spinks' luck is in stark contrast to that of his brother, Michael, though they were both boxers. They won Olympic gold medals in Montreal and when Michael defeated Larry Holmes in 1985, the Spinks boys became the first brothers to become world heavyweight champions. Michael invested his money in a $5 million estate in Delaware and secured his future. Leon says they're close, and that he could always ask Michael for help, but that's not his style. "I can make it myself," he says.

Spinks wishes things had gone differently, but he's a hero to the locals. In Chicago, he hands out food, drink and clothes to the homeless. Even if he had never been heavyweight champion of the world, they would still love him. The fact is that, after his tough childhood, he might have been one of them if he hadn't taken up boxing. Local children come up to him all the time, thrilled to be in his presence. It makes everything worthwhile for Spinks. "I tell them I was heavyweight champion and if they eat healthy, stay off drugs and grow up real strong, maybe one day they might become the champ, too."

67

Grammar | conditional sentences

5 **a** Read examples 1–7 in the Active grammar box. Are they about Leon Spinks or Zhou Xiaoguang?

b Match examples 1–7 to descriptions a–g in the Active grammar box.

c Find three or four sentences with conditionals or *wish* in the final paragraphs of the articles on pages 67 and 154. What type of conditional are they?

Active grammar

1 *If he/she hadn't trusted others, he/she wouldn't have lost so much.*

2 *If it hadn't been for his/her large family, he/she might not have needed to work when so young.*

3 *He/She might still be producing cheap goods today if he/she hadn't seen the industry's potential.*

4 *He/She probably wishes that he/she had saved some of the money.*

5 *If he/she happens to meet some children, he/she tells them about past glories.*

6 *Should he/she be travelling by night, he/she probably won't catch a night train!*

7 *Supposing his/her family offered financial help – he/she wouldn't accept.*

a) *wish* (or *if only*) + Past Perfect to talk about regret

b) Third Conditional to talk about a hypothetical situation in the past

c) Third Conditional with *if it hadn't been for* to talk about how a negative result would have occurred without an event or a certain person's actions taking place

d) Mixed Conditional to talk about a hypothetical present result of a past action

e) *should* (+ somebody/something) used in formal sentences as a replacement for *if*

f) Other phrases (*supposing, provided, as long as,* etc.) can be used as a replacement for *if.*

g) *if* + *happen to* (or *should happen to*) used with First Conditional sentences to emphasise that something is unlikely to occur or will occur by chance

Other words/phrases can be used instead of *if* in conditional sentences, e.g. *provided that, as long as, supposing.*

***Supposing** you could start a new company, what type of business would you choose?*

6 Rewrite the sentences (1–8) so the meaning is the same. Use the words in brackets.

I'll renew the contract if the conditions stay the same. (provided)

Provided that the conditions stay the same, I'll renew the contract.

1 Would we get to the bank in time if we left immediately? (supposing)

2 I failed the exam because the last question was so difficult. (if the last question ... passed the exam)

3 I didn't have my credit card with me, so I didn't buy any presents. (I would ...)

4 The business isn't doing well because there is so much competition. (if only ... better)

5 You can call me if you have any problems. (should)

6 Thanks to Dr Hyde, I survived the operation. (if it ... might not)

7 They fell out over money and their marriage broke up. (if they ... married now)

8 In case you arrive late, just ask for me at the desk. (should you ...)

Pronunciation | contractions (2)

7 **a** 🌐 1.28 Listen to sentences 1–3. Which words are represented by the underlined contractions: *have, had* or *would*?

1 If I'<u>d</u> gone to university, I'<u>d</u> 've probably got a better job.

2 I'<u>d</u> probably be happier now if I'<u>d</u> moved to Australia.

3 If I hadn't got this job, I'<u>d</u> 've probably got into debt.

b Listen again and repeat. Pay attention to the contractions.

Speaking

8 Work in pairs and discuss the questions.

1 What would you do if only you had more time?

2 If you happened to find £100, what would you do with it?

3 Supposing you could do any job in the world, what would you do?

4 Is there anything which you wish you had done when you were younger?

5 How might things be different now, if you had made a different decision at some point in your life?

see Reference page 75

Vocabulary | finance and philanthropy

9 **a** Read the definition of *philanthropy*. What philanthropists do you know about?

> **philanthropy** (*n*) [U] the practice of giving money and help to people who are poor or in trouble

b Read the article below. Which of the philanthropists have you heard of?

Great philanthropists

John D. Rockefeller once said, 'Giving away money intelligently is more difficult than making it.' He should know – he <u>gave $530 million to charity</u> in his lifetime. Rockefeller's entrepreneurial spirit blossomed early. Aged 12, he lent $50 to a farmer. The following year he got the money back, and <u>charged interest</u>! Decades later, when his three-year-old grandson died of scarlet fever, Rockefeller began <u>investing heavily in</u> medical research. He founded the Rockefeller Institute in 1901, and later his doctors flew around the world providing vaccines for children.

The best-known philanthropist today is Bill Gates, whose foundation has <u>dedicated billions of dollars to</u> projects in over 100 countries. While Gates gives away more money than anyone else in the world, there are many other great but lesser-known philanthropists. Marcos de Moraes, chairman of Brazilian drinks company Sagatiba, <u>funds programmes</u> to keep children off the streets. His Instituto Rukha, founded in 2004, <u>aims to eradicate</u> child labour. Texan oil heiresses Helen and Swanee Hunt <u>make large donations to</u> women's causes. They ask rich women across the US to write million-dollar cheques which are then fed into numerous causes such as <u>promoting welfare</u> for women. On the other side of the world, Indian businessman Sunil Mittal has <u>amassed a fortune</u> in the telecoms industry and is now <u>putting it back into</u> the fight against illiteracy. He has opened over 200 schools and invested in teacher-training and community libraries. His catchphrase is: 'give back what you take'.

10 Work in small groups and discuss the questions.

1 Do you admire the actions of any of the people in the article? Why/Why not?
2 Do you think that, as in Rockefeller's case, tragedy sometimes inspires generosity?
3 Do you believe in giving money to charity? Which causes do you/would you support and why?

11 Work in pairs. Look at the <u>underlined</u> expressions from the article. What do you think they mean? Which expressions have a similar meaning?

12 **a** Complete each sentence with one word.

1 Anyone who amasses _____ fortune is probably either a genius or a criminal, or both.
2 Dedicating millions of dollars _____ a cause is great, but real heroes dedicate their lives.
3 The trouble with _____ money to charity is that most of it never gets to the people who need it.
4 Philanthropists who _____ huge donations set a great example to the developed world.
5 It's better to invest _____ local causes where you can see the results more easily.
6 The rich should _____ their money back into the community, where it came from.

b Work in pairs. Which statements from exercise 12a do you agree with?

13 Read the Lifelong learning box and do the exercises.

Words that are verbs and nouns

❗ Many words connected to business and finance can be verbs and nouns.

fund   charge   launch   experience   profit   recruit   share   benefit

Complete the sentences below with a word from the list above.

1 a The new _____ was excellent at his job.
  b It's getting harder to _____ workers for this business.
2 a He's the philanthropist who will _____ our organisation.
  b She donated money to the _____ for disabled war veterans.
3 a The new law will _____ everyone in this business.
  b The biggest _____ of the job is that we get free healthcare.

Use the other five words from the list above to write pairs of sentences with gaps (one with a noun and one with a verb). Give your sentences to another student to complete.

Lifelong learning

Vocabulary | describing a job

1 Work in pairs. What is important in a job? Make a list of the five most important things for you.

2 Check the meaning of the words/phrases from the box. Did any appear on your list?

> job satisfaction   recognition   good salary
> promotion prospects   travel opportunities
> supportive colleagues/boss   pension plan
> freedom/autonomy   flexible working hours
> professional/personal development
> perks and benefits   working environment
> convenience of location   challenging tasks

Speaking

3 Complete the How to... box using words from the box below.

> about   absolutely   could   main   do   really

How to... express priorities

| Saying it's very important | My (1) _____ priority is ...
The essential thing for me is ...
This is (2) _____ vital!
I couldn't (3) _____ without ... |
| Saying it's not important | I'm not (4) _____ bothered/
concerned (5) _____ this.
This isn't a major priority.
I (6) _____ do without ... |

4 Work in pairs. Discuss which things from exercise 2 are priorities and which are not. Try to use language from the How to... box.

Reading

5 Read the article and answer the questions.

1. How does *Fortune* magazine get the results for its annual list?
2. What makes the winners special?
3. What is Wegmans' philosophy?
4. Why does a manager say that the company is run 'by 16-year-old cashiers'?

100 BEST COMPANIES TO WORK FOR

Every year, *Fortune* magazine publishes a list of the '100 Best Companies to Work For'. How does the magazine choose the companies? Firstly, it uses a survey: 350 employees answer 57 questions about their company. Secondly, *Fortune* looks at important features of companies: for example, pay, benefits, and communication between workers and management. Finally, the magazine compares the results to find its Top 100.

To a certain extent, the results are guesswork, but the companies on the list, by and large, have many things in common: they pay their employees well, they allow workers to make decisions, and they offer a comfortable workplace. Broadly speaking, however, the winners tend to offer something above and beyond the norm. J.M. Smucker, a jam company, gives its workers free muffins and bagels for breakfast; at Griffin Hospital, employees get free massages; a bank called First Horizon National gives its employees time off to visit their children's classrooms. Wegmans Food Markets sent one worker on a ten-day trip to London, Paris and Italy to learn about cheese. This is not unusual for the New York-based company, which is well-known for the scholarships it gives its employees to further their education. At W.L. Gore, workers decide on their colleagues' salaries. Surprisingly enough, the most important thing for employees is not money. It is freedom to develop ideas. Timberland offers a six-month paid sabbatical for employees who have 'a personal dream that benefits the community'.

Let's not forget that all these companies are businesses whose priority is making money. They have to make a profit. And do they? Seemingly, the answer is a big 'yes'. The number one company, Wegmans, makes a fortune. The company, which has a motto, 'Employees first, customers second', is one of the 50 largest private companies in the US, with annual sales of $3.6 billion, according to *Forbes* magazine. Apparently, being good to your employees is no obstacle to making money.

How much of Wegmans' success is due to the company's policies? 'Up to a point, the success is because of the freedom they give us,' says one employee. 'On the other hand, no company gets rich just by being nice. Wegmans has great marketing strategies and it's well-positioned within the community. I've been here for 15 years. Looking back, I'd say that the company's innovations for customers, such as the Shoppers' Club electronic discount programme in the 1990s, have been just as important as the benefits to staff.'

But the employee benefits are striking. Fundamentally, Wegmans believes in professional development. As well as scholarships, the company gives its employees business opportunities. For years, one employee made delicious cookies for her colleagues. Eventually, she started selling the cookies in Wegmans. 'I just asked the manager,' she says. 'With hindsight, I should have asked earlier. I could have made more money!'

The staff's freedom to make decisions is another thing you won't find everywhere. Essentially, Wegmans wants its workers to do almost anything to keep the customers happy. Believe it or not, an employee once cooked a Thanksgiving turkey in the store for a customer because the woman's turkey, bought in Wegmans, was too big for her oven. One manager says, 'We're a $3 billion company run by 16-year-old cashiers.'

Grammar | sentence adverbials

6 **a** Read the article on page 70 again. What purpose do the <u>underlined</u> sentence adverbials serve?

b Choose the correct options in rules A and B in the Active grammar box.

c Complete the table in the Active grammar box with the <u>underlined</u> sentence adverbials from the article.

d Add any other adverbial phrases that you know to the table.

Active grammar

A. Sentence adverbials show how the sentence fits in with the rest of the text and frequently go at the <u>beginning/middle/end</u> of a sentence. This makes the link to the previous sentence clear, though adverbials can go in other positions.

B Sentence adverbials show the speaker's attitude and feelings, and are usually separated from the rest of the sentence by a <u>full stop/comma</u>.

Adverbial functions	Examples
Basic ideas	*fundamentally* *essentially*
Unexpected points	
Generalisations	
How something appears	
Contrast	
Reflection on the past	
Partial agreement	

see Reference page 75

7 Choose the sentence adverbial in *italics* which does not fit the context.

We want our workers to be happy. Fundamentally/Essentially/⟨With hindsight⟩ this means helping them to foster a sense of pride in their work.

1 We believe in giving our employees as much autonomy as possible.
Broadly speaking/Apparently/By and large, we try not to interfere unless really necessary.

2 Our employees don't complain if they have to work at weekends.
On the other hand/Seemingly/However, they do expect to be paid overtime for this.

3 We believe in second chances, because employees learn from their mistakes. *Believe it or not/Surprisingly enough/Broadly speaking*, our company has never dismissed a worker.

4 Employees like to set their own system *up to a point/apparently/to a certain extent* but we don't let workers pay themselves huge amounts.

5 Some employees' salaries were getting too high too fast. *Believe it or not/Looking back/With hindsight*, we should have introduced a pay cap earlier.

6 We studied some large companies. It is *apparently/seemingly/surprisingly enough* difficult, but not impossible, to change the whole culture of a company.

Speaking

8 Work in pairs and discuss the statements below.

1 It's a good idea for employees to set their own salaries.

2 Employees shouldn't have to wear uniforms.

3 Employees should be allowed to evaluate their bosses formally.

4 In future, everyone will work flexitime.

5 Working at weekends will become normal for every profession.

Listening

9 Work in pairs and discuss the questions.

1 Do you know any companies with particularly favourable/poor working conditions?

2 What effect do/did they have on the employees and on the company results?

10 a 🔵 1.29 Listen to an interview with a company director. What do you think of the conditions he describes?

b Listen again and make notes on the topics below.

- type of business
- staff
- incentives
- salaries
- atmosphere
- personal involvement

c Work in pairs and compare your notes.

11 Work in small groups and discuss the questions.

1 What do you think of the ideas introduced at Piranha Recruitment? Would you like to work for the company? Why/Why not?

2 If you were the director of a new company, what ideas would you introduce to help retain your staff?

Vocabulary | expressing quantity

12 a Complete the phrases (1–10) with words from the box.

> most   many   plenty   majority   awful
> handful   few   much   deal   bit

1 as _____ as (a surprisingly large number)
2 a little _____ more (a little more)
3 a great _____ of energy (a lot of energy)
4 _____ of benefits (lots of benefits)
5 not _____ of an expert (not really an expert)
6 for the _____ part (generally)
7 an _____ lot of time (a surprisingly large amount of time)
8 the vast _____ (most of)
9 quite a _____ staff (a considerable number of staff)
10 only a _____ of people (very few people)

b 🔵 1.30 Listen and check.

c Listen again. Mark the stressed words. Which words are pronounced as weak forms?

d Practise saying the phrases, paying attention to stress and weak forms.

13 Rewrite the sentences below using the words in brackets.

1 The government spends a lot of money on defence. (The government ... great)

2 Not as many people turned up to see the race as had been expected. (Surprisingly ... few)

3 The customers generally appreciate our top-quality service. (For ... most)

4 It isn't a huge fee if you consider the amount of work involved. (It ... much)

5 There are more than enough bottles on the rack. (There ... plenty)

6 Three or four people asked questions at the end. (Only ... handful)

7 Most of the workers joined the strike. (The vast ...)

8 The crowds were huge. (There ... awful)

14 a Complete the sentences below using phrases from exercise 12a.

> I'd like to ... this course by ...

I'd like to get the most out of this course by doing a little bit more homework.

1 I think the government wastes ... on ...

2 ... of people in this country ...

3 ... of road accidents could be avoided if ...

4 There are ... women in top management positions because ...

5 I spend ... my time ...

6 There are not ... as there used to be.

b Work in pairs and compare your sentences.

1 Read the dialogue below. What are the two meanings of *fortune*?

A: Thanks to my good <u>fortune</u>, I picked the correct lottery numbers.

B: Yes, you won a <u>fortune</u>, didn't you?

2 Match the <u>underlined</u> phrases (1–9) to <u>underlined</u> phrases with a similar meaning (a–i).

1 I could never afford that watch. It <u>costs a fortune</u>.

2 He's got six cars and a yacht! You know, he's <u>worth a fortune</u>.

3 If you're careful you <u>can live on</u> £150 a week, even in London.

4 I'm not <u>well off</u> but I still have a good lifestyle.

5 That shirt only cost me £15. It was <u>a bargain</u>.

6 I had a rather expensive holiday. Now I'm <u>broke</u>.

7 Great meal! Shall we <u>split the bill</u>?

8 It's my birthday so I <u>treated myself to</u> a bottle of champagne.

9 That business closed down. The owners were always <u>in debt</u>.

a That house was <u>dirt cheap</u>. It's really spacious and it only cost £150,000.

b I'm not <u>rich</u>, but I get by on my salary.

c Neither of us have much money so let's <u>go halves</u>.

d He can't <u>afford</u> a holiday. He's a bit hard up.

e We're <u>in the red</u> at the moment, but the company's finances will improve in June.

f I'm glad you like my new car. It <u>cost me an arm and a leg</u>.

g She's <u>splashed out on</u> new clothes. Look at her!

h You should have let him pay! He's <u>rolling in it</u>!

i I can't go out tonight. I'm <u>skint</u>.

3 Work in pairs and discuss the questions.

1 Which phrases from exercise 2 are generally more colloquial: 1–9 or a–i?

2 Are phrases 1–9 more formal or more neutral?

3 Do you have similar phrases in your language?

4 Look at the photos above. Which phrases from exercise 2 could you use to describe them?

5 **a** Work in pairs and discuss the questions.

1 In your home town, how much money does a person need to live on per month?

2 When was the last time you treated yourself to something?

3 What would you splash out on if you suddenly got some money unexpectedly?

4 Do you know anyone who has been in debt or skint? What happened?

5 Where's the best place to look for bargains in your opinion?

6 Which businesses in your home town are worth a fortune?

7 Do you usually go halves when you go out with people? Are there ever any occasions when you don't go halves? What does it depend on?

8 Are most students in your country hard up? Why?

b Compare your answers with other students.

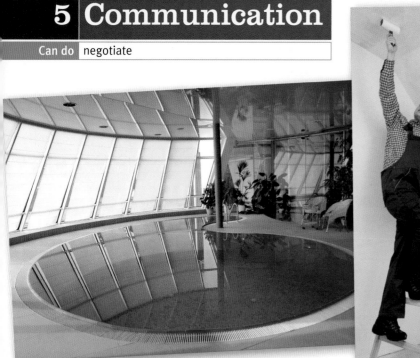 

1 **a** 🔊 1.31 Listen to two people discussing what they would do if their company suddenly had a fortune ($1,000,000) to spend. What ideas do they have?

b How are the speakers' characters different? Listen again and check.

2 **a** Work in small groups. What would you suggest if your company/university/school suddenly had a fortune to spend?

b Compare your ideas with other groups. Which group has the best ideas?

3 Read the profile of Fortune Foods below and answer the questions.

1 What are the company's main strengths?
2 What are the main problems for employees?

4 **a** Work in two groups. Fortune Foods has just received a donation of $2,000,000 from a philanthropic ex-employee! Read the instructions below and decide what the company should do with the money.

1 Group A: you represent the employees. Read the information on page 150.
   Group B: you represent the company management. Read the information on page 149.
2 Prepare your arguments and what you would like to negotiate with the other group.
3 Work with the other group and discuss what the company should do. Try to reach a joint decision.

b Discuss the questions with your group.

1 How did the negotiations go?
2 What did you decide to do in the end?
3 Was everyone happy with the decision?

Company Profile

The company: Fortune Foods

Produces: quality food for parties.

Strengths: the company has an excellent reputation and is growing. The clients are rich businesses.

Problems: workers often stay late at night to finish preparing food. They are stressed. The factory is in a part of the city with poor roads and heavy traffic. It is difficult to reach.

Financial Situation: Fortune Foods made a profit last year.

Emphasis

Passive constructions can be used to emphasise information at the beginning of a sentence:
*The suspect **was arrested** by police.*

'What' clauses

You can change the order of a sentence to put a clause at the beginning which would not normally be there:
***What she thinks she's doing**, I don't know!*

Cleft sentences

Sentences introduced with *what* can be used to emphasise different parts of the sentence:
***What annoys me is** her selfishness.*

We can also use introductions with *it is/it was* to emphasise a later part of the sentence:
***It was me** who spotted the mistake.*

Adding words/phrases for emphasis

*She used her **own** ingredients.*
*We were **very** pleased indeed.*
*They aren't **in the least bit** scared.*
*I haven't thought about it **at all**.*
*Some people were **even** asking for discounts.*
*It was **utterly** pointless us being there.*

Conditionals (review)

To talk about something that is always true, use
if + Present Simple + Present Simple:
***If** you **go** into business with relatives, it **tends** to put a strain on your relationship.*

To talk about a possible, real situation in the future, use *if* + Present Simple + modal verb:
***If** we **find** a bank, we **could change** some money.*

To talk about a hypothetical or unlikely situation in the future, use *if* + Past Simple + modal verb (*would, might, may, could, should*):
***If** they **asked** me to go back, I **wouldn't hesitate**.*

To talk about a hypothetical past situation, use
if + Past Perfect + modal verb (*would have, could have, should have, might have*):
***If** he **had taken** his phone, I **could've called** him.*

To talk about regrets, use *if only/I wish* + Past Perfect:
***If only** I **hadn't told** him about Johnny.*
*I **wish** I'**d thought** of looking it up on the Internet – it **would've saved** so much time.*

Mixed conditionals

These may express a hypothetical present result of a past action:
***If** we **hadn't answered** the ad, we **wouldn't be** here now.*

Other phrases can be used with, or instead of, *if* in conditional sentences:
provided that, as long as, if only, should you happen to, supposing, if it hadn't been for

Sentence adverbials

These are adverbial phrases which comment on part of a sentence. They can be used to: show the speaker's attitude towards a subject; organise information; rephrase information; change the subject; summarise or generalise information, etc. They are usually separated from the rest of the sentence by a comma.
***Broadly speaking**, we all agree.*

Common adverbials: *fundamentally, essentially, broadly speaking, however, surprisingly enough, seemingly, apparently, up to a point, on the other hand, looking back, with hindsight, believe it or not*

> ### Key vocabulary
>
> **Fortunes**
> come into a fortune   haggle   stock market
> high-income   rise   priceless   pay on commission
> go bankrupt
>
> **Business**
> launch a company   make a living   recruit
> profit-share   hands-on work experience
> start-up funds   fringe benefits   publicity
> make a profit   break even   bail (something) out
>
> **Finance and philanthropy**
> philanthropy   philanthropist   give (money) to charity
> charge interest   invest in (something)
> dedicate (billions of dollars) to a cause
> make a donation   promote welfare   amass a fortune
> put (money) back into (something)
>
> **Describing a job**
> job satisfaction   recognition   perks and benefits
> promotion prospects   supportive colleagues/boss
> travel opportunities   freedom/autonomy   salary
> professional/personal development   pension plan
> flexible working hours   convenience of location
> working environment   challenging tasks
>
> **Expressing quantity**
> as many as   a little bit more   a great deal of
> plenty of   not much of   for the most part
> an awful lot of   the vast majority of   quite a few
> only a handful of
>
> **Idioms (1)**
> cost a fortune   worth a fortune   live on
> well off   bargain   broke   split the bill
> treat myself to   in debt   dirt cheap   get by
> go halves   hard up   in the red   rolling in it
> cost an arm and a leg   splash out on   skint

Listen to the explanations and vocabulary.

ACTIVEBOOK

see Writing bank page 159

5 Review and practice

1 Rewrite the sentences with the correct words in brackets. There may be more than one possible answer.

He was offered the job but he didn't accept. (*surprisingly enough/broadly speaking*)

He was offered the job but <u>surprisingly enough</u>, he didn't accept.

1 They explained how the project would be too difficult to manage and I agree. (*on the other hand/to a certain extent*)

2 They didn't know who I was talking about. Georgia left the company years ago. (*Principally/Apparently*)

3 I decided to leave and change careers. I'm not sure that I made the right decision. (*Essentially/With hindsight*)

4 The new arrangements have worked out well. (*By and large/Primarily*)

5 The new minister was faced with an impossible task. (*however/seemingly*)

2 Complete the sentences with the correct clauses (a, b or c). There are two possible answers for each sentence.

1 If he'd planned to give the money back, why ...
   a didn't he contact the police?
   b hadn't he contact the police?
   c would he contact the police?

2 Supposing you lost your job tomorrow, ...
   a what are you going to do?
   b what would you do?
   c you could call me.

3 He can come with us provided that ...
   a he pays for his own meals.
   b he would pay for his accommodation.
   c he doesn't drive the car.

4 If you happen to find my bag, ...
   a could you call this number?
   b just put it on the side.
   c I'd be really surprised.

5 If it hadn't been for Mary, ...
   a you will still be waiting.
   b we would never have found you.
   c everything would have been fine.

3 Rewrite the sentences to be more emphatic using the words in brackets.

1 We weren't at all surprised to hear that she got the part. (bit)

2 I couldn't believe it when they told me to leave! (what)

3 It was very hot soup. (indeed)

4 I think it is surprisingly warm here. (actually)

5 She makes a lot of her clothes. (own)

6 It is not certain that the game will take place. (means)

7 Rachel complained about the service. (it)

8 They have done nothing to put the problem right. (all)

4 Rewrite the <u>underlined</u> words correctly.

1 Those charity workers are always <u>etsegpirn</u> me for money.

2 Handling the takeover was one of the most <u>glanhingcel</u> tasks of his career.

3 The head of department's duty was to <u>cuexete</u> the strategy.

4 Increasing sales has to be our main <u>trioripy.</u>

5 The job has excellent <u>morotipon</u> prospects.

6 Come on! Let's <u>salhps</u> out on an expensive hotel.

7 I'm sending her some money. She's a bit <u>drah</u> up at the moment.

8 Why don't you <u>retat</u> yourself to something nice?

9 Within a few months of opening, he had declared <u>kracynpbut</u>.

10 He doesn't worry about money. He's <u>ginlorl</u> in it!

5 Complete the text with words from the box.

> vision   charity   mind   remarkable   wealthy
> worth   design   fortune   venture   founded

Anita Roddick, who (1) _____ The Body Shop, kept her promise to give away her entire £51 million (2) _____ to (3) _____ . One of the UK's best-known and most (4) _____ entrepreneurs, she started her business (5) _____ in 1976 with her husband. Their strategy, (6) _____ and excellent product (7) _____ meant that the business, selling body scrubs and ethical beauty products, was a fantastic success. Dame Anita was soon (8) _____ a huge fortune. Later she said she had found business life 'boring' and hoped to achieve peace of (9) _____ by sharing her good fortune with those who had not been so lucky. 'The worst thing is greed,' she once said. 'I do not know why people who are extraordinarily (10) _____ are not more generous. I don't want to die rich. Money doesn't mean anything to me.'

Lead-in

6

1 Look at the photos. What sort of 'power' is represented in each? Can you think of any other types of 'power'?

2 **a** Which words can collocate with *power*? Which words can collocate with *powerful*? Write the words from the box in the table. Some may go in both columns.

> tool   nuclear   speech   medicine   spending   argument
> economic   solar   brain   influence   world   political
> people   army   consumer

power	powerful
power tool	*a powerful tool*

b Can you add more words to each column?

3 Work in pairs. Check you understand the <u>underlined</u> phrases below. Discuss the questions.

1 Do you think people <u>have</u> enough <u>power over</u> the decisions that affect their lives?
2 Should more women be in <u>positions of power</u>?
3 Can you think of any countries which are growing in <u>economic power</u>?
4 In what circumstances should police be given <u>special powers</u>?
5 What political changes often occur when a new leader <u>comes to power</u>?
6 Who <u>holds the power</u> in your family/school/workplace?

Reading

1 Read about a TV programme below. Choose the best summary.

1 How modern architecture has been influenced by ancient buildings
2 How architecture is used as a symbol of political status
3 How the Romans invented many architectural techniques

Architecture of Power

No one knew better than the Romans how to gain political influence through the use of engineering and architecture. The Romans built roads, bridges, aqueducts, forums, amphitheatres and baths in order to win over the minds of the cultures they were conquering. It's hard not to be impressed by a power which provides you with clean water to wash in, a road to the capital city, a way to travel across previously impassable rivers, and incredible public buildings.

Architecture has played an important part in public life throughout history, whether as homage to an individual, or as a monument to an institution or ideology. Architecture has always been a potent symbol of wealth, status and power. From castles to cathedrals, from the pyramids to skyscrapers, architecture has always served to glorify the ideal of the time. 'Architecture of Power' explores some of the world's most famous buildings and structures to see what we can learn about their history.

2 Work in pairs and discuss the questions.

1 According to the TV programme, how did the Romans use architecture to increase their power?
2 How has architecture been used through history?
3 Can you think of examples of 'powerful architecture' where you live?
4 If you had money to invest in your town/ city, what would you build?

The Pentagon

The Eiffel Tower

The Forbidden City

Vocabulary | power

3 Complete definitions a–d and example sentences 1–8 with the correct form of words from the box.

> win   gain   impressed   part   by   play   over
> important   be

a _____ : to obtain or achieve something
1 Radical left-wing parties _____ control of the city.
2 We are hoping to _____ a better understanding of the process.

b _____ _____ : to get someone's support/friendship by being nice to them
3 The party wanted to _____ _____ undecided voters.
4 He took her out to restaurants and the theatre, and she was completely _____ _____ .

c _____ _____ _____ : feel admiration and respect for
5 We _____ very _____ _____ the standard of her work.
6 We _____ _____ _____ your presentation.

d _____ an _____ _____ in: to have a big effect
7 Diet _____ an _____ _____ in helping people live longer.
8 Everyone from the cleaners to the management _____ an _____ _____ in this year's financial success.

Sydney Harbour Bridge

The Great Pyramid

Hassan II Mosque

The Millennium Dome

Listening

4 **a** Look at the photos. Work in pairs and guess which structure:

1 is large enough to house the Eiffel Tower?
2 was built to celebrate a king's 60th birthday?
3 was constructed by 400,000 men?
4 is known as the 'coathanger'?
5 takes 20 minutes to walk around?
6 is one of the largest palaces in the world?
7 was built in 1889?

b 🔊 2.01 Listen and check your answers.

5 **a** Listen again and make notes about each structure (size, date built, etc.).

b Work in pairs. Compare your notes and discuss the questions.

1 What does the speaker say about each structure?
2 Which structures do you think are the most impressive or interesting?
3 Which have you visited/would you like to visit?

Grammar | articles

6 **a** Work in pairs. Write some rules for when we use the definite, the indefinite, or no article.

b Check your ideas with the Reference on page 89.

c Find examples of each type in audioscript 2.1 on page 172.

d Choose the correct option to complete rules A–C in the Active grammar box.

Active grammar

A Use *a/an/the/no article* to introduce something new/unexpected. It indicates that the reader or listener does not know what we are talking about.

I bumped into _____ old friend. (This is news.)

B Use *a/an/the/no article* to indicate 'common ground'. It may refer the reader/listener to shared experience or general knowledge. The context is important for establishing exactly which noun is being referred to.

I went to see _____ house this morning. (I told you about this house. This is shared experience.)

C Use *a/an/the/no article* to refer to something in general.

I enjoy talking to _____ taxi drivers. (taxi drivers in general)

see Reference page 89

7 **a** Complete the article with *a*, *an*, *the* or – (no article).

The Sagrada Familia in (1) _____ Barcelona is one of (2) _____ Gaudí's most impressive works. This enormous church, as yet unfinished, is in some respect (3) _____ summary of everything that Gaudí designed before. (4) _____ architectural style of the Sagrada Familia has been called 'warped Gothic', and it's easy to see why. The contours of (5) _____ stone façade make it look as though the Sagrada Familia is melting in (6) _____ sun, while (7) _____ towers are topped with brightly coloured mosaics which look like (8) _____ bowls of fruit. Gaudí believed that (9) _____ colour is life, and, knowing that he would not live to see (10) _____ completion of his masterpiece, he left coloured drawings of his vision for future architects to follow.

For nearly 30 years, Gaudí worked on the Sagrada Familia and other projects simultaneously, until 1911, when he decided to devote himself exclusively to (11) _____ church. During (12) _____ last year of his life, Gaudí lived in (13) _____ studio at the Sagrada Familia.

Tragically, in June, 1926, Gaudí was run over by (14) _____ tram. Because he was poorly dressed, he was not recognised and (15) _____ taxi drivers refused to take a 'vagabond' to the hospital (they were later fined by (16) _____ police). Gaudí died five days later, and was buried in the crypt of the building to which he had devoted 44 years of his life, (17) _____ as yet unfinished Sagrada Familia.

b Work in pairs. Explain the use or non-use of articles in exercise 7a.

8 Find the mistake (or mistakes) in each sentence and correct them.

1 She really enjoys the sport and plays the tennis a lot.
2 If the Mr Hart phones, can you tell him I'm in meeting?
3 There is a cold weather, especially in north.
4 Go down the Forest Street and turn left into New Road.
5 The violent crime is definitely on increase.
6 I went to one restaurant there years ago.
7 The life in London is getting more and more expensive.
8 Katia is ideal candidate for job. She has a great deal of the experience.
9 Maurice has the cold and won't be coming back to work this week.
10 It's without doubt best hotel in an area.

Speaking and writing

9 Work in pairs. Think of two important buildings. What do you know about them? Make notes.

10 Look at audioscript 2.1 on page 172 and complete the How to... box.

How to... describe architecture	
Use superlatives	The Great Pyramid is (1) _____/ probably the most ... It is (2) _____ _____ Australia's best known, and most photographed ... It is (3) _____ to be/It is the largest/ tallest ...
Provide details (size/ description, etc.)	It is built from metal/stones ... The base is ... (4) _____/Covering an area of more than ... metres squared It is over 1km round, and 50m high. It (5) _____ ... of ground floor space. Standing 134m high/above ...
Describe reason for building/ purpose	It was built to (6) _____ the anniversary/as a memorial for/in order to/in honour of ... Built to house/as office space ...

11 **a** Choose one of the buildings/structures you thought of in exercise 9. Write a paragraph about it using your notes and phrases from the How to... box.

b Work in groups and take it in turns to describe the building/structures. Which do you think have been most influential? Why?

Listening

1 a Work in pairs and discuss the questions.

1 What gadgets are the people in the photos using? Why do you think they are so popular with teenagers?

2 Where do you think big companies go to find out how teenagers use technology?

3 What do you think the next big technological development will be?

b 🔘 2.02 Listen and check.

2 a Work in pairs. Discuss ways to finish the sentences.

1 Microsoft began the trend for …

2 Kids drive technology because …

3 Kids want technology that can be …

4 Text messaging caught on because …

5 Teenagers influenced the ThinkPad because …

6 Collaborative computing will be useful because …

7 Converse trainers sent their market researchers to …

b 🔘 2.02 Listen again and check.

Vocabulary | fashions and fads

3 a Match the underlined phrasal verbs in 1–8 to definitions a–h.

1 Using teenagers really to find out what's in and what isn't, what the market wants …

2 … anywhere they thought trends might kick off.

3 They experiment and they automatically home in on the new.

4 Anything bigger than a few inches is out.

5 Text messaging caught on because kids wanted to pass notes to each other during class.

6 … all of these things came about because of the needs of kids.

7 And what's coming up on the horizon?

8 … if you want to keep up with the latest style of trainers, who do you ask?

a start

b know the most recent developments

c focus/direct their attention towards something

d is going to happen in the near future

e is fashionable at the moment

f became popular and fashionable

g is unfashionable at the moment

h happened

b Look again at the phrasal verbs in exercise 3a.

1 Which two phrasal verbs are exact opposites? Are they formal or informal?

2 Which has a literal meaning connected with football?

4 Find five mistakes with phrasal verbs in the article below and correct them.

A new trend is catching off. Budding basketball star, Mark Walker, can shoot the ball into the basket 18 times in a row. On his website, which is sponsored by Reebok, he faces the camera and says, 'I am the future of basketball. I am Reebok.' Mark Walker is three years old. Big business has always homed in at talented youth – the phenomenon really kicked up with Michael Jordan – but now it appears that talent isn't necessary. Horton Chesleigh is even younger than Mark Walker and he is already associated with a brand. His parents, Sean and Deanna, agreed to name him after a character from a Ruffles potato crisps ad. How did this situation go about? The food company agreed to donate $50,000 towards little Horton's education. So, will personal branding become popular? Will we be seeing branded kids walking the streets? Maybe. Jim Nelson had the orange, blue and black logo of an Internet company tattooed on the back of his shaved head. In return for showing the tattoo for the next five years, he gets $7,000. Who knows what's coming off next? Kids called 'Coke' and 'Big Mac'?

5 Work in pairs and discuss the questions.

1 What's the best way to keep up with developments in your job or hobby?

2 Are there any interesting events coming up in your life?

3 What trends have caught on recently (in fashion, music, food, etc.) where you live?

4 How do global trends come about? Can you think of any examples?

5 Think of one piece of technology/clothing that used to be 'in' but is now 'out'.

Speaking and listening

6 Work in pairs. Look at the photos and answer the questions.

1 How old are the people?
2 What are they doing?
3 Can you think of any problems associated with their behaviour?
4 How would you deal with these problems?

7 Work in groups. Which things (1–6) do you think teenagers aged 15–17 should be allowed to do?

1 watch however much TV they want
2 stay up late whenever they want
3 decorate their room in whatever way they want
4 go wherever they want at night
5 socialise with whoever they want
6 wear whatever they want

8 **a** ⬤ 2.03 Listen to two parents and two teenagers. Which things from exercise 7 do they talk about?

b What were their opinions? Listen again to check.

Grammar | *whatever, whoever, whenever, etc.*

9 **a** Look at examples 1–2 in the Active grammar box and choose the correct option in rule A.

b Look at rule B and examples 3–5 in the Active grammar box. Which mean(s) 'I know what you are doing and I want you to stop'? Which mean(s) 'I don't care what you are doing, but I want you to stop'?

c Look at rule C. Match uses a–b with examples 6–7.

Active grammar

A *Whenever, whoever, whatever, etc. <u>are conjunctions that join two clauses together/mean the same as 'if'</u>.*

1 *Teenagers shouldn't be allowed to watch **however** much TV they want.*

2 *Teenagers should be able to socialise with **whoever** they want.*

B We use *whenever, whatever, whoever,* etc. when 'it doesn't make any difference when, what, who, etc.' or when we don't have to be specific. They also mean 'we don't know the exact details of when, what, who, etc.' *What, who, when,* etc. are a little different to *whatever, whoever, whenever,* etc.

3 *Stop **what** you are doing now!*

4 *Stop **whatever** you are doing now!*

5 ***Whatever** you are doing, stop it now!*

NOT: ~~What you are doing, stop it now!~~

C We can use *however* in two different ways:
   a) as a conjunction that means 'but' or 'on the other hand'.
   b) with an adjective or adverb, meaning 'even if'.

6 *He's brilliant. **However**, he's also annoying.*

7 ***However** hard he works, he'll never get promoted.*

---

see Reference page 89

10 Complete the sentences with *whenever*, *however*, *whatever*, *whoever* or *wherever*.

1 _____ you do, don't lose these keys!

2 Send me an email _____ you have time.

3 Carry your documents with you _____ you go.

4 _____ is at the door, tell them I'm busy.

5 _____ you travel – train, car or bus – it will take you at least three hours.

11 Complete the second sentence so that it means the same as the first. Use three words in each space.

1 If it's the last thing you do, make sure you turn off the power.

_____ , don't forget to turn off the power.

2 Even if you're a good swimmer, Thorpe is better than you.

_____ are at swimming, Thorpe is better.

3 Call me any time you feel down.

_____ down, give me a call.

4 It doesn't matter where we go – they always follow us.

_____ , they're always close behind.

5 I'll see her as soon as I can.

_____ , I'll see her.

6 It doesn't matter who we employ – he'll have to be a genius.

_____ , he'll have to work miracles.

7 No matter how you fix this photocopier, it keeps breaking down.

_____ the photocopier, it always breaks down again.

8 Those children can do anything, and it turns out successful.

_____ do, they make a success of it.

Pronunciation | emphasis using *however*, *whatever*, etc.

12 a 2.04 Listen to sentences 1–8 from exercise 11. Which syllable is stressed in *whatever*, *however*, etc.?

b Listen again and repeat, paying attention to stress and intonation.

13 a Think of two pieces of advice for a teenager with *whatever*, *whoever*, etc.

b Work in pairs. Take turns to tell each other your advice, paying attention to stress and intonation.

Speaking

14 a Read some quotes about 'the best age'. Which do you agree with?

Childhood is the time of your life. Everything is new and wonderful and whatever mistakes you make, you're forgiven.
(Suleiman, 25)

The best thing about being a teenager is the freedom. You can be friends with whoever you want, you don't have to work and you don't have any responsibilities except school.
(Ravi, 18)

The worst thing about being a teenager is that you have no power. Everyone tells you what to do. When I was 15 I couldn't wait to leave home and make my own decisions.
(Marissa, 19)

The best age is your 30s, when you're old enough to do whatever you want and young enough to have the energy to do it.
(Mphelele, 38)

Middle-age is when people become powerful. Most business and political leaders are in their 40s, 50s and 60s. After that, it's all downhill.
(Joanne, 27)

When you're old, you see things differently. You're more patient and tolerant whenever there are problems to deal with. You also realise the important things in life are family and friends.
(Riccardo, 70)

b Write six sentences giving your opinions about the ages in exercise 14a. Start each sentence with the <u>underlined</u> phrases at the beginning of each quote.

Childhood is when you have the most fun and the fewest worries.

c Read the Lifelong learning box. Work in groups and follow the instructions.

Planning to speak

! 1 If you have to speak for a long time, then use the 'three Ps'.

Prepare – decide what your main points will be.

Predict – think about what other people will say or ask you.

Practice – spend a few moments alone, rehearsing (silently!) what you will say.

2 Using the 'three Ps', prepare to talk about the sentences you wrote from exercise 14b.

3 Discuss your opinions. Do you agree about the best age?

Lifelong learning

6.3 Charisma

Mohammed Ali

Kate Middleton

Lady Gaga

Reading

1 a Read the definition of 'charisma' below. Can you think of any famous charismatic people? Do you think the people in the photos are charismatic? In what ways?

> **charisma** /kəˈrɪzmə/ *n* [U] the natural ability to attract and influence other people

b Work with a partner and discuss these questions.

1 Who is the most charismatic person you know? In what ways are they charismatic?

2 Are there any dangers connected with being charismatic?

3 Is charisma something you can learn or do you have to be born with it?

2 Read the article and choose the best title.

1 Five Ways to Learn Charisma

2 How to be a Great Leader

3 The Mystery of Charisma

According to actress Joan Collins, <u>while</u> Bill Clinton's looking at you, he "eats you up with his eyes. I don't know whether it's magic or a trick, but it's the best act I've ever seen." Of course, Bill Clinton and Barack Obama have it. Lady Gaga and Mohammed Ali have loads of it, too. And most agree that Kate Middleton, Prince William's wife, has it too. Charisma. **Hard as we try** to understand it, the formula remains elusive. All we can do is watch the masters at work and learn from them.

Perhaps the most charismatic of them all is Nelson Mandela. Colleen Dawson's grandson was in the same class as Mandela's grandson. <u>During</u> one parents' night, an interesting event occurred. The evening was progressing as usual, and the parents sat down to discuss their childrens' progress with the teachers, <u>at which point</u> Mandela suddenly walked in. Dawson recalls that the room went quiet. Instead of the normal chit chat about homework and behaviour, all eyes turned to Mandela. <u>On finding</u> himself the centre of attention, the great man put the teachers and parents at ease and quietly began to speak about the importance of teaching. He found common ground for everyone present – education – and his charisma shone through.

Even though charisma is usually associated with politicians, businesspeople and celebrities, scientist Richard Feynman proved that people in other fields can have it. <u>You had no sooner begun</u> a conversation with Feynman than you'd be struck by his love of the subject. **Despite** the fact that Feynman's field was theoretical physics – not exactly a crowd-pleaser – he had such enthusiasm for the mysteries of the universe that he infected everyone within earshot. The Nobel Prize-winning scientist was a larger-than-life figure, and very charismatic. One ex-student recalls, "<u>He'd hardly started</u> his lecture when you'd notice the whole audience on the edge of their seats."

Most of the great leaders in history possessed an innate magnetism that's now called 'star quality'. Alexander the Great, William Churchill, and Martin Luther King had extraordinary charisma. Lifestyle writer Elena Hawthorne says, "Some people seem to be born with charisma. Look at the likes of Richard Branson or Angelina Jolie. They just seem to have a lust for life that's contagious. But, for the mortals among us, I think there are techniques that anyone can learn: the importance of body language and the way you use your voice." Other experts in the field say that, **much as** charisma can be learned, it can't be faked. Personal development coach Robin Wills says, "It isn't about techniques like making eye contact or touching people on the shoulder. **Although** those things can help, charisma is really about having a genuine interest in people and communicating it through enthusiasm and by really listening."

3 Work in pairs and answer the questions.

1 Does the writer believe there's a simple way to become charismatic?

2 What did Mandela discuss? Why?

3 Does the writer believe charismatic people are associated with particular professions?

4 Why did people want to listen to Feynman?

5 Why does Hawthorne think there's hope for normal, uncharismatic people?

4 Find the phrases from the box below in the article. Work in pairs and discuss what you think they mean. Use the context to help you.

> the formula remains elusive   a crowd-pleaser
> he infected everyone within earshot   a larger-than-life figure
> on the edge of their seats   star quality

Grammar | link words of time and contrast

5 **a** Look at the six underlined time clauses in the article on page 84. Match them to descriptions 1–3 in the Active grammar box.

b Match *when*, *whilst* and *by which time* to descriptions 1–3 in the Active grammar box.

c Look at the five contrast clauses in **bold** in the article. Match them to descriptions 4–6 in the Active grammar box.

d Match *in spite of*, *while* and *difficult as it was* to descriptions 4–6 in the Active grammar box.

Active grammar

There are many words/phrases we use to link ideas in sentences.

Time clauses

(1) It happens soon after another thing.	(2) It happens at the same time as something else.	(3) It comes at the end of a long, continuous sequence of action. It often introduces a moment of change in the sequence OR the result of this sequence.
on finding		

Contrast clauses

(4) phrases that are always followed by a clause (with a verb)	(5) can be followed by a noun phrases or *-ing* form	(6) phrases that use adjective/adverb + *as* + subject + verb to emphasise the contrast

see Reference page 89

6 Complete the texts below using the words/phrases from the boxes. Some of the phrases can't be used.

Two charismatic women

> despite   much as
> by which time   on being
> when   although   during
> hardly had she begun
> hard as she tried

(1) _____ King William IV died in 1837, his daughter Victoria became Queen of England, (2) _____ she was just 18 years old. (3) _____ her reign when she married Albert, and together they had nine children. When he died, Victoria wore black for the rest of her life and was hardly seen again in public. (4) _____ this, she is remembered as a successful leader. (5) _____ her reign, Britain's Empire grew extremely strong, and British society changed in many ways. She died in 1901, (6) _____ she had reigned for 63 years.

> despite   hard as
> she had no sooner
> even though   when
> by which time   much
> on getting the job

Until she was six, Oprah Winfrey lived on a farm with her grandmother. (7) _____ her family's poverty, she had access to books, and she read and preached in church. She got her lucky break (8) _____ , aged 17, she was offered a job at a radio station, (9) _____ she lacked experience. Her talk show later became *The Oprah Winfrey Show*, which is watched by over 20 million people a day. (10) _____ as she enjoyed her TV success, Winfrey's real ambition was to act, and in 1985 she starred in *The Color Purple*, for which she received an Oscar nomination.

Vocabulary | personal characteristics

7 Match the adjectives (1–8) to the underlined words/phrases (a–h) with the opposite meaning.

1 charismatic
2 inspirational
3 dignified
4 aloof
5 idealistic
6 tireless
7 trustworthy
8 resolute

a 'She's a bit <u>lacking in drive and energy</u>.'
b 'He <u>wavers in the face of problems</u>.'
c 'He's very <u>approachable</u>. He always has time to talk to people.'
d 'He's <u>corrupt</u>.'
e 'She is rather <u>nondescript</u>.'
f 'She's very <u>down-to-earth</u> and practical.'
g 'She's <u>not very inspiring</u>.'
h 'She <u>lacks gravitas</u>.'

Pronunciation | stress shift on long adjectives

8 **a** 🔊 2.05 Look at the root words and their adjectives. Listen and <u>underline</u> the stress.

1 charisma (n)
charismatic (adj)
2 ideal (n)
idealistic (adj)
3 inspire (v)
inspirational (adj)

b Complete the 'rules'.

1 Adjectives that end in -ic (*romantic, acrobatic, ecstatic, pathetic*, etc.) tend to have the stress on the syllable before the letters _____.
2 Adjectives that end in -tional or -sional (*professional, international, dysfunctional, irrational*, etc.) tend to have the stress on the syllable before the letters _____.

9 Work in pairs and discuss the questions.

1 What do you know about the people in the photos? Which adjectives would you use to describe them?
2 Can you think of any other famous people who could be described using the adjectives or the phrases above?
3 Think of qualities which would be important for the occupations below.

• a politician   • a teacher   • an actor   • a businessperson

Mark Zuckerberg

Lionel Messi

Angelina Jolie

Shakira

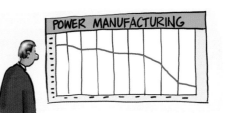

1 a Look at the pictures and make a story.

b Read the story. Were your ideas the same or different? How?

Mr Power's story

1 For ten years, I owned a manufacturing company, but I really <u>had my hands full</u> with it. I never had time to enjoy myself. So I sold the company and retired. But after a few years, I heard that the company needed a new Chief Executive. Bored with retirement, I decided to reapply for my old job. I got it, and I found the job easy. After all, I <u>was an old hand</u> at it.

2 Back in my old job, I thought: 'This is great. I've <u>landed on my feet</u> again.' But soon I <u>was rushed off my feet</u>. There was too much to do and no time for golf or even to visit my holiday home in Monaco. What's more, the company's results were down.

3 We had a meeting, at which <u>it all came to a head</u>. The shareholders said, 'You're wasting company money on your expensive cars and yachts.' 'Rubbish!' I replied. 'I've got a good head for business, and I know what we can and can't afford.'

4 'I only <u>have</u> the company's <u>interests at heart</u>,' I told them. But they said that if results didn't improve, I'd be out. And my <u>heart</u> really <u>sank</u> when they demanded that I return my sixth Ferrari and sell the house in Barbados that I'd felt was necessary to keep senior executives (me) happy.

5 Unfortunately, results didn't get better, so we had another meeting. 'You have to <u>face the music</u>,' said one of the shareholders. 'Your time as Chief Executive has been a disaster.' I'm sure they were about to fire me when I decided to <u>save face</u>. I resigned. Now I'm retired again. Here I am in my beachfront home in Brazil.

2 Match the <u>underlined</u> idioms in the story to the phrases (a–j) with a similar meaning.

Paragraph 1: hands

a have a lot of difficult tasks to do

b very experienced at doing something

Paragraph 2: feet

c be extremely busy

d get into a good situation because you're lucky

Paragraph 3: head

e be naturally good at commercial matters

f reach such a bad situation that something has to be done

Paragraph 4: heart

g to want what is best for someone or something

h suddenly feel very disappointed

Paragraph 5: face

i avoid losing the respect of other people

j take responsibility for something bad

3 Work in pairs and discuss the questions.

1 Do you have a good head for business?

2 Are you rushed off your feet at work/school?

3 Are you an old hand at anything? If so, what?

4 Are you the type of person who always lands on your feet?

5 When was the last time your heart sank?

6 Do you have your hands full at home/school/work?

7 Can you think of a time when you wanted to save face? Did you succeed?

8 When was the last time you had to (or told someone else to) face the music?

1 Look at the picture of nine passengers on a plane. One of these people is a spy, one is a criminal, one used to be famous, one will be famous, one is a doctor, one is a lawyer, one has a dark secret, one is a journalist and one is a soldier. Who is who? Guess the identities and label the picture.

2 Work in groups. Choose a different passenger each. Imagine you are that passenger and write a short profile by completing the phrases below.

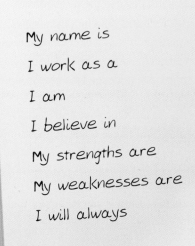

My name is

I work as a

I am

I believe in

My strengths are

My weaknesses are

I will always

3 Imagine that the plane crashes. Everyone survives and you all wake up on a desert island. You decide to start a new community. Your character wants to be leader. Think about questions 1–4.

1 What ideas do you have to run the community? What is your manifesto?
2 How will you persuade the others that you should be leader?
3 What experiences do you have that will be useful?
4 What are your beliefs?

4 Take it in turns to present your manifesto and argue your case for becoming the leader of the new community.

5 Elect a leader and explain your choice to other groups.

Articles

Definite article

Classes: **The** *arctic fox is known to inhabit the area.*

National groups: **The** *French are unhappy about the new policy.*

Other groups: **The** *Green Party has staged a protest.*

Unique objects: **The** *sun was setting on the horizon.*

Titles: **The** *President has yet to make the decision.*

Musical instruments: *She learned to play* **the** *harp.*

Geographical names: rivers (**the** *Seine*), oceans (**the** *Pacific*), compass points (**the** *North*), collective countries (**the** *UK*), mountain ranges (**the** *Alps*). NOT: lakes (~~the Lake Erie~~), single mountains (~~the Mount Everest~~), continents (~~the Asia~~), countries (~~the Germany~~)

Shared knowledge or experience:

We'll meet them in **the** *café. (= the café by our work – shared knowledge)*

Indefinite article

Jobs: *Martha is* **a** *dentist.*

Measuring: *It costs £150* **a** *week. (= per week)*

Introducing something new: *There's been* **an** *accident!*

No article (zero article)

Names: *Tom Cruise is my favourite actor.*

Streets: *They live on Harvard Street.*

General countable plurals: *I love cats.* NOT: ~~I love the cats.~~

whatever, whoever, whenever, etc.

Whenever, however, whatever, etc. are conjunctions. They join two clauses together. We use them when it doesn't make any difference *when, what, who*, etc., or we don't have to be specific, or we don't know the exact details of *when, what, who*, etc.

Come **whenever** *you can.*

(= it doesn't matter exactly when you come)

What, who, when, etc. are a little different to *whatever, whoever, whenever*, etc. Compare:

Repeat **what** *you just said!*

Repeat **whatever** *you just said!*

Whatever *you just said, repeat it!*

NOT: ~~What you just said, repeat it!~~

Whoever *you saw was probably the criminal.*

NOT: ~~Who you saw was probably the criminal.~~

However has two meanings. Compare:

However *you go, whether by train or car, it takes a day.*

It takes two days by car. **However,** *if you go by train, it takes only a day.*

The second *however* contrasts two statements.

Link words of time and contrast

There are many words/expressions which allow us to link our ideas and narratives in different ways. To link things happening at the same time, use *while, whilst, when* and *as*.

As *the plane took off, she felt free.*

To link things that happen when other longer actions are finishing/have finished, use *by which time* or *at which point*.

I reached the end, **by which time** *I was tired.*

To link things that happen immediately after the previous action, use *hardly + when, on + -ing* form and *no sooner + than*.

On hearing *about the crash, he ran straight to the hospital.*

To link things that contrast with previous information, use *though, although* and *even though* + verb phrase.

Although <u>he's short</u>, *he's good at basketball.*

We can also use *despite* and *in spite of* + noun phrase or *-ing* form.

In spite of <u>my poor exam results</u>, *I still managed to get a good job.*

We can use adjective/adverb + *as/though* + subject + verb to add emphasis to the contrast. Typical examples are *much as* (*I like*) and *hard though* (*we tried*).

Much as I love *television, even I can't watch for more than three or four hours a day.*

Key vocabulary

Power

nuclear speech medicine spending argument economic solar brain influence world political people army consumer   have power over position of power   special powers   come to power hold power   gain control   win over be impressed by   play a part in

Fashions and fads

be in   be out   kick off   home in on   catch on come about   come up with   keep up with

Personal characteristics

charismatic inspirational dignified aloof idealistic tireless trustworthy resolute nondescript   waver in the face of   approachable corrupt   down-to-earth   inspiring (lacking in) drive and energy   (lack) gravitas

Idioms (2)

have your hands full   be an old hand (at something) land on your feet   be rushed off your feet it all comes to a head   have a good head for business have (someone's) interests at heart   your heart sinks face the music   save face

---

Listen to the explanations and vocabulary.

ACTIVEBOOK

see Writing bank page 160

1 Complete the text with *a*, *an* or *the*. Change the punctuation if necessary.

The Shanghai World Financial Centre

This 492m-high building consists of two elements that correspond to Chinese concept of earth as square and sky as circle. Hole in top also has practical use – to relieve pressure of wind on building. Glassy tower is being built just blocks away from 420m Jinmao Tower in district of Shanghai that has been designated Asian centre for international banking. Tower's lower levels will be used for offices, and its upper levels for hotel, art museum and restaurants.

2 Complete the dialogues with *whatever*, *whoever*, *whenever*, etc. The same word can be used more than once.

1 **A:** Why do you like Italy?
   B Because _____ you go in Italy, you can find amazing architecture.
2 **A:** What's so different about that school?
   B: There are no compulsory subjects. You can study _____ you want.
3 **A:** We can buy the black one or the blue one. Which would you like?
   B: _____ you prefer. I don't mind.
4 **A:** What time shall I come to your house?
   B: Come _____ you can make it.
5 **A:** How will you manage to get time off work?
   B: It'll be OK – they're quite flexible. I'll talk to _____ is on duty.
6 **A:** Will it be quicker if we take the bus or the train?
   B: _____ you travel, it takes over two hours.

3 Complete the sentences (1–6) with the correct form of verbs and particles from the boxes to complete the sentences.

> come   be   home   catch   keep   kick

> in (x2)   up   on (x2)   off   about   with

1 We _____ _____ _____ the latest developments by reading magazines.
2 The new series _____ _____ just three weeks ago – its first episode was a great success.
3 I don't think that new type of phone will ever _____ _____. It's too ugly.
4 I've lost touch with the music scene. I've no idea what _____ _____ any more.
5 This extraordinary situation _____ _____ because our marketing men had a great idea.
6 Hi-tech companies are increasingly _____ _____ _____ teenagers as their number-one consumer.

4 Make idioms from the words from the boxes. Then complete the sentences (1–10) with the idioms.

> head   hands   feet   a   your   have   came
> full   my   land   on   to

1 The problem had been developing for a long time, when it finally ...
2 Sorry, I can't help you tonight because I ...
3 So you found a great job and a nice house! You're so lucky! You always ...

> hand   face   heart   feet   an   off   at
> old   rushed   her   interests   save

4 I knew all the rules of the game already because I was ...
5 She's too busy to attend the meeting. She's ...
6 I want you to do really well. I only have your ...
7 It was an embarrassing situation but, by being honest about it, they managed to ...

> face   head   heart   a   the   his   sank
> business   music   for   good

8 I thought he would make a good managing director, because he has ...
9 When he saw that he'd failed the exam, ...
10 She committed the crime, and now that she's been caught, she has to ...

5 Find and delete any unnecessary words in the text.

1 An hour with the Body Earth Power Group was
2 enough for me. No sooner but had Carin Brook
3 entered than everyone became silent. Much as I
4 tried to keep my mind open – and despite of the
5 fact that I have been known to do a bit of tree-
6 hugging myself – I couldn't help thinking that
7 this was going to be a waste of time. Brook, even
8 and though she is tiny, had a charismatic presence.
9 We started stretching in order to 'feel the Earth's
10 rhythm', but it didn't last long. I'd hardly but lifted
11 my hands up when she told us all to sit down, close
12 our eyes and 're-visualise ourselves from above'.
13 Hard as though I tried, I just couldn't imagine what
14 the top of my head looked like, and in the spite of
15 her promptings to 'relax', the hard floor was getting
16 very uncomfortable. Luckily, four o'clock came,
17 by which the time I was desperate for a nice soft
18 chair and a cup of tea.

Lead-in

1 Look at the photos. Work in pairs and discuss the questions.

1 Where are the animals?

2 Are they being used by people? If so, how?

3 Do you approve of the way they are being used? Why/Why not?

2 Write the words from the box into the table.

> mammal fur trade carnivore tame natural habitat stalk
> animal rights breed (v) breed (n) hibernate sanctuary
> nature reserve endangered reptile animal testing exotic
> rare cage lay eggs nest predator over-hunting/fishing

1 Types of animal (noun)	2 Describes animals (adjective)	3 Where animals live	4 Things animals do	5 Animal issues

3 Work in groups and discuss the questions.

1 Think of examples of the types of animal in column 1.

2 What animals can the adjectives in column 2 describe?

3 Which animals do the things in column 4?

4 What do you know about the issues in column 5? How do you feel about them? What solutions are there?

Grammar	relative clauses
Can do	explain procedures

Reading

1 a Match words 1–6 to words a–f.

1	natural	a	the human eye
2	carried to	b	lives
3	animal	c	safety
4	rescue	d	disaster
5	save	e	instincts
6	invisible to	f	team

b The phrases in exercise 1a are all from the article on the right. Look at the headings. What do you think the article is about?

c Read and check your predictions.

2 Work in pairs and answer the questions.

1 What was strange about the elephants' and the flamingos' behaviour?

2 What do animals typically do before natural disasters occur?

3 How do we know what the sharks did before Hurricane Charlie?

4 What specific ability allows animals to predict natural disasters?

5 Why can't people predict natural disasters, according to Rupesh Kaneira? What other reason does the article give?

6 What are the similarities and differences between the 'rescue dogs' and the 'rescue rats'?

7 How do rescue teams know that the rat has found someone?

8 In what particular conditions would a rat be much better than a robot in a rescue situation?

3 Work in pairs and discuss the questions.

1 What differences between humans and animals does the article describe?

2 Do you believe in 'sixth sense' or 'animal instinct'?

3 The article says that, when disasters occur, we hope to use animals in two ways. What are these ways? Are they ethical?

4 Do you think the ideas for using animals will be successful? What problems might there be?

Animals to the rescue

Watching animals could warn us of danger ...

During the tsunami disaster of 2004, over 300,000 people died. No one has counted the number of animals killed, but we know that it wasn't many. All over the region, before the disaster struck, animals were behaving strangely.

Shortly before the tsunami, in Khao Lak, Thailand, 12 elephants that were giving tourists rides became agitated. They suddenly left their usual habitat, carrying four surprised Japanese tourists to safety. On the eastern coast of India, flamingos, which should have been breeding at that time of year, suddenly flew to higher ground. Of the 2,000 wild pigs that inhabit an Indian nature reserve, only one was found dead after the tsunami.

The idea that animals are able to predict disasters is nothing new. In fact, it has been well documented over the years. Twelve hours before Hurricane Charlie hit Florida in 2004, 14 electronically tagged sharks left their natural habitat and stayed in deeper waters for two weeks. The sharks, which were being observed by US biologists, had never done this before. They escaped the hurricane. In the winter of 1975 in Haicheng, China, snakes which would normally have been hibernating were seen on the ground. Days later there was an earthquake which measured 7.3 on the Richter Scale.

Unlike human beings, wild animals perceive a great deal of information about the world around them. Their senses are sharper and they can feel even the smallest changes in the environment. In other words, they see natural warnings that are invisible to the human eye. Ancient people probably had similar 'animal instincts', which they needed to survive, but these have been lost to us as modern technology leads us further away from the dangers that nature poses.

The real question is, can we use the reactions of animals to save ourselves from natural disasters? Animal behaviour expert, Rupesh Kaneira, believes we have no choice. 'The technology which we rely on isn't always perfect, and in poorer countries it isn't even available. Animals know the environment better than any of us. When they run for their lives, we must follow.'

And rats could rescue us from disaster ...

In the earthquake-prone regions of the world – Japan, Los Angeles, Turkey – rats will soon be our new best friend.

In the aftermath of an earthquake, rescue teams send in dogs which are trained to smell people. No one knows how many lives they have saved, but there are, of course, drawbacks: dogs are big and they can't get into small spaces. Now a new research project is using a smaller animal to save lives: the rat.

How does it work? Firstly, the rat is trained to smell people. When this happens, the rat's brain gives off a signal, similar to what happens when a dog smells a bomb. So, the trained rats are sent into the wreckage. On their back is a very small radio, which is connected to the rat's brain. The rescuers, at a safe distance, monitor the radio signals. When the rat's brain activity jumps, the rescuers know that someone is alive.

Of course there are already robots which can do this job, one of which looks and moves like a snake, but rats are better because they can smell more efficiently than robots, whose noses don't work well when there are other smells around. Rats also crawl efficiently in destroyed buildings – something which robots are not as good at – and they don't need electricity. What's more, rats have a survival instinct: they get out when it isn't safe.

Grammar | relative clauses

4 Complete the tasks (1–6) in the Active grammar box.

Active grammar

1 Read the examples (a–g) below and underline the relative clauses.

2 Which examples contain defining relative clauses (essential information)? What type of information is described in the other relative clauses?

3 In which type of relative clause (defining or non-defining) can we use that instead of *who* or *which*?

4 When do we use commas with relative clauses?

5 Which clause contains a dependent preposition? Where does the dependent preposition go in the relative clause? Find another example in the final paragraph. Where can the preposition go in formal English?

6 Find a sentence in the final paragraph of the article that contains the structure '___ of which'? What other words sometimes come before *of which*? (e.g. *all of which* ...)

a) ... *12 elephants that were giving tourists rides became agitated.*

b) ... *flamingos, which should have been breeding at that time of year, suddenly flew to higher ground.*

c) *The sharks, which were being observed by US biologists, had never done this before.*

d) *Of the 2,000 wild pigs that inhabit an Indian nature reserve, only one was found dead.*

e) ... *there are already robots which can do this job.*

f) ... *rats are better because they can smell more efficiently than robots, whose noses don't work well ...*

g) *The technology which we rely on ...*

5 Do sentences a and b in each pair below have the same meaning? If not, how are they different? Which are wrong?

1 a Monkeys whose DNA is similar to humans are often used in research into the brain.

  b Monkeys, whose DNA is similar to humans, are often used in research into the brain.

2 a Guide dogs were first used by soldiers who had been blinded in war.

  b Guide dogs were first used by soldiers, who had been blinded in war.

3 a Seals, whose blubber is used for fuel and food, are hunted by Inuits.

  b Inuits hunt seals whose blubber is used for fuel and food.

4 a The tiger shark is one of the few sharks that attacks people.

  b Most sharks are not dangerous, but one exception is the tiger shark, which attacks people.

5 a The funnel spider's web, which is extremely fine, was used to cover wounds.

  b The funnel spider's web, that is extremely fine, was used to cover wounds.

6 Add the phrases a–d to questions 1–4. Add commas where necessary.

a which take animals from their natural habitat

b which is done only for sport and not for food

c about which there has been much debate in the fashion industry

d which is being destroyed

1 Should hunting be allowed?

2 Should zoos be banned?

3 Should the Amazon rainforest be protected against industry? If so, how?

4 Should the use of fur for clothing be banned?

Speaking

7 Read the questions in exercise 6 again. Work in pairs and discuss the questions. Think of arguments for and against each issue.

I think hunting which is done for sport should be banned because it's inhumane.

see Reference page 103

Listening

8 **a** 🔘 2.06 Listen to two people explaining how to do something. Write true (T), false (F) or doesn't say (DS).

1 You need to make some plans before you even buy your rabbits. ☐
2 Rabbits eat almost any type of food. ☐
3 You should be vaccinated. ☐
4 You should have at least two rabbits in a hutch. ☐
5 Lots of people choose their dog because it looks cute. ☐
6 The speaker thinks it's a bad idea to keep a dog outside. ☐
7 The owner's lifestyle is an important consideration in choosing the breed of dog. ☐
8 The speaker knows a lot of dog owners. ☐

b Listen again and check.

Pronunciation | *to*

9 **a** How is *to* pronounced in these clauses?

1 The first thing you need to do …
2 So you need to plan well …
3 You have to make sure they like the food they're given …
4 It's best to get it from a farmer …

b 🔘 2.07 Listen and check.

10 **a** Underline the prepositions in extracts 1–4 below. Which are weak forms? How are they pronounced?

1 A lot of people, for example, just go for the cutest dog they can find.
2 The first thing you've got to do is to ask yourself a number of questions.
3 … the next thing is to think about what type of dog.
4 … if you spend most of your time at home watching TV, get a less active dog.

b 🔘 2.08 Listen and check.

Speaking

11 Complete the How to… box by with the words from the box below.

> easy   without   step   any   doesn't   first
> it   be   piece   the

How to… explain procedures

Prefacing with a general statement	*It can* (1) _____ *a bit tricky at* (2) _____ *.* *It's pretty straightforward.* *It's really* (3) _____ *.* *It's a* (4) _____ *of cake.*
Sequencing	*Firstly …/* (5) _____ *first thing you've got to do is …* *Then/Secondly, …/The next* (6) _____ *is to + infinitive …* *Once you do/'ve done this …* *Finally,*
Addressing the listener	*You do this …/Do this …* *One does this* (formal/usually written English)
Conditions/ what can go wrong	(7) _____ *doing this, it won't work.* *If it* (8) _____ *work, you should …*
Checking it's understood	*OK?/Got* (9) _____ *?/* (10) _____ *questions?*

12 **a** A friend is going to stay in your house while you go on holiday. Think of three things they will have to do (use your washing machine, feed your pet, water your plants, etc.). Complete paragraphs 1–3, explaining how to do them.

1 It's really easy. You can do it by _____ the _____ into the _____ . The next step is to _____ . Once you've done this, all you need to do is _____ . Any questions?

2 It's pretty straightforward. What you have to do is _____ . Without doing this the _____ can't _____ . Then you _____ , and finally the _____ should work perfectly. If it doesn't, _____ ! OK?

3 It can be a bit tricky the first time. You put the _____ in the _____ and then you _____ . If it doesn't _____ , then it means you need to _____ . Got it?

b Work in pairs. Take turns to explain your procedures. Ask your partner questions if necessary.

Vocabulary | descriptive language

1 a Match words 1–7 to words a–g to make collocations.

1	spectacular	a	level
2	permanent	b	town
3	tourist	c	settlement
4	below sea	d	landscape
5	active	e	land
6	ghost	f	volcano
7	inhospitable	g	site

b Look at the photos (A–D). Work in pairs and describe them using the collocations from exercise 1a.

2 Complete the sentences with collocations from exercise 1a.

1 The world's most popular _____ is the area around the Eiffel Tower, Paris.

2 Mount Etna in Sicily, Italy, is the world's most _____ .

3 Antarctica is the only continent on which there is no _____ . It is too cold!

4 The Dead Sea is the lowest point on Earth. It is 418 metres _____ .

5 Walhalla, Australia, is a rare example of a _____ that came back to life. Originally a gold-mining town, it was abandoned when the gold ran out, but is now popular with tourists.

6 Some of the world's most _____ can be found in Cappodochia, Turkey.

7 The Atacama Desert, Chile, is an _____ . Few people can survive its dry climate.

Speaking

3 Work in pairs and discuss the questions.

1 What's the hottest place you have been to?

2 What problems could you have visiting a very hot place? Think about animals, accommodation, health, etc.

4 Work in pairs. Imagine you are taking a trip in the desert for a month. What would you take with you? Decide on five things from the box below.

> candle and matches   mobile phone
> sleeping bag   tent   mirror   laptop
> compass   map   hat   gun   umbrella

Listening

5 **a** ⊙ 2.09 Listen to the first part of David Hewson's story. Answer the questions.

1 What does David need from the bureaucrat's office?

2 What is the bureaucrat's attitude to David's trip? How do we know?

3 The bureaucrat has a sense of humour. What does he say that shows this?

b Work in pairs and discuss the questions.

1 What will the journey be like?

2 What do you think the Danakil Depression, the world's hottest place, looks like?

3 How do you think David will feel when he arrives?

c ⊙ 2.10 Listen to the second part of the story. Were your predictions correct?

6 Work in pairs and discuss the questions.

1 Why do you think David wanted to make this journey? What was his motivation?

2 Why do explorers go to extreme places?

3 Why do you think David is disappointed with the Danakil Depression?

4 How would you feel if you were him? Would you like to go there? Why/Why not?

5 'It is better to travel than to arrive.' Do you agree with this proverb?

7 **a** Look at audioscripts 2.9 and 2.10 on page 173. What things/people do the words from the box describe?

'Drone' describes the noise of a fan.

Verbs	drone zig-zag crumble
Adjectives	warped vibrant hunched

b Work in pairs. Try to define the words from exercise 7a. Check with your teacher or a dictionary.

'Drone' means make a dull, low, continuous sound.

c Now think of other things you can talk about using the adjectives from exercise 7a.

Vibrant – 'the colours were vibrant', 'Barcelona has vibrant nightlife', 'She has a vibrant character.'

8 Read the Lifelong learning box. Work in pairs and discuss the question.

Read on!

Reading descriptive writing is a good way to develop your vocabulary. Writers often use unusual images and metaphors, and these creative uses of language can extend your understanding of English.

Read these literary descriptions of natural places. <u>Underline</u> any interesting imagery or metaphors. Do you have similar expressions in your language?

1 Looking east from the heart of Santiago, you see the mountains looming over the city like giants.

2 As our camels stumbled over the edge of the dune, we saw the desert sands stretched out in front of us.

3 The sea rears up, a wild horse under a starless sky.

Lifelong learning

Grammar | verb patterns (2)

9 Complete the tasks in the Active grammar box.

Active grammar

Some verbs can be followed by both the infinitive or the *-ing* form. Sometimes the meaning changes.

mean

1 Which <u>underlined</u> verb phrase means 'intended'? Which means 'involved'?

Going to the Danakil Depression <u>means walking</u> into hell on Earth.

David <u>meant to write</u> a book after his trips.

remember

2 Which <u>underlined</u> verb phrase describes 'a responsibility or something that you need to do'? Which describes 'a memory of the past'?

He <u>remembers experiencing</u> a feeling of emptiness when he arrived.

They tell you … to <u>remember to drink</u> even when you're not thirsty.

regret

3 Which <u>underlined</u> verb phrase means 'a feeling of sadness about something in the past'? Which is used in a formal apology?

I <u>regret to inform</u> you that your application for a visa has been turned down.

I didn't <u>regret going</u> to the Danakil Depression.

stop

4 Which <u>underlined</u> verb phrase means 'paused in order to do something'? Which means 'completely finished something'?

We <u>stopped to visit</u> a ghost town.

David <u>stopped looking</u> for vegetation and wildlife once he realised nothing survived in the Danakil Depression.

try

5 Which <u>underlined</u> verb phrase describes an experiment to see what will happen (as a solution to a problem)? Which describes an effort to do something difficult?

They had <u>tried to build</u> a railway.

He <u>tried drinking</u> more water but he still felt absolutely terrible.

go on

6 Which <u>underlined</u> verb phrase means 'continued an action'? Which means 'did something after finishing something else'?

They waved and <u>went on riding</u>.

David Hewson <u>went on to write</u> a book.

---

see Reference page 103

10 Complete each sentence (1–12) with two words. Use patterns from the Active grammar box.

1 I don't remember _____ photo, but it has turned out really well, one of my best!

2 After six hours of driving, we _____ have a break by the roadside.

3 We _____ visit the cathedral, but it was closed that day.

4 Even after I told her to be quiet, she went _____ loudly.

5 She regrets _____ so early this morning. Now she's really tired.

6 Getting fit means _____ smoking and drinking completely. You'll also have to go to the gym.

7 I didn't mean _____ the window. I lost control of the ball!

8 I remembered _____ traveller's cheques this time. Last time, I forgot and I lost all my money.

9 She used to send letters regularly, but she _____ to me last year. We're not in touch any more.

10 After leaving Oxford with a law degree, she _____ to become a famous lawyer.

11 We regret _____ you that you have not been accepted by the college.

12 If you have problems sleeping, you should _____ hot milk before you go to bed.

11 a Choose the correct words in *italics*.

1 For me, a holiday means *to lie/lying* around on a beach.

2 I can remember *to go/going* on a long journey when I was a child.

3 I try *spending/to spend* time in places of natural beauty whenever I can.

4 I'll never stop *travelling/to travel* even when I'm old.

5 I admire people like David, who went on *to explore/exploring* places even though it was very uncomfortable for him.

6 I've never regretted *to go/going* anywhere because you can always learn something from different places and cultures.

b Work with a partner. Discuss which sentences from exercise 11a are true for you.

Reading

1 **a** Work in pairs. Discuss which statements (1–6) you think are true.

1 It is illegal to sell wild animals such as gorillas and tigers.

2 You can buy a gorilla online for $900.

3 You can't buy a giraffe online because it is too tall to ship anywhere.

4 The most popular wild animals sold online are snakes.

5 Some websites sell clothes and nappies for your pet monkey.

6 Wild animals are being sold online by criminal gangs.

b Read the article to find out.

2 **a** Choose the best words in *italics* in the sentences (1–6).

1 The animals are marketed as if they are *useful around the home/dangerous/toys*.

2 The writer is concerned about *all animals/rare animals/the effects of animals on children*.

3 The IFAW was surprised *at the size of the illegal market for wild animals/to find endangered species for sale/at the way the traders treat the animals*.

4 After buying the animal, many people *abandon it/can't look after it/treat it like a doll*.

5 'Monkey moms' are the people who *buy the animals on the Internet/sell the animals on the Internet/hunt the animals*.

6 The online animal trade is one cause of *economic problems in poor countries/violent crime/illegal hunting*.

b Read the article again to check.

3 Work in pairs and discuss the questions

1 Do any of the facts in the article surprise you?

2 Should people have wild animals as pets? Give reasons.

3 Why do you think monkeys seem to be so popular as pets?

4 What can the IFAW do to stop the illegal trade? Is it possible to stop illegal Internet sales in general?

ANIMALS ONLINE

They are marketed as the perfect birthday present for animal-loving children, or a classy addition to the image-conscious suburban home. But the products being sold over the Internet are not
5 soft toys or unusual knick-knacks, but potentially dangerous live animals from the world's most endangered species.

Monkeys, tigers and chimps can be bought and sold for as little as a few hundred dollars, despite
10 international bans on their sale. The illegal online trade in rare and exotic wildlife is now worth billions of dollars, according to a report by the IFAW (the International Fund for Animal Welfare). Indeed, IFAW researchers discovered well over 9,000
15 live animals and products made from endangered species for sale on internet auction sites, in chat rooms and on the small-ads pages. The scale of the trade is astonishing.

So what exactly would it cost and what
20 would you have to do to buy a wild animal? The researchers say you wouldn't have to do a great deal. Want a gorilla in your living room? It's yours for $9,000. For those with a little more headroom, giraffes can also be bought. Got-PetsOnline.com
25 offered a 'sweet natured' two-year-old giraffe for $15,000. Or how about a pair of rare giant tortoises from Madagascar? These are a little pricier at $24,000, plus airfare to Kuala Lumpur. This may be because there are only 200 mature specimens
30 of these creatures alive in the wild. All the others appear to be in storage awaiting a buyer.

However, it is monkeys that make up the large majority of Internet sales, and experts are particularly concerned at the way they are
35 marketed and traded on the net. A number of websites describe them as if they are little more than large hairy dolls. These websites offer 'accessories' such as nappies, feeding bottles and clothes to go with the monkey. The traders
40 even have a 'cute' name for themselves: 'monkey moms'. They call the animals themselves 'monkids'. Virtually none of these websites explain how to look after the animals.

When the IFAW undercover investigators
45 contacted some of the US traders, they were told it would be possible to export monkeys to the UK – a blatant breach of EU law. There is also concern that demand for monkeys and chimps is fuelling the illegal trapping and trading of wild species. Where
50 there were approximately two million chimpanzees in the wild a century ago, there are as few as 100,000 left, and some estimates suggest there may be a maximum of 70,000 by 2020.

Phyllis Campbell-McRae, director of IFAW UK,
55 says, 'Trade on the Internet is easy, cheap and anonymous. Criminal gangs are taking advantage of the opportunities provided by the Web. The result is a cyber black market where the future of the world's rarest animals is being traded away. Our
60 message to online shoppers is simple – buying wildlife online is as damaging as killing it yourself.'

Grammar | *as ... as* and describing quantity

4 **a** Read rule A in the Active grammar box. Find three examples of *as* + adjective + *as* in the article (lines 9, 51 and 61). Which meaning (1 or 2) does each example have?

b Look at phrases a–h and answer the questions.

1 Find their opposites in the article and write them in the Active grammar box.

2 Which phrases are often followed by *of*?

3 Which phrases use numbers (e.g. *as much as 20*)?

4 Which four phrases <u>can't</u> be used with countable nouns?

Active grammar

A

as + adjective + *as*

This structure can be used in two ways:

1 to say two things are equal

2 as a way of showing surprise about a statement.

B

Other ways of describing quantity

a) *as much as* → _____ (line 9)

b) *well under* → _____ (line 14)

c) *not very much* → _____ (line 21)

d) *a tiny minority* → _____ (line 33)

e) *virtually all* → _____ (line 42)

f) *precisely* → _____ (line 50)

g) *as many as* → _____ (line 51)

h) *a minimum* → _____ (line 53)

---

see Reference page 103

5 **a** Find mistakes in six of the sentences and correct them.

1 Pet rabbits usually live for approximately eight years, but small minority live longer.

2 Hamsters can give birth to as many of 20 offspring at a time.

3 A larger majority of parrots are able to repeat domestic human speech.

4 The life of a housefly is as short as two days.

5 Koala bears spend virtually of all their lives asleep: 18 hours per day.

6 Horses usually die at around 20 or 25, but can live a greater deal longer.

7 Tortoises can live to over well 100 years, a great deal longer than humans.

8 Dogs remain pregnant for a minimum of 53 days and a maximum of 71.

b Work in pairs. Discuss whether you think the sentences in exercise 5a are true or false. Then check on page 149.

Pronunciation | *as*

6 **a** ⊙ 2.11 Listen to three sentences. How is the word *as* pronounced?

b ⊙ 2.12 Listen to three questions and answer them with *I'm as ...* and the prompts below. Pay attention to the pronunciation of *as*.

blind – bat (I'm as blind as a bat.)

1 free – bird

2 strong – ox

3 quiet – mouse

Speaking

7 Work in groups. Read the quotes and discuss the questions (1–3).

> "The greatness of a nation and its moral progress can be judged by the way its animals are treated."
> *Mohandas Gandhi, statesman*

1 Is it important to treat animals well or should we only worry about our own species?

> "Don't make the mistake of treating your dogs like humans or they'll treat you like dogs." *Martha Scott, writer*

2 Why do some people love their domestic pets? What is your country's attitude to animals in the house?

> "All the good ideas I ever had came to me while I was milking a cow." *Grant Wood, artist*

3 Can caring for animals help people in other ways besides providing food?

Vocabulary | buying and selling

8   **a** Work in groups and discuss the questions.

1 What products can you think of that are made using animal parts? Look at the photos to help you.

2 Which of these have you bought in the last six months?

3 Do you think it is ethical to use animal parts in all of the products in the photos?

b Match the phrases (1–10) to phrases with a similar meaning (a–j).

1 It's in excellent condition
2 It's the latest model
3 It's second-hand
4 It's available now
5 It's hand-crafted
6 It's brand new
7 It features ...
8 It has some wear and tear
9 It's unique
10 It comes in a wide range of (colours/sizes)

a It's one of a kind
b It's used
c It's on the market
d It's not in perfect condition (it's been used a lot)
e You can choose from a selection of ...
f It's made by hand
g It's still in its packaging
h It's as good as new
i It includes ...
j It's state of the art

c Work in pairs. Look at the phrases in exercise 8b again for a few minutes. Take turns to say one of the phrases 1–10. Without looking, your partner says the phrase with a similar meaning.

Speaking

9 Work in pairs. Look at the photos and discuss which phrases from exercise 8b you could use to describe the things you see.

10 Work in pairs. Take a possession from your bag. Think of a way to make it sound wonderful and 'sell' it to your partner. Try to use some of the phrases from exercise 8b.

This pen really is one of a kind. It's the latest model used by some of the biggest names in business!

1 a Correct sentences 1–7 by adding a suffix to one word. You may need to omit some letters from the original word.

Humans use more and more land to plant crops and extend cities. This <u>signs</u> a great threat to the habitat of a number of species.

Answer: *signifies*

1 Elephants are hunted for their ivory tusks. This highly profit business is illegal.

2 There are only about 400 gorillas left in central Africa. The destroy of their forest habitat has led to this situation.

3 Jaguars are hunted illegal for their fur, which is used for coats, handbags and shoes.

4 The disappear of dinosaurs is a great mystery. Some people believe it happened because of a dramatic climate change.

5 Giant pandas are depend on the greenery in their habitat. As this gets eroded, they struggle to survive.

6 We need to emphasis responsible care of the environment in order to preserve natural resources.

7 In the short term, people hunt animals for their beautiful fur. It is only after – when these animals become extinct – that we regret it.

b What type of words did you create by using the suffixes (nouns, adjectives, adverbs and verbs).

2 Read the Lifelong learning box and follow the instructions.

Break it up!

! When you come across very long words that you don't understand, try breaking them up. Look for prefixes and suffixes that can help you to guess the meaning. Example: *non-refundable*. What does *non-* mean? What type of word usually ends in *-able*? What is a *refund*? Where might you see the word *non-refundable*?

Lifelong learning

1 Work in pairs. Make sentences using the words below. If you don't know the meaning of the words, try breaking them up.

unforgettably   demotivating   intolerable anti-hero   immortality

2 Compare your ideas with other students.

---

3 Work in groups. Add one example for each suffix in tables 1–4 using the words from the boxes.

1 Forming abstract nouns

> sad   global   retire   tend

suffix	examples
-ation/-isation	*nationalisation, compilation, _____*
-ment	*enjoyment, harassment, _____*
-ness	*kindness, emptiness, _____*
-cy	*redundancy, accuracy, _____*

2 Forming nouns – types of people

> motivate   psychology   enter   door

suffix	examples
-er/-ar/-or	*baker, burglar, aviator, _____*
-ant/-ent	*assistant, opponent, _____*
-ist	*biologist, pianist, _____*
-man, -woman, -person	*spokesman, businesswoman, _____*

3 Forming verbs

> satire   tolerance   test   broad

suffix	examples
-ate	*motivate, captivate, _____*
-ise/-ize	*characterise, idealise, _____*
-ify	*simplify, clarify, _____*
-en	*lighten, enlighten, _____*

4 Forming adjectives

> phenomenon   Poland   permanence   hope

suffix	examples
-al/-ical	*manual, practical, _____*
-ant/-ent/-ient	*tolerant, urgent, _____*
-ish	*selfish, childish, _____*
-ful	*selfish, childish, _____*

4 Do the crossword on page 151.

Fact File

Paradise island has 50 square kilometres of land which can be developed.

The land has some hilly areas and a little forest.

The land and climate are good for growing vegetables, fruit, etc.

There is a lot of wildlife on the island.

There are two natural springs on the land. This is very good for people's health.

The island nearby is becoming more popular with tourists.

1 Look at the photo and read the notes about Paradise Island.

2 Work in small groups. Paradise Island belongs to you. Make a list of all the things you could do with the land.

3 ⊙ 2.13 Listen to two people discussing what they could do with the island. Were their ideas the same as/similar to yours?

4 **a** Work in groups of three. Read and memorise your roles.

Student A: look on page 148.
Student B: look on page 150.
Student C: look on page 152.

b Discuss what to do with the island. You must agree on at least two points (but if you can't agree on one thing, you can combine some of your ideas).

c Report back to the class. What did you decide to do with the island?

Relative clauses

Defining relative clauses make it clear who/what we are referring to. They cannot be omitted from the sentence. Don't use commas before the relative pronoun.

*That's the town **where** I lived ten years ago.*

That can replace *who* or *which*. If the relative pronoun is the object of the clause, *that/which* can be omitted.

*They're playing the song **which** Jenny wrote.*
*= They're playing the song **that** Jenny wrote.*
*John ate the cake **(that/which)** we bought yesterday.*

Whose can refer to people or things.

*I saw the man **whose** wife won the prize.*

Non-defining relative clauses give extra information. This information can be omitted. Use a comma before and after non-defining relative clauses unless they end the sentence. *That* cannot replace *who* or *which*. The relative pronoun cannot be omitted.

*I went climbing at the weekend, **which was fun**.*

Relative clauses with verbs + dependent prepositions usually have the preposition at the end of the clause.

*That's the company **(which)** I worked **for**.*

But in formal English, we can put the preposition at the beginning of the clause.

*That's the company **for which** I worked.*

A common pattern is (*one/some/all/either/neither*, etc.) ... *of which/whom*. This pattern is slightly formal.

*I saw two women, **neither of whom** was wearing a red woollen coat.*

Verb patterns (2)

Some verbs can be followed by the infinitive or *-ing* form. Sometimes the meaning changes.

Abstinence means not drinking. = involves
I didn't mean to break the door. = didn't intend
She dreads going to the dentist. = strongly dislikes
I dread to imagine the mess. = don't want to (because I imagine it will be terrible)

Some verbs of perception (*hear, watch, feel, observe*, etc.) don't change their meaning when followed by different verb forms. Compare:

1 *I **saw** the camel **eat** the leaves.*
2 *I **saw** the camel **eating** the leaves.*

Sentence 1 describes a finished action. Sentence 2 describes an action that may be unfinished.

as ... as and describing quantity

We use *as ... as* to say that two things are similar.

We use *as ... as* with adjectives, adverbs, *much/many*.

*I'm **as strong as** an ox.*
*The motorbike costs **as much as** a car.*

We can put a clause after the second *as*.

*She doesn't talk to me **as much as** she used to.*

We often put *possible, ever* or *usual* after the second *as*.

*I got here as quickly **as possible**.*
*You're looking as beautiful **as ever**.*

We use *as ... as* to show something is surprising.

*The meal cost **as much as** $400 per person!*

We can use different phrases to talk about surprising or extreme numbers.

***As many as/As few as** one million people are using the product.*
***Well under/Well over** 50% of my friends use Facebook.*

We can use different phrases to avoid saying an exact number.

***Virtually all/Approximately half** of us attended the course.*
***A tiny minority/A large majority** of people voted for him.*

Key vocabulary

Animals and their environment

mammal   fur trade   carnivore   tame   stalk
natural habitat   animal rights   breed   hibernate
sanctuary   nature reserve   endangered   reptile
animal testing   rare   exotic   cage   predator
lay eggs   nest   over-hunting/fishing

Descriptive language

tourist site   permanent settlement   ghost town
spectacular landscape   below sea level
active volcano   inhospitable land

Buying and selling

in excellent condition   as good as new
the latest model   state of the art   second-hand
used   available now   on the market   hand-crafted
brand new   made by hand   still in its packaging
features   includes   some wear and tear
not in perfect condition (used a lot)   unique
one of a kind   come in a wide range of (colours/sizes)
choose from a selection of

Listen to the explanations and vocabulary.

ACTIVEBOOK

  see Writing bank page 161

1 Complete the text with the phrases from the box.

> which trains   when they   that will   who spend
> who trained   who work   which has

One great problem for prison inmates, most of their time locked up, is how to develop self-esteem and find a purpose to their days. One idea, _____ been piloted at a prison in Washington, US, is to get the inmates to train dogs _____ eventually help disabled people. The project has been a great success. The relationship between the inmates and the warders at the prison has improved considerably. Many of the inmates, _____ leave the prison, go on to work with animals.

In another scheme, Pilot Dogs, a company _____ dogs for the blind in Ohio, US, put five dogs into the hands of prison inmates, _____ the dogs successfully.

2 Rewrite the sentences using _of which_, _whom_ and words from the box.

> one   some   all   none   either   neither

I left messages for Dave and Lena. They didn't return my calls.

I left messages for Dave and Lena, neither of whom returned my calls.

1 I tried on ten pairs of shoes. Just a single pair fitted me perfectly.
2 She called her classmates. Nobody had done the homework.
3 We found two good candidates. Both of them could have done the job.
4 We test-drove six cars. Every one of them cost over $20,000.
5 Sixteen people came camping with us in 2006. A group of them returned the following year.
6 I worked with the two children. They didn't speak any English.

3 Choose the correct words in _italics_.

1 I meant _to say/saying_ something to you earlier, but now I've forgotten what it was.
2 She's such a crazy dresser. I hate _to think/thinking_ what she's wearing tonight!
3 I always dread _to speak/speaking_ to the boss – she's so scary!
4 He remembered _to lock/locking_ the door this time. Last time, we got robbed!

5 We regret _to tell/telling_ you that your application has been unsuccessful.
6 Sorry, I can't stop _to talk/talking_! I'm late!
7 She tried _to drink/drinking_ hot chocolate before bedtime, but she still couldn't sleep.
8 Despite a difficult start, he went on _to become/becoming_ the world's greatest athlete.

4 Complete the sentences with words from the box.

> approximately   none   as   much   well
> large   maximum   virtually   precisely   deal

1 Apparently you can buy a leopard for _____ little as $10,000 on the net.
2 A _____ majority of the public voted to keep the old currency – nearly 90 percent.
3 Sorry, but there's not a great _____ we can do about your problem.
4 There are _____ 6,000 people in the hall, but we don't know the exact number.
5 I spent _____ all my money on the entrance fee. I only have £1 left for food.
6 We will meet at _____ six o'clock. Don't be late.
7 This lift holds a _____ of eight people.
8 He's huge! He must be _____ over two metres tall.
9 You can earn as _____ as $200,000 a year, if you work hard enough.
10 Virtually _____ of the team had ever played there before.

5 Add four missing words to each advertisement.

Eco-car for sale, in excellent _____ . This state _____ the art vehicle runs on water-power, and is _____ latest model. There is some wear _____ tear on the seat. Ring Jerry for further details.

Cat boxes for sale. Perfect for large or small cats. Plenty of space and beautiful decoration. You can choose from a selection _____ styles and a wide _____ of colours. These wooden boxes were made _____ hand, and painted individually. They are _____ of a kind. £20 per box.

Animal Magic books on _____ market, as good _____ new. Just $2.50 per book. Buy the books in a set of four and receive a generous discount. The books are _____ perfect condition (some of them are still _____ their packaging).

Lead-in

1 Look at the photos. Work in pairs and discuss the questions.

1 What can you see in the photos?
2 Which issues are represented?
3 Do you think they are important? Why/Why not?

2 Make nouns from the words/phrases (1–10).

1 biotechnological
2 censor
3 poor
4 democratic
5 globalise
6 global warm
7 immigrant
8 identity thief
9 space explorer
10 pollute

3 Which nouns are associated with the words/phrases in the box? There may be more than one answer.

> unemployment   depletion of the ozone layer   identity (ID) cards
> cloning   the right to vote   freedom of speech   giant corporations
> cost and safety issues   multiculturalism

4 Work in pairs and discuss the questions.

1 Which issues have been in the news recently? What do you think of them? Do any of them affect you personally? Which issues are the most/least important, in your opinion?
2 Do you think the problems associated with these issues are exaggerated in the media? Are any of the problems underestimated?
3 Which issues will become more important in the future? Why?

Vocabulary | contrasting opinions

1 a Read the opinions (1–6) and check you understand the underlined phrases. Then match them with the photos (A–F).

1 It does more harm than good. It pollutes the environment and uses too much oil.

2 It's a waste of space. It mostly shows repeats or ads, and it ruins your eyes.

3 It's overrated. You can't trust the information because anyone can publish things on it.

4 It's deadly. It's a threat to people and the environment, especially when accidents happen, causing radiation levels to rise.

5 They've been disastrous for humanity. The gas from these destroys the ozone layer.

6 We can do without them. No one really needs to have conversations every five minutes.

b Read the opinions (a–f) and check you understand the underlined phrases. Which opinion in exercise 1a does each one contrast with?

a It's underrated. It lets us find information quickly by using search sites and also helps us keep up with current affairs.

b We can't do without them. They're essential for talking to people while you're on the move.

c It's indispensable. It gives us up-to-date images and news, films and all kinds of programmes.

d It's been a force for good. It means we have more freedom to visit other places.

e It's invaluable. It's a sustainable source of energy that will provide energy for many generations

f They've had big benefits for humanity. They make daily activities, such as putting on deodorant and repelling insects, easier.

2 a Work in pairs. Take turns to give an opinion on one of the things in the photos. Respond to each others' opinion.

A: *In my view ...*

B: *On the other hand ...*

b Can you think of anything that you wish had never been invented? What would you replace it/them with (if anything)? Give reasons.

Reading

3 a Read the statements. Write true (T) or false (F).

1 It takes hundreds of years to produce oil. ☐

2 There is enough oil on Earth for about 50 more years. ☐

3 Most of our rubbish is either buried underground or thrown into the sea. ☐

4 Internet fraud is the fastest-growing criminal activity. ☐

5 We can predict the illnesses that people will have by studying their genes. ☐

b Read the article on page 107 and check your answers.

4 Choose the correct answers in *italics*.

1 The writers of the text *think the bicycle is the greatest invention/are interested in things that haven't been invented yet.*

2 According to the text, *a teenager suggested a way to produce oil/solar power might provide a source of energy to replace oil.*

3 The text says *there is too much rubbish for the space available/the rubbish is poisoning the environment.*

4 Two inventors are trying to find ways to *use our rubbish productively/reduce rubbish.*

5 Protection against ID theft will involve *microchips in every object we own/technology 'reading' the human body.*

6 The main invention in medicine will be *a way to predict the illnesses a person is vulnerable to/a pill that will enable people to live forever.*

5 a Work in pairs. What do you think of the article? Does it have any good ideas?

b Look at this example of humour from the article. Can you find other examples?

If that happens, we'll need another invention: a new pensions system.

FUTURE INVENTIONS

The editors of Future World Magazine look at the inventions we will need for a brighter future.

1 Everyone has their favourite invention. Some of us even make lists of them. One survey recently named the toilet as the world's greatest ever invention. Another survey, which asked for Britain's greatest invention, named the bicycle, which received twice as many votes as the World Wide Web. That's the past, but what about the future? What inventions will shape our lives? J.B.S. Haldane, a British scientist and not one of life's optimists, once made his prediction for the future. He warned that whatever hadn't happened would happen and no one would be safe from it. Whether you agree or not, one thing is beyond doubt: human beings need to invent a few things pretty quickly. Here is our own list.

2 Number one is a new source of power. Oil is running out. A teenager, in a recent letter to a newspaper, wrote that it would take over a hundred years to produce fresh oil. He was wrong by a few million years. Once our oil is gone, it's gone forever. We have about 50 years' worth left, less if rates of industrialisation accelerate. A hundred million new cars will need lots of oil. At a recent conference about the world's future, scientist Hilary Craft said we had already found the answer: solar power. She suggested that we could expect enormous mirrors in the sky that would reflect sunlight and provide the world's electricity. We wait with bated breath.

3 Number two on our list is a waste processor. Throughout most of history we just threw the rubbish out the back door. If the jungle didn't swallow it, wild animals would get it. Once the jungles disappeared, we started burying our waste underground or chucking it into the sea. Now we're running out of space. If we want to avoid choking the Earth, we'd better find a way to recycle more effectively. According to inventor Ray Kurzweill, tiny self-replicating microscopic robots will convert rubbish into new sources of energy. Another inventor, Clara Petrovic, said she was working on a prototype that would convert waste into bricks and other building material.

4 Number three on our list is biological ID. Criminal investigator Alexis Smithson said that in the past, thieves had always taken objects. Now they steal your identity. ID theft is the fastest-growing type of crime. So how will we stop it? You can expect to have tiny microchips injected into your body; scanners will read your genetic information to check your ID. Or worse, you may need to provide skin cells whenever you go shopping. Imagine scratching yourself at the checkout every time you buy the groceries. Supermarkets will never be the same.

5 Finally, medicine. In the past, a cold killed you. In 1347–1350, the Black Death killed half of Europe's population. Now we are examining people's genes for signs of future illness. Find the disease early enough and you can prevent it. Glen Hiemstra of Futurist.com recently claimed that somewhere on planet Earth there is a young child who will be the first person to live forever. If that happens we'll need another invention: a new pensions system.

Grammar | reported speech

6 Complete the tasks in the Active grammar box.

Active grammar

1 Find one example of reported speech in paragraphs 1–4 of the article. What actual words did they say? What happens to the verb tenses when we report speech?

2 Sometimes, instead of repeating the verb and shifting the tense, we use a reporting verb. Which example from paragraph 5 doesn't shift the tenses back and uses a reporting verb?

3 We often use a reporting verb to paraphrase the meaning.

'Let's go home.'
→ She **thinks** we should leave.
'Why don't we discuss it with everyone?'
→ He **suggested** that we talk it through with everyone.
'It was my mistake.'
→ He **admitted** that it was his fault.

4 Match reporting verbs 1–8 with reporting verbs a–h. Are there any differences in meaning/formality?

1 *admit*	a) *maintain*
2 *remember*	b) *imply*
3 *tell*	c) *presume*
4 *answer*	d) *respond*
5 *suggest*	e) *confess*
6 *threaten*	f) *recollect*
7 *insist*	g) *inform*
8 *assume*	h) *warn*

see Reference page 117

7 Delete the incorrect words in *italics*.

1 I *warned/informed/threatened* them that ID theft was common.

2 He *suggested that they discuss/suggested discussing/implied discussing* immigration at the meeting.

3 She *insisted/maintained/informed* that technology would solve the problem.

4 He *admitted/told/confessed* that he knew nothing about developments in biotechnology.

5 I don't *remember visiting/recollect visiting/remember to visit* the lab when I was a child.

6 We must *tell/inform/suggest* the audience about the research into global warming.

8 Work in pairs. Report the dialogues using verbs from the boxes. Leave the main (non-reporting) verbs in the same tenses if possible. In one sentence, change a positive adjective to a negative one.

~~admit~~ suggest remember confess warn

Mike: I never recycle anything because I'm too lazy.

Mike admitted that he never recycles anything because he's too lazy.

Sarah: If we don't start recycling, the consequences will be serious for the planet.

David: So why don't we start a recycling group in the community?

Sarah: Wait a minute. There's one already.

Mike: There was. I started one, but then it became really hard work, so we stopped.

respond threaten imply assume

David: No one drives if they can walk these days, do they?

Mike: What? I drive everywhere.

Sarah: Do you think that's good for the environment?

Mike: If you two don't shut up about the environment, I'll kick you out of my flat.

Speaking and listening

9 Look at the pictures (A–G). Work in pairs. Discuss what you think these new inventions are and what they do.

10 a 🔊 2.14 Listen to seven people answering the question: 'Which new invention would you most like to see?' Match the speakers (1–7) to the pictures (A–G).

b Read the sentences and write true (T) or false (F).

1 Speaker 1 probably hates housework. ☐
2 Speaker 2 wants to go back in history in order to see different civilisations. ☐
3 Speaker 3 is fed up with the terrible weather. ☐
4 Speaker 4 probably doesn't like cooking. ☐
5 Speaker 5 might be a student. ☐
6 Speaker 6 wants a machine that will instantly move his body to another place. ☐
7 Speaker 7 probably doesn't enjoy getting up in the morning. ☐

c Listen again and check.

11 Complete the How to... box using the words from the box below. Look at audioscript 2.14 on page 173 to check.

a see tricky question about

How to... stall for time (when you're asked a difficult question)

That's a good (1) _____ .
Let me (2) _____ .
That's (3) _____ .
I'd have to think (4) _____ that.
That's (5) _____ difficult question.
Well, ...

12 a Work in pairs. Look again at the pictures (A–G) and discuss the questions (1–5). Try to use language from the How to... box.

1 Which of the inventions do you think is/are a good idea? Why?
2 What other invention(s) do you think might help the world?
3 What other invention(s) do you think might help you at work or at home?
4 What invention couldn't you do without?
5 Are there any modern inventions that are overrated?

b Work with another partner. Report your original partner's opinions.

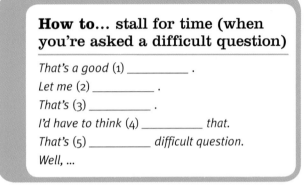

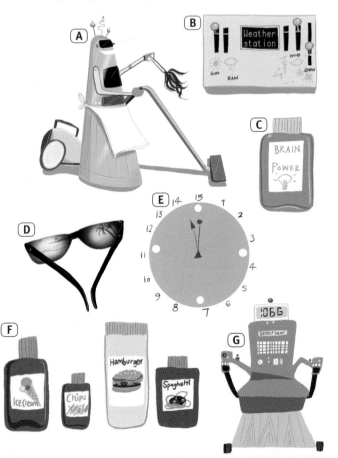

Listening

1 Work in pairs. Look at the photos and discuss the questions.

1 What type of people do you think Thomas and Elise are?
2 What are they like?
3 What do they do?
4 Where do they live?
5 What do you think are their most valued possessions?

2 🔊 2.15 Listen to Thomas and Elise talking about their work/life habits. How do their opinions and lifestyles differ?

3 a Choose the best answers (a, b or c).

1 What made Thomas change his lifestyle?
   a He received an important email.
   b He couldn't enjoy Rome because he was obsessed with work.
   c He went to the coast and fell in love with the sea.
2 Why does he think people carry technology around with them?
   a Because they wish they were in the office.
   b Because it helps them feel less stressed.
   c Because they are worried they will miss important pieces of information.
3 What has Thomas learned from living by the sea?
   a That human actions and money aren't so important.
   b That you can't make much money there.
   c That he should have left his city job much earlier.
4 Why does Elise carry around so much technology?
   a Because she doesn't have an office.
   b Because she is frightened of missing out on important news.
   c Because she travels a lot.
5 What does she believe about her future?
   a She won't do the same job for more than three and a half years.
   b She will never have a completely relaxing lifestyle. She doesn't want one.
   c Her lifestyle will probably get worse, especially her health, so she will slow down.

b Listen again and check.

Vocabulary | lifestyles

4 a 🔊 2.15 Listen again and read audioscript 2.15 on page 174. What do expressions 1–10 mean?

1 tearing my hair out
2 life in the fast lane
3 a wake-up call
4 the be-all and end-all
5 go with the flow
6 work around the clock
7 burn out
8 golden opportunity
9 have itchy feet
10 the buzz

b Match expressions 1–10 from exercise 4a to definitions a–j below.

a the excitement
b to be too exhausted to continue working
c a way of life that's full of excitement, activity and danger
d an excellent chance to do something
e the most important thing
f getting into a panic because of frustration, or feeling anxious or upset about something
g an event that makes you realise you must change
h to have a strong desire to go somewhere new or do something else.
i to work very long hours
j to accept a situation in a relaxed way, and not try to change it

5 Work in small groups and discuss the questions.

1 Do you agree that 'the world is one stressed-out place'? What are the main causes of this stress?
2 Do you live life in the fast lane or do you tend to go with the flow? Give examples. Why do you think you prefer one way to the other?
3 Do you think people in your country/industry/ profession work hard compared with others? Do a lot of people burn out?
4 Do you ever get itchy feet? If so, where do you want to go and what do you want to do? What, for you, would be a golden opportunity?

Grammar | the continuous form

6 **a** Look at the examples (a–f) in the Active grammar box. Match them to the headings below.

1 Present Continuous
2 Past Continuous
3 Present Perfect Continuous
4 Past Perfect Continuous
5 Future Continuous
6 a present participle clause

b Read rule A in the Active grammar box. Complete 1–4 by matching them to examples a–f.

c Read rule B in the Active grammar box. Can you think of any examples?

d Read rule C in the Active grammar box. Write four common stative verbs for each category (1–3).

Active grammar

a) *I'd been having dinner with a client all evening.*

b) *I was tearing my hair out trying to get internet access.*

c) *After leaving my job, I moved to the coast.*

d) *The waves will be rolling in every morning long after we're gone.*

e) *I've been working in an investment company for about four years.*

f) *In fact, the statistics are getting worse – I think it's under three years now.*

A We can use the continuous form to describe activities:

1 actions that are background events (possibly finished) before another event (sentences a, b and _____).

2 actions that are temporary/incomplete or we want to stress the duration (usually a long time) (sentence _____).

3 actions that are repeated (sentence _____).

4 actions that are in the process of changing (sentence _____).

B We can also use continuous forms (especially the Past Continuous) to sound more tentative and less direct in suggestions, offers, inquiries, etc.

C 'Stative' verbs are not usually used with the Present/Past/Future Perfect Continuous.

1 Verbs of personal feeling: *like*, ...

2 Verbs of thought: *know*, ...

3 Verbs of the senses: *appear*, ...

---

see Reference page 117

7 **a** Rewrite the sentences (1–8), changing the verb forms into the continuous. Does this change the meaning? If so, how?

1 I've read that book.
2 He gets bored.
3 I'll work till about 8 p.m. tonight.
4 She hit me.
5 The first chapter is written.
6 What music do you listen to?
7 He had lost his hair.
8 The coach leaves at 11 p.m.

b Are the responses (1–8) to the simple or continuous form of the sentences in exercise 7a? Could they be replies to both?

1 Was it good?
   = *reply to 'I've read that book' (simple form)*

2 Why don't you take him to the park?
   = *reply to 'He's getting bored' (continuous form)*

3 What are your plans after that?
4 How long did this go on for?
5 How long did it take?
6 It's the first time I've heard it. I don't know the name of the singer.
7 I know. I thought he looked completely different, totally bald.
8 Can you ask the driver to make it 11.30? The tour party needs a bit more time to see the palace.

8 Complete the text with the correct form of the verbs from the box. Use the continuous form if both forms are possible.

> urge   go back   grow   work   begin   drive
> seem   advocate   ponder   quote

At the beginning of last month I looked out of my window and saw the telltale signs: increased traffic, early-morning crowds, glum faces. Yes, that's right, the children (1) _____ to school and parents (2) _____ a new work year. And I asked myself an old question: do we have the work/life balance right?

A new generation of economists (3) _____ the century-long assumption of economics: that men and women are motivated by more – more profit, more possessions, more work. Is the hectic pace of life what we really want? (4) _____ 14-hour days long into our old age? And will it make us happy?

The number of people in mid-career who (5) _____ ready to abandon the desperate climb up the corporate ladder (6) _____ . And now, several journalists and social commentators (7) _____ us to go slower and enjoy life.

Tom Hodgkinson, in *How to Be Idle*, says that prominent literary figures (8) _____ the idle life for centuries. He (9) _____ Bertrand Russell, Samuel Johnson and others. Carl Honoré's *In Praise of Slow* also suggests that slowing down may be the best way, and he provides a telling anecdote. He recalls a time recently when he (10) _____ extremely fast in Italy because he was late for a Slow Food meal. The irony of it!

9 Read the Lifelong learning box and do the exercises.

Lifelong learning

Keeping motivated

! 1 Work in pairs. Which of these statements sounds like you? Are there any advantages/disadvantages to each way of learning?

a) As a student, I like the idea of 'In Praise of Slow'! I take my time when I learn new information.

b) I'm a fast learner. I try to learn as much as I can as quickly as possible.

c) I try to set myself specific learning goals (e.g. learning 30 new words in a week).

2 Learning goals can be motivating and can help us to manage our time. What type of learning goals would you/do you like to set yourself? Think about the ideas below and add some of your own.

*take an exam   learn X words per week
listen to the news in English
write emails in English regularly
read a work of English literature
conduct a meeting in English
understand English-language films/TV*

Speaking

10 Read the profile of Dana Kolansky. Is she an idler or a striver?

<u>Profile of Dana Kolansky</u>
Dana is a shop assistant and part-time anthropology student.
Before getting a job as a shop assistant, she had been working in a bar.
After finishing work she usually goes jogging.
At the moment she's reading a book on anthropology.
In the last few days, she has been studying for an exam.
Recently, she's been learning German as a hobby.
This weekend she'll be working on a paper for her MA, playing squash with a friend and going dancing with her boyfriend.

11 a Look at the profile outline below. What questions will you need to ask to complete it?

Profile of _____ (name)
_____ is a _____.
Before -ing _____, _____ had been _____.
After finishing work/her daily studies _____ usually _____.
At the moment _____ is reading _____.
In the last few days _____ has been _____-ing _____.
Recently _____ has been _____-ing.
This weekend _____ will be _____-ing.

b Work in pairs. Interview each other.

c Is your partner an idler or a striver? Choose one or two pieces of information to tell the class.

Reading

1 Work in pairs and discuss the questions.

1 What is happening in the photos?

2 Have you ever been in any situations like these? What happened? How did you resolve the problem?

2 **a** Read the problems (A and B). What advice can you think of? What advice would you give?

b Read the advice (1–4) to Silvana/Jake's problems. Was your advice similar? Do you agree with the suggestions?

ADVICE.COM

http://www.advice.com

A *My friend's kids are too spoilt!*

My closest school friend has two healthy, normal children aged seven and nine. The trouble is, they are incredibly spoilt. Every time they come round, they jump on furniture and break things. They even set the kitchen on fire once. Even worse is my friend's reaction. When I try to say something to her, she gives me dirty looks and says, 'That's kids for you!' I don't know what to do.

Silvana

B *Too much exaggeration?!*

I got a job recently in a very good company. During the application process I exaggerated a few details on my CV. The thing is, I really wanted the job. I knew I could do it, and felt that adding a few things to my CV would give me a better chance. Recently, a colleague of mine who had done the same thing got caught. He had said he had experience in certain areas, but he didn't. They fired him. What really worries me is that my company is now promising to check up on all the employees. I am seriously nervous, even though I am doing a good job and my boss likes me. What should I do?

Jake

1

Dear Silvana,

When our friends have children, it often creates a barrier because the dynamic changes. What you need to do is to put yourself in your friend's shoes. She's used to their behaviour. You're not. She deals with them every day. You don't. She loves them unconditionally. You love them as long as they're as quiet and well-behaved as china dolls. The fact remains that you need to find a solution. One thing you could try is giving the children rewards for good behaviour: a bar of chocolate if they keep their feet off the furniture. This way, it emphasises positive behaviour. What might also work is having some games available for the children. Most bad behaviour is because of boredom, so maybe there's not enough for the children to do in your house. Good luck!

Faisal P

2

Dear Jake,

I can understand why you fooled the company (you wanted the job). Why you insist on fooling yourself I really don't know. You didn't 'exaggerate'. You didn't 'add a few things' to your CV. You lied. There are no other words for it. The first thing you must do is admit it to yourself. The second thing you must do is go straight to your boss, explain exactly what you did and why you did it. The truth is, if your boss values you and your work, you may get away with it.

Penelope

3

Dear Silvana,

There's not much you can do. They're her kids, not yours. But you don't have to put up with that kind of behaviour in your house. Why don't you arrange to visit them in her house? That way, if the kids start acting up, you can go at any time. And try to see your friend without the kids, in a restaurant once a month, or arrange something special just for the two of you. The point is, she was your friend before the kids, and she can still be your friend now.

Gertrude Jarvis

4

Dear Jake,

The fact of the matter is that 19% of all job applicants claim skills they don't have, 28% exaggerate the pay from their former jobs, and millions of people claim to have had experiences like working in the rainforest on 'community projects' that no one can verify. Don't worry about it. Look at it from the company's point of view. Do they really want to go to the trouble of firing you and finding a replacement when they don't really need to? What they really care about isn't the morals or ethics of you embellishing your CV – it's your ability to do the job. That's why your mate got fired. Relax, man! You're safe.

Anthony

Grammar | fronting

3 **a** Look at rule A in the Active grammar box. Rewrite example 2 using fronting to emphasis the word *why*. Then check with website answer 2.

b Find other examples of fronting in website answers 1, 3 and 4.

c Look at rule B in the Active grammar box. Find other examples of fronting phrases in website answers 1–4.

Active grammar

A We sometimes move the object, verb, adverb or adjective to the front of a sentence in order to give it more emphasis.

1 *My friend's reaction is even worse*
→ ***Even worse** is my friend's reaction.*

2 *I really don't know why you insist on fooling yourself.* → _____

B We often use fronting phrases (*the trouble is …/the question is …/the fact of the matter is…/the fact remains that …*) to emphasise the importance of what we are going to say.

3 *The trouble is, they are incredibly spoilt.*

4 *The thing is, I really wanted the job.*

---

see Reference page 117

4 Rewrite the sentences (1–6) starting with the words in brackets, so that the meaning stays the same.

1 She didn't discipline them – that was the problem. (The)

2 I'm not sure how long he hoped to get away with this lie. (How)

3 I don't know how she manages with those kids. (How)

4 Their behaviour was completely unacceptable. (Completely)

5 My colleague lost his job because his work was so bad. (So)

6 I really didn't know why they wanted to check up on me. (Why)

5 **a** Work in groups of three. Read about a problem.

Student A: turn to page 148.

Student B: turn to page 150.

Student C: turn to page 152.

b Take turns to explain your problems and give advice. Try to use fronting expressions.

Pronunciation | fronting

6 **a** 2.16 Listen to sentences 1–3 from exercise 4. Which words are stressed?

b Listen again and repeat.

7 **a** Write three more sentences about the situations you discussed in exercise 5.

b Work in small groups. Take turns to say your sentences. Pay attention to stress and intonation.

Listening and speaking

8 **a** Work in pairs and discuss the questions.

1 What can go wrong with everyday machines?

2 Do you have any recent experiences of machines going wrong?

b 2.17 Listen to three people complaining about problems with machines. What machine are they talking about in each case and what's the problem?

9 **a** Read the How to... box. Are the expressions followed by a verb + *-ing*, an infinitive with *to* or an infinitive without *to*?

How to... describe problems

It keeps (1) _____ .
I can't get it to (2) _____ .
It's always (3) _____ .
I don't know how to make it (4) _____ .
I'm having problems (5) _____ .
This … seems (6) _____ .
It won't (7) _____ .

---

b 2.17 Listen again and check.

10 **a** Work in pairs. Imagine there is a problem with an item of technology in your home. Take turns to describe it (without mentioning the name of the item) using language from the How to... box.

b Take turns to guess what your partner is talking about and come up with a solution if possible.

Vocabulary | cause and effect

11 **a** Read what eight people say about issues at work or in their life as a student. Are any of the comments true for you?

1 Exams are a <u>major source</u> of stress for me and my friends at the end of every year. (Maria-Angeles, student)

2 Email has <u>brought about</u> wonderful changes in the way we work but some people send far too many unedited ones. (Sharifa, office worker)

3 The biggest <u>cause of</u> stress in my job is dealing with uncooperative people. Working the city centre around midnight is always a challenge. (Harry, police officer)

4 My major worry is keeping my customers happy. The rising cost of oil <u>results in</u> higher prices for them, so this is a big issue for me. (Hamid, taxi driver)

5 The decisions I make have <u>far-reaching implications</u> for individuals and society, so I need to get it right every time. (Conrad, judge)

6 We have a huge <u>influence on</u> children so we must always be at our best, no matter how we're feeling. (Jemima, teacher)

7 The things we make sometimes <u>give rise to</u> huge social movements and real progress, but we spend most of our lives alone, unrecognised, fiddling with small machines. (Paul, inventor)

8 I have no idea where my creativity <u>stems from</u>, but when it periodically dries up, it's extremely stressful. (Kimberly, fashion designer)

b The <u>underlined</u> phrases in exercise 11a all describe cause or effect. Which are nouns and which are verbs? Write them in the table.

nouns	verbs
It has its <u>origins</u> in ... The <u>result</u> is ... It has its <u>roots</u> in ...	They <u>influence</u> many people ... It <u>breeds</u> confidence ...

12 Delete the incorrect words in *italics*.

1 Unemployment is a major *source/cause/root* of worry for me.

2 The rivalry has its *implications/roots/origins* in an old argument.

3 This invention *brought about/influenced on/gave rise to* a social movement.

4 The idea *stems from/has its origins in/results in* ancient philosophy.

5 Boredom and alcohol can sometimes *rise/breed/result in* violence.

6 The new law *has implications for/results/will influence* the development of business.

13 **a** Complete the sentences so they are true for you.

1 ... influenced me a lot, because ... .

2 ... is sometimes a source of stress to me.

3 ... resulted in me learning English.

4 My family's roots are in ... .

5 ... has serious implications for my future.

6 I hope to have an influence on ... .

b Work in pairs. Compare your sentences.

Speaking

14 **a** Think of a problem or issue (e.g. stress, bad neighbours, unemployment, unhealthy lifestyles, annoying emails, pollution, etc.). Make notes about the topics below.

- the causes of the problem/issue
  unhealthy lifestyles: too much junk food, sitting all day
- the effects it has had on you/others
  unfit, get sick more often
- some solutions
  change diet, do daily exercise

b Work in groups and discuss your ideas.

c Report back to the class. Which are 'hot topics' and what solutions did your group come up with?

1 Choose the correct words in *italics*. Then complete the tables with the words from the boxes.

1 There have been a number of claims (1) *with regard to/regarding/to be precise* the Internet. It is a great tool for information-sharing, and some search engines, (2) *notably/namely/in terms of* Google, have long been household names.

> ~~regarding~~ in terms of notably namely
> in particular with regard to to be precise

Introducing a topic	Being specific
regarding	

2 Originally, the Internet was used by academics. (3) *Nevertheless,/However,/Furthermore,* criminals recognised its usefulness immediately. The Internet crosses international boundaries. (4) *What's more,/However,/Furthermore,* it allows anonymity.

> furthermore nevertheless on the other hand
> what's more and yet however in addition

Contrast	Saying more

3 It is necessary to (5) *hint at/highlight/underline* some of the problems: besides various scams, the music industry's sales have suffered because of piracy on the Web. We can't be sure but reasonable estimates would (6) *suggest/focus on/hint at* further losses in the near future.

> highlight hint (at) imply point out
> emphasise infer stress underline
> focus on suggest

Verbs of direct focus	Verbs that focus indirectly

4 If we try to (7) *evaluate/appraise/generate* the Internet's effect, it is possible to (8) *assess/formulate/construct* a balanced thesis: it has great benefits because it is free and open, and drawbacks in that it makes crime simpler.

> generate assess construct evaluate
> appraise formulate

Verbs for judging	Verbs which mean 'create'

5 (9) *To sum up,/In conclusion,/In chronological order,* the Internet has become a tool for good and bad deeds, just like all other technology.

> to sum up for X days/hours running
> in order of + (age, importance, etc.)
> in alphabetical/chronological order in conclusion

Arranging data	Finishing

2 Choose the correct words in *italics*.

There are many differences between academic writing and literary writing. In academic writing every point contributes towards the thesis. (1) *Furthermore,/Regarding* the purpose of academic writing is usually to inform rather than entertain. (2) *Namely/In terms of* style, academic writing is more complex, and longer, more abstract words are used. (3) *Nevertheless/On the other hand,* fiction tends to (4) *emphasise/infer* the things that happen. Another difference is that academic writing is explicit about how parts of the text relate; everything is signalled, whereas writers of fiction leave 'gaps' where things are (5) *implied/stressed* but not (6) *inferred/pointed out* overtly. These gaps allow readers to use their imagination. A further difference is that academic writers have responsibility; (7) *with regard to/in particular*, they must provide evidence for their claims. Writers of fiction, (8) *and yet/however*, are free to (9) *construct/appraise* fictitious worlds.

3 Work in pairs. Ask and answer the questions using language from exercises 1 and 2.

1 Will you need to read or write academic texts in English now or in the future?

2 Are there any academic texts which you found particularly memorable or useful?

3 Is formal English easier or more difficult for you to understand than spoken English? Why?

1 **a** Read the statements (a–j). Can any of them be used to describe the photos?

a Travel is the greatest form of education.

b Marriage is an old-fashioned idea and it's not necessary these days.

c Money can't make you happy.

d The dominance of any one culture is bad for the world.

e Modern technology has not made the world a better place.

f Rich countries should always give money to poor countries.

g Space exploration is a waste of money.

h As you become older, you become wiser.

i Nature gives us the best things in life.

j Childhood is the happiest time of life.

b Read the statements from exercise 1a again and give them a number from 1–5 (1 = completely disagree, 5 = completely agree).

c Choose five topics which you would like to discuss.

2 **a** Work in groups. Compare the topics you have chosen but do not give your opinions about the issues yet. Decide which five you will discuss.

b When you have agreed on the topics you are going to discuss, compare the numbers you gave for each statement. Discuss your opinions, giving reasons and examples.

c Report back to the rest of the class. Which issues did you talk about and what were the main views/opinions on each?

Reported speech

Reporting verbs show the function of the original piece of speech.

'You can't leave the office before 6.00.' (She informed him that he couldn't leave the office before 6.00.

Reporting verbs use different patterns. The majority use a verb + (*that*) clause. Other examples are as follows.

verb + *that* clause: *accept, recollect, respond, imply, insist, presume, maintain, suggest, answer, confess, remember, conclude, state, boast, repeat*

verb + object + *to* + infinitive: *persuade, remind, tell, advise, urge, warn, expect, force, invite, order*

verb + object + *that* clause: *inform, advise, remind, tell*

verb + *to* + infinitive: *agree, refuse, propose, decide*

verb + *-ing*: *deny, regret, suggest, mention*

verb + object + preposition + *-ing*: *blame (someone) for, congratulate (someone) on, thank (someone) for*

Often when reporting speech, we shift the tense 'back' (e.g. if the speech was in the Present Simple, we report their words in the Past Simple).

Continuous forms

We use continuous tenses to talk about:

background actions that are in progress at the moment we describe:

*When I woke up, **it was raining**.*

actions that are temporary or incomplete:

*She**'s working** for me at the moment.*

actions that are repeated:

*I**'ve been training** every day for the last month.*

actions in the process of change:

*Costs **are rising**.*

Sometimes we use the Past Continuous to sound more tentative and less direct.

*I **was wondering** if you could help me.*

'Stative' verbs are not usually used with the Present/Past/Future Continuous. Some common stative verbs are as follows.

verbs of personal feeling: *like, love, hate, want, prefer, dislike, wish*

verbs of thought: *know, believe, imagine, mean, realise, understand, doubt, feel (have an opinion)*

verbs of the senses: *hear, sound, appear, taste, see, smell, resemble, seem*

verbs of fixed situations: *depend on, contain, belong to, own, involve, include, possess*

Some stative verbs have a continuous form but the meaning may be a little different.

*I **feel** he deserves the prize. (belief)*

*I**'m feeling** sick. (sense)*

*I **see** your point. (understand)*

*I**'m seeing** the boss tomorrow. (plan to meet)*

Fronting

In informal English, we sometimes begin a sentence with the complement (object, verb, adjective or adverb). This gives the complement more emphasis.

***Intelligent she may be**, but kind she isn't!*

We sometimes use *what* or another question word.

*I don't know **what** she's doing here!*

→ ***What** she's doing here I don't know!*

Fronting can provide a link to previous information.

*Her first book was bad. **Much better was her second**.*

We can front verbs and adjectives with *as* and *though*.

***Tired though I was**, I didn't stop running.*

There are a number of common 'fronting phrases' which show the importance of what follows.

***The trouble is**, he's so lazy.*

***The question is**, can we get her to join us?*

***The fact of the matter is**, you're not good enough.*

Key vocabulary

Issues

biotechnology censorship poverty democracy globalisation global warming immigration identity theft space exploration multiculturalism unemployment depletion of the ozone layer cloning the right to vote freedom of speech giant corporations pollution

Contrasting opinions

It does more harm than good   It's a waste of space It's overrated   It's underrated   We can do without it It's been disastrous for humanity   It's deadly It's had big benefits for humanity   It's indispensable It's been a force for good   It's invaluable We can't do without it

Lifestyles

tear my hair out   life in the fast lane   wake-up call the be-all and end-all   go with the flow work around the clock   burn out   golden opportunity have itchy feet   the buzz

Cause and effect

a major source of (stress)   a cause of far-reaching implications   has its roots in an influence on   bring about   give rise to result in   influence   stem from

Academic English

in terms of   in particular   with regard to furthermore   nevertheless   and yet   in addition on the other hand   imply   emphasise   infer stress   generate   assess   formulate   notably for (X) days/hours running   to sum up in alphabetical/chronological order

Listen to the explanations and vocabulary.

ACTIVEBOOK

see Writing bank page 162

1 Find seven mistakes in the text and correct them.

'We propose to adopt a new measurement of people's lives. Recently it was explained us that the kingdom of Bhutan measures its citizens' wellbeing by Gross National Happiness instead of Gross National Product. The country encourages people think about quality of life, not just money. In many countries tourism is blamed for destroy the local culture. While the Bhutanese are not accusing anyone of deliberately harm the environment, in Bhutan, tourism is strictly limited. We suggest to adopt this same idea. We urge people to considering spiritual wealth, as well as money. This approach is guaranteed to opening our eyes to a better way of life.'

2 Complete the questions with the words in brackets.

1 A: _____ (think) of doing a PhD?
   B: Yes, I was. It seemed like a good idea, but I didn't have enough money.

2 A: _____ (wear) those weird clothes?
   B: Because I'm supposed to be at a fancy dress party in ten minutes.

3 A: _____ (go) when I saw you this afternoon?
   B: To the bank. But it was closed by the time I got there.

4 A: _____ (play) basketball?
   B: For about ten years. But I only play once a week nowadays.

5 A: _____ (live) there long before they kicked him out?
   B: Yes, he had. Nearly 20 years. That's why he was so upset.

6 A: _____ (not/understand) the task?
   B: Because I hadn't been listening when you gave the instructions.

7 A: _____ (stay) since you left the hostel?
   B: In my sister's flat, but I'll only stay there until I find my own place.

8 A: _____ (see) what I mean?
   B: Not exactly. Can you explain it again?

3 Put the words in the box in the correct place in texts 1–3.

would   problem   is   matter   what   why   surprises

1
My family is going to visit my mother-in-law next week. The is, we can't stand her cooking! I want to be culturally sensitive – she is from another country – but the fact of the is that the kids and I just can't eat her meals. Quite we're going to do I have no idea.
Marlene

2
What me is her cultural insensitivity. The thing, she has to adapt to you, too. Why not take her out to nice restaurants because that's what daughters-in-law do in your country?
Veronica

3
You're complaining about this I really don't know. All over the world, people are starving. You're lucky enough to have food, so just pretend you like it. If you're desperate, one idea be to train the kids to say 'Mmm, delicious'.
Ayodele

4 Complete the sentences.

1 Carl Honoré had a great _____ on the Slow Life Movement. Many people followed his ideas.
2 The modern work ethic has _____ in more stressful lifestyles. It does more _____ than good.
3 Twenty-two percent of UK citizens suffer from work-related stress. The _____ of this are very serious.
4 Stress at work _____ rise to absenteeism, which is disastrous _____ business.
5 Honoré wants to _____ about a great revolution in lifestyles. His work is a _____ for good.
6 Many people's sense of satisfaction stems _____ their job. Most of us _____ do without work.
7 Violence, job insecurity and overwork are the major _____ of worry in the US.
8 Honoré's philosophy has its _____ in the lifestyles of our ancestors, who didn't work so hard.

5 Some lines in the text below have one extra incorrect word. Write the extra words in the spaces. Tick (✓) if there is no extra word.

With a regard to the type of language used by academics in their   ____
publications, there are a number of tendencies that we wish to point   ____
out. Firstly, we must emphasise to the lack of clarity in much academic   ____
writing. Of the 400 papers evaluated, over 300–317 really to be precise   ____
were considered 'difficult' in their terms of sentence and paragraph   ____
construction. What's the more, the writers tend to use deliberately obscure ____
vocabulary. While this study focused up on scientific writing, we believe ____
that its findings can be widely applied. Nevertheless, we must also   ____
underline the fact that there is some outstanding writing, too. To sum them up, ____
we need to consider a number of factors. In an order of importance ...   ____

9

Lead-in

1 Work in pairs. Look at the photos and discuss the questions.
1   Which of the arts are represented?
2   Can you think of any other examples of 'visual' arts?
3   Which do you prefer and why?

2 **a** Look at the sentences below. Which refer to books/film/theatre/art/architecture? There may be more than one answer.
1   It was a/an spectacular/dreadful/appalling performance.
2   The scenery was breathtaking/disappointing/stunning.
3   It's an absolute masterpiece/not one of his best/his finest piece.
4   The acting was stereotyped/poor/over the top.
5   It's a fantastic/difficult/heavy read.
6   The style is contemporary/traditional/gothic.
7   The special effects were astonishing/incredible/awful.
8   He is famous for his landscapes/portraits/sculptures.

b Work in pairs. Describe the photos with the words from exercise 2a.

3 Work in pairs and discuss the questions.
1   How often do you go to the theatre/the cinema/museums or other buildings of interest? How often do you read novels?
2   Talk about paintings, buildings, films, novels, etc. that you like or dislike. Use vocabulary from exercise 2a.

My favourite painting is Picasso's Guernica. *I think it's an absolute masterpiece.*

I didn't really enjoy Iron Man. *In my opinion, the special effects were rather disappointing.*

Reading

1 Work in pairs and discuss the questions.

1 What do you think the people in the pictures have in common?

2 What do you think are their areas of special interest and achievements?

2 Read the texts to check or find out more.

The Yellow Emperor

The first sovereign of civilised China, Huang Ti, or the Yellow Emperor as he became known, is now recognised as the common ancestor of the Chinese people. Living in a time of constant warfare between tribes, Huang Ti strove to improve the virtues of people, pacifying by strengthening his army and unifying the tribes. He introduced the idea of military discipline, invented the compass to improve his military strategy, and used carts in warfare.

Once he had established peace, he created civilised systems for his people. Among the many inventions attributed to him are the calendar, mathematics (he invented numbers and a system for measuring length and weight), music (he invented the flute using bamboo), writing (he invented Chinese characters), boats, carts, bows and arrows, etc.

His scientific interests also led him to author *The Inner Book of Simple Questions of the Yellow Emperor*, the founding classic of Chinese medicine. His queen is also famous for having been the first to raise silkworms to make clothes with silk.

Leonardo da Vinci

As a painter, his legacy of works is indisputably less extensive than other master painters. As an anatomist, he failed to publish his research. As a sculptor, he left us not a single verified sculpture. As a mathematician, he had no significant input into the development of the theories of mathematics. As a scientist, his records are disorderly. As a musician, he left little record of his music. As an architect, he left no notable buildings for us to visit. And yet he is popularly held as one of the most important figures of the Italian Renaissance. In the words of Sigmund Freud, 'Leonardo da Vinci was like a man who awoke too early in the darkness, while the others were all still asleep.'

Most people recognise the 'Mona Lisa' or the 'Last Supper' as examples of this artist's extraordinary capabilities. However, he was not just an artistic genius, but he was also a genius in the fields of architecture, engineering and science. His sketchbooks, with notes often written in mirror form, were full of ideas for his inventions. Some were improvements to existing machines, others were new and ranged from a primitive tank to a human-powered flying machine. These books were to stun the world when they were discovered centuries after his death.

Rachel Carson

Environmentalism has existed in various forms for centuries, but Rachel Carson's influence in the field is unsurpassed. She made a vital contribution to the environment and her work is still influential today, half a century later.

Brought up on a farm in Pennsylvania, USA, she spent her childhood exploring the land and writing animal stories. After completing her Master's degree at Johns Hopkins University, Carson wrote a radio show which explored marine life. But it was her work in the 1940s that cemented her reputation. A fire ant eradication program caught her attention and she became immersed in the science of pesticides and environmental poisons. After working on her ideas for several years, she published *Silent Spring* in 1962. The nascent environmental movement drew inspiration from the work, and President John F. Kennedy demanded the testing of chemicals mentioned in it.

As with all revolutionaries, she came under criticism. One biochemist wrote, 'If man were to follow the teachings of Miss Carson, we would return to the Dark Ages.' On one occasion, a former Secretary of Agriculture concluded that, because she was unmarried, she was 'probably a communist'. However, the scientific community and the public soon realised that her claims were accurate.

3 Read the texts again and answer the questions.

1 Who was concerned about the impact of humans on the environment?
2 Who wrote notes and ideas in a type of code?
3 Who had ideas for military artillery?
4 Who influenced a President?
5 Who wanted people to have a better quality of life?
6 Who was interested in medical science?

4 Work in pairs. Which of the people you read about achieved the most, in your opinion? Which would you most like to have met? Why?

Grammar | dependent prepositions

5 **a** Look at the underlined dependent prepositions in the texts. Write them in the table in the Active grammar box.

b Look at the phrases from the box below. Add them to the table in the Active grammar box.

> hope for   make observations about   succeed in
> devote your life to   improve on   (be) obsessed with
> a solution to   admiration for   specialise in   the quality of
> of all time   in later life   in recognition of ...

c Match definitions a–f to phrases from the Active grammar box.

a spend your life trying to do something.
b thought to have been achieved/accomplished by someone.
c to think about something all the time.
d be completely involved in something.
e do/make something better.
f feeling of great respect/liking for something/someone

Active grammar

verb + preposition	range _____ ... (to ...) work _____ ... attribute _____ ...
verb + object + preposition	draw inspiration _____ ... made contributions _____ ...
noun + preposition	in the fields _____ ... ideas _____ /_____ ... the development _____ ...
adjective + preposition	(be) famous _____ ... (be) immersed _____ ...
prepositional phrases (beginning with a preposition)	in a time _____ ... _____ one occasion

6 Choose the correct words in *italics*. What do you think is the name of this visionary scientist?

Widely regarded as the greatest scientist of the 20th century, or even (1) *of all/in all* time, this man devoted his life (2) *in/on/to* science. He made major contributions (3) *from/to/for* the development of quantum mechanics, statistical mechanics and cosmology, and in recognition (4) *for/of/about* his work, he was awarded the Nobel Prize for Physics in 1921.

In 1905, while working alone in a patent laboratory, obsessed (5) *in/with/from* relativity, he eventually succeeded (6) *to/in/with* finding a solution (7) *to/at/of* a problem he had been working (8) *in/for/on*. He developed his own theory of relativity, which disproved things that Newton had previously established. Later in the same year he made further observations (9) *in/about/for* the universe and how it is made up and improved (10) *on/to/with* his own theories until he developed the theory which he became famous (11) *of/about/for*: $E=mc^2$. (12) *In/At/To* later life, he realised both the positive and negative implications of his work as nuclear energy and atomic bombs were developed.

7 Complete the sentences with the correct prepositions.

1 The Yellow Emperor succeeded _____ bringing civilised life to his people.
2 Einstein had great admiration _____ the work of Newton.
3 Newton spent his time absorbed _____ his work.
4 Leonardo da Vinci made observations _____ nature in his sketchbooks.
5 Newton specialised _____ the field of mathematics.
6 Mozart was famous _____ being able to re-create a piece of music after hearing it only once.
7 At one time, van Gogh was obsessed _____ painting sunflowers.
8 Shakespeare made a major contribution _____ world literature.

see Reference page 131

8 **a** Think of one or two other famous 'visionaries' or inspirational people. Make notes about them using prepositional phrases from the Active grammar box.

b Work in pairs. Describe the people you made notes on. Ask your partner questions to find out more information.

Do you think she's the most important ... of all time?

What did she do in later life?

Listening

9 Work in pairs. Discuss the questions.

1 Do you know of any people living today who could be called geniuses? Why are they thought of as geniuses?

2 When do you think geniuses do their best work: when they are under pressure or when they are relaxing?

10 **a** ● 2.18 Listen to a radio interview about geniuses. Make notes on the topics below.

• discoveries made outside the laboratory

• the psychology of high achievers

• Can only creative people be geniuses?

b Work in pairs and compare your ideas.

c Listen again to check.

11 Work in pairs and discuss the questions.

1 Did you find any of the information in the interview surprising?

2 Have you experienced finding the solution to a problem by 'sleeping on it'?

3 Do you pursue any creative hobbies or interests? Did you use to?

4 What do you do to take your mind off a problem?

Speaking

12 Look at the words/phrases from the box below. Write them in the correct row in the How to... box.

> without a doubt   it's not 100 percent certain
> undeniably   questionable   unquestionably
> irrefutable   debatable   it's not clear-cut

> ### How to... describe certainty/ uncertainty
>
> | certainty | *indisputable* |
> |---|---|
> | uncertainty | |

13 Choose the correct words in *italics*.

1 It's *debatable/without a doubt* whether Leonardo da Vinci was a genius.

2 It's *not 100 percent certain/undeniably* what or who killed Mozart.

3 The novel is *not clear-cut/indisputably* his greatest work.

4 The Yellow Emperor was *not clear-cut/unquestionably* a great leader.

5 It's not *clear-cut/irrefutable* why Leonardo wrote in mirror form.

6 Mozart was *not 100 percent certain/irrefutably* exceptionally gifted.

7 The story about Newton's discovery under the apple tree is *questionable/without a doubt*.

8 The impact of Einstein's theories are *without a doubt/irrefutable*.

14 Work in small groups and discuss the statements. Try to use language from the How to... box.

1 Genius is an overused term. Many so-called geniuses had one good idea and got lucky.

2 Being a genius doesn't guarantee you success in life. Other things are more important.

3 Genius is 10% inspiration and 90% perspiration.

4 It's better to know a little about a lot of different things, rather than a lot about only one thing.

A La Familia   B Daniel   C Giulietta Coates

Vocabulary | describing art

1 Work in pairs. Discuss what sort of art you like and dislike.

2 **a** Check you understand the underlined words.

1 This is an abstract painting by Mondrian.

2 This painting is really striking. It stands out.

3 I don't like avant-garde art. I can't understand it.

4 Don't you find her work really calm and tranquil?

5 I love colourful art, like Matisse's work.

6 That painting is rather plain, isn't it?

a So you prefer more traditional stuff?

b I prefer monochrome images.

c No way! I think her work is very disturbing.

d Oh, I think that one's a bit dull. It's not my type of thing at all.

e I think it's stunning. I noticed it at once!

f He also did a lot of figurative work, didn't he?

b Match the underlined words in sentences 1–6 with their opposites in a–f. Which are used to show personal opinions? Which describe facts?

Listening and speaking

3 **a** Look at the pictures above and read the text. Which picture do you like best/least? Which do you think should win the competition?

Every year, at the National Portrait Gallery in London, there is a competition for the best portrait. The winner is decided democratically: everyone who visits the exhibition can vote for their favourite portrait. The prize is £25,000.

b 🔊 2.19 Listen to three people discussing the pictures. Which do they talk about in each conversation? Which words/phrases helped you decide? Which picture do they think should win?

4 🔊 2.20 Listen to the next part. Which picture actually won? What does the speaker think of the winner?

5 **a** Write the sentences from the box below in the correct place in the How to... box.

> It's really not my taste.   It's not my cup of tea.
> I've always admired her work.
> I'm a big fan of his stuff.
> He's one of my all-time favourites.
> I can't relate to this type of thing.

How to... say what you like/dislike

saying what you like	*I'm really into her work.*
saying what you don't like	*It's not my (kind of) thing at all.*

b 🔊 2.21 Listen to the sentences from exercise 5a. Mark the stress.

c Work in pairs. Tell your partner about a picture you like (or don't like).

Grammar | discourse markers

6 **a** Look at the <u>underlined</u> phrases 1–5 in the Active grammar box. Write them in the table.

b Add the phrases from the box below to the table in the Active grammar box.

> anyway, what I was going to say was   more or less   frankly
> mind you   as a matter of fact   as far as … is concerned
> in fact   as for   as regards/regarding

Active grammar

Discourse markers are words/expressions which help us to organise what we want to say or write. They also show our attitude to the subject.

1 … <u>as I was saying</u>, it really does look like a photo …

2 … the expression on her face <u>is kind of</u> intense …

3 … <u>it sort of</u> looks like a photo …

4 … <u>to be honest</u>, it's not really my taste …

5 … <u>to tell you the truth</u>, I still wouldn't want it hanging on my bedroom wall.

focusing on the main topic or returning to a previous line of discussion	introducing an opinion or criticism
softening an opinion or criticism	making additional (often contrasting) points

see Reference page 131

7 Complete the statements below with one word.

1 _____ be honest, Salvador Dalí's work isn't my cup of tea.

2 Caravaggio had a very difficult life. Anyway, _____ I was going to say was he is my favourite artist.

3 I love those old Renaissance paintings. To tell you _____ truth, I don't like modern art at all.

4 Nek Chand must be one of the world's greatest artists. _____ any rate, he's the best in India!

5 I think the 'Mona Lisa' is overrated. As _____ matter of fact, I don't think it's Leonardo's best painting.

6 As far as modern sculpture is _____ , Henry Moore is undoubtedly the greatest.

7 Georgia O'Keefe's paintings of flowers are kind _____ interesting. I love the colours she uses.

8 _____ I was saying, Lee Krasner's art was overshadowed by that of her husband, Jackson Pollock.

8 Read the dialogues about art and choose the best options in *italics*.

1 A: *To be honest/ As far as it's concerned/ Regarding*, I don't like Impressionism much.

B: Neither do I. *As for it/ What I was going to say/ At any rate*, I think it's been overexposed.

2 A: Pollock's technique of dripping paint onto canvas was *as for/ anyway/kind of* strange.

B: I agree. *More or less,/ Mind you,/As regards* his work did revolutionise modern art.

3 A: I love performance art. *Sort of/ Regarding/As a matter of fact*, David Blaine's my hero.

B: David Blaine? The magician? *Anyway, what I was going to say was/Frankly,/As I was saying*, I think he's crazy!

4 A: I love Spanish art. *Kind of/ In fact/As for* Picasso, I think he was the greatest of all time.

B: Well, yes, he *more or less/ as regards/to tell you the truth* invented modern art.

5 A: *As far as it's concerned/ Regarding/Anyway* photography, Cindy Sherman is currently the most famous artist.

B: Really? *In fact/As I was saying/ To tell you the truth*, I've never heard of her.

Speaking

9 Work in pairs and discuss the questions.

1 Do you have a favourite artist or style (e.g. modern abstract paintings)? Why do you like this in particular?

2 Are there any types of art you don't like? Why?

3 Why do you think people are willing to pay a lot of money for certain works of art? Do you think art is overpriced, generally?

Reading

10 **a** Look at the cartoon. What is happening?

b Read the article and answer the questions.

1 Why was the painting so badly protected?
2 What type of people are art thieves, according to Charley Hill?
3 What are Vermeers and Gainsboroughs and what happened to them?
4 What did Hill have to do to find 'The Scream'?
5 Who is Stephane Breitwieser and why is he unusual among art thieves?

11 Work in pairs and discuss the questions.

1 Would you like Charley Hill's job? Why/Why not?
2 Do you think Hill's book sounds interesting?
3 What type of person do you think Stephane Breitwieser might be?
4 What type of people collect art? Do you think it would be an enjoyable hobby?

12 **a** Read the Lifelong learning box and answer questions 1–4 below.

Guess first

! Use contextual clues to help you with difficult vocabulary. Think about the following points when you don't know a word or phrase.

- Which words surround the unknown word?
- What is the general meaning of this part of the text?
- Can you guess by thinking of similar words in the same family or similar words in your own language?

If you can't guess, and the word seems important, use a good dictionary.

Lifelong learning

---

1 What does *thugs* (line 11) mean?
2 What words come before *thugs* in the article? How does the article describe the people who steal paintings? How does this help us guess the meaning of *thug*?
3 Does *thug* have other words in its 'family'?
4 What does the dictionary entry below tell us about the pronunciation?

thug /θʌg/ n [C] a violent man: *He was beaten up by a gang of young thugs.*

b Try to guess the meaning of words 1–7 below using the advice from the Lifelong learning box.

1 aesthetes (line 9)
2 mastermind (line 10)
3 hideout (line 11)
4 track down (line 13)
5 stuffed (line 16)
6 crack a case (line 25)
7 haul (line 44)

Now you see it ...

No wonder the man in Munch's 'The Scream' is screaming. He keeps getting stolen. The famous painting went missing in 1994 and again ten years later, both times from museums in Norway.
5 Apparently, security was extremely poor. Officials thought the painting was so famous that it wouldn't be stolen. Wrong.

The world of art theft is not, as one might presume, populated with stylish aesthetes,
10 masterminding their operations from tax-free hideouts. Art thieves are thugs, according to a book by Charley Hill. Hill was an undercover policeman whose job was to track down stolen paintings. He says that the people who steal paintings were usually
15 stealing wheels from cars a few years earlier. He describes priceless Vermeers being stuffed into the back of cars, Gainsboroughs being passed around by drug dealers with dirty hands and a particularly nasty end to one of Henry Moore's huge sculptures.
20 The bronze, 'King and Queen', a masterpiece by Moore, was too heavy for the thieves to move, so they took out a chainsaw and cut off the heads, thinking those might be worth something.

Hill's is an adventure story fit for any James Bond
25 fans. A number of years ago he cracked a case in which 11 valuable paintings had been stolen from Russborough House near Dublin. In order to rescue 'The Scream', Hill posed as a buyer for the J. Paul Getty Museum in LA: bow tie, big suit, even bigger
30 Mercedes. He also had to learn everything about the painting, or should we say paintings: there are four versions of 'The Scream'. He even memorised the patterns of wax droplets left on one version of the painting when Munch blew out a candle one night.

35 The artworks usually turn up, sometimes many years later, though the police don't always catch the thief. Even rarer is when a gentleman thief – one who steals art for personal pleasure only – is caught.

Stéphane Breitwieser, a 32-year-old from France,
40 was recently found guilty of stealing 239 artworks from 172 museums around Europe while working as a waiter. His spree lasted eight years before he was caught. He said he had done it for the love of art even though his haul was worth over $1 billion – not
45 bad for a waiter.

Speaking

1 Work in pairs. Look at the photos from a travel magazine. How do they make you feel? What do they remind you of? What do you think the story behind each photo is?

Vocabulary | vision

2 a Read an opinion of what makes a good photograph and check you understand the underlined words. Do you agree? Which photo do you think the writer would like best?

> I like photos to be really <u>evocative</u>. They need to move me. Of course a photo needs to be technically good so it isn't blurred or unbalanced or too dark, but it also needs to be <u>intriguing</u>. I want to be led into a story. Really good photos make you want to know what's going on. I don't really like standard, touristy photos. I find them too <u>clichéd</u>. I think pretty pictures are fine for photo albums but not as art. I like to see something <u>quirky</u> or unexpected in a piece of art. It doesn't have to be completely <u>breathtaking</u> but it needs to be <u>novel</u>.

b Match the underlined words/phrases from exercise 2a to phrases 1–6 with a similar meaning.

1 It's an overused stereotype.
2 It brings to mind other ideas, images, etc.
3 It's a little bit unconventional.
4 It breaks new ground.
5 It piques my curiosity.
6 It makes me sit up and take notice.

Reading

3 Work in pairs and discuss the questions.

1 What's the best way of recording holidays and memories (taking photos, writing about them, buying postcards, shooting videos, etc.)? How do you record your memories?
2 What type of person makes a good photographer or travel writer?

4 a Work in pairs.

Student A: read the article on page 148 and make notes on the topics below.

Student B: read the article on page 152 and make notes on the topics below.

• the best time to do it
• stories
• the local culture
• learning from professionals

b Tell your partner about the main ideas in your article.

5 Discuss the questions.

1 What do you think of the advice in your article? Was it interesting, obvious, surprising, etc.?

2 Are the articles for amateurs, or people who want to make a living doing these things?

3 Which sounds easier: being a photographer or being a travel writer?

4 Would you like to be a travel writer or a photographer? Why/Why not?

5 Do you know of any famous photographers or travel writers? What do you think of their work?

Grammar | unreal past

6 Read the Active grammar box and do the exercises.

Active grammar

wish/if only

If only I'd taken a better picture.

1 Find more examples of these forms in articles A and B from exercise 4a.

2 What verb form follows *wish/if only* to talk about (a) the present? (b) the past?

it's high time/it's about time

3 Find examples of these forms in the articles from exercise 4a.

4 Does *It's high time/It's about time* mean something should be happening now, but it isn't? Or does it mean that something is happening on time?

5 What verb form follows *It's high time/It's about time*?

would rather/would sooner

6 Find examples of these forms in the articles from exercise 4a.

7 What verb form follows *would sooner/would rather* if the person speaking and the subject are (a) the same? (b) different?

*I **would rather** go.* (The person speaking and her subject is *I*).

*I **would sooner** they left.* (The person speaking is *I*, but the subject is *they*).

what if/suppose (or supposing)

***Suppose** you had taken that job as a photographer? Would you be happier now?*

8 Find more examples of these forms in the articles from exercise 4a.

9 What verb form follows *what if/suppose* to talk about an imaginary situation in the (a) present? (b) past? (c) future?

---

see Reference page 131

7 Find the mistakes in six of the sentences and correct them.

1 It's high time we went on a photography course.

2 They'd rather we didn't use flash photography in the museum.

3 This scenery is so beautiful. If only I brought my camera.

4 I'd sooner you wouldn't write that down, please.

5 It's about time you go to bed.

6 What if you'll get ill when you go abroad?

7 I wish I can speak the language better. I'd ask them about their lives.

8 Suppose you woke up earlier yesterday. Would you have seen the sun rise?

8 Complete the second sentence so that it has a similar meaning to the first. Use the correct form of the verbs in brackets.

1 We should start writing our journals.
It's high _____ writing our journals. (begin)

2 What if you had the chance to become a travel journalist?
Suppose someone _____ a job as a travel journalist? (offer)

3 Please stop taking photos!
We'd rather _____ photos inside the building. (take)

4 I should have sent in my story for the travel writing competition.
If only _____ the competition, I might have won! (enter)

5 I'd love to be able to take good photos.
I wish _____ good photographer. (be)

6 We should select the photos for my new travel book together.
I'd sooner _____ photos together. (choose)

7 You should finish writing that article soon.
It's about _____ that article. (complete)

8 I'm nervous about my camera jamming at the vital moment.
What if _____ at the vital moment? (jam)

9 **a** Think about a hobby or something you have wanted to do for a long time. Complete the sentences so they are true for you.

- It's high time I ...
- It's about time ...
- I wish ...
- If only ...
- I'd sooner ... than
- Suppose ...

b Work in small groups and compare your sentences.

Speaking

10 a Work in pairs. Suppose someone offered you a job as a travel writer in the Caribbean, but it meant you had to live on a tiny island for two years. Would you accept?

b Complete the How to... box with words from the box below.

> I'd   way   unlikely   suppose   to   doing   wouldn't

How to... respond to hypothetical questions

positively	It's highly likely (1) _____ agree.
	I would probably agree (2) _____ that.
	I would consider (3) _____ that.
	I (4) _____ I might do that.
	I'd definitely do that
negatively	I probably (5) _____ accept.
	It's (6) _____ I'd be able to do that.
	There's no (7) _____ I would do that.

c ● 2.22 Listen and check.

Pronunciation | emphasis (2)

11 ● 2.23 Listen to the sentences (1–4). Where does the intonation rise to show emphasis?

1 I'd definitely do that!
2 I suppose I might do that.
3 It's unlikely I'd do that.
4 There's no way I'd do that.

Speaking and writing

12 a Work in pairs. Choose three of the situations below to discuss. Extend the discussion for as long as possible, using language from the How to... box.

1 What if you were offered a free place on either a photography course or a creative writing course? Which would you accept?

2 Suppose you could have one of the following talents: to write great novels, paint great pictures or sing brilliantly. Which would you choose?

3 What if a time machine was invented which meant you could travel to any one period in the past? Would you use it? Which period would you choose?

4 Suppose a film director asked to make a film about your life? Would you accept? Who would you like to act as you?

5 Suppose you had the opportunity to travel around the world for a year. Would you go?

6 What if someone asked you to participate in a reality TV show? Would you agree?

b Think of two more hypothetical questions to ask your partner. Start your questions with *What if ...?/Suppose ...* .

13 Work in pairs. Choose one of the situations from exercise 12a. Imagine that it really happened. Write the story in about 150 words.

1 **a** Work in pairs. Read the text and discuss what new job was created and why. Who got the job?

Visionary thinker wanted!

A few years ago, a committee at my university department held a (1) *reunion/meeting* to discuss a new post for a 'visionary' thinker. A number of the professors were (2) *sympathetic/friendly* to this idea, because, like me, they felt that our educational goals were far too (3) *sensitive/sensible* and boring; no one took risks any more because everyone wanted to (4) *fit into/suit* the current way of thinking. We also felt it would be a great (5) *possibility/opportunity* for an original thinker to come and (6) *prove/test* his or her ideas to see if they (7) *at the moment/actually* worked, while getting paid.

We hired a freelancer to do the (8) *propaganda/advertising*, and this is where we got a big surprise. The freelancer, a lady called Anousha Jalal, came up with a brilliant campaign to advertise the (9) *vacancy/vacation*. It really was a (10) *classic/classical* piece of advertising copy. In fact, her work was so imaginative and interesting that we asked her to (11) *assist/attend* an interview for the job. She wasn't sure if she wanted it, but (12) *in the end/at the end*, after lots of phone calls and emails, she had an interview and got the job.

b Read the text again. Choose the correct words in *italics*.

2 Match the words in *italics* from exercise 1a to definitions 1–12.

1 **a** when a group of people come together to discuss important issues
b when people come together a long time after they last saw each other

2 **a** willing to support someone's ideas or actions
b willing to be nice to other people (help and talk to them)

3 **a** does what is correct and doesn't take chances
b easily offended/someone who considers the feelings of others

4 **a** be appropriate/feels right
b belong in a category

5 **a** something that might happen in theory
b a real chance to do something

6 **a** use/check something to find out if it's successful
b find evidence that something is true

7 **a** in reality/in truth
b now

8 **a** false information that an organisation gives to the public to influence them
b publicity for a product/service

9 **a** holiday (US English)
b something is available (job/room in a motel)

10 **a** a style of music
b a timeless masterpiece

11 **a** help
b go to an event

12 **a** after a period of time (and maybe after discussion/debate)
b the last part of something (a book, a film, year, etc.). It is often followed by *of*.

3 Complete the sentences with the words in *italics* from exercise 1a.

1 There's a _____ for a manager at that company. It's the type of job that would _____ you.

2 We would be grateful if you could _____ us in setting up the class's 20th anniversary _____ .

3 Going to the Mozart Conference will be a great _____ to learn more about _____ music.

4 _____ of the book, the hero decides to be _____ ; he forgets his crazy dream of being a billionaire.

5 There were high hopes for the 'Wonder Drug'. _____ end, scientists _____ that it didn't work.

6 Joan's not studying _____ , but there's a _____ that she'll do a PhD next year.

7 I found it difficult to _____ that class. The other students weren't _____ at all.

8 The huge signs promoting government policies were just _____ . None of it was _____ true.

4 Choose a few of the commonly confused words that you had problems with. Write your own sentences using the words.

5 Work in pairs and discuss the questions.

1 Are there any confusing words in your own language? Are they confusing for native speakers or only for foreigners?

2 Do you know any strategies for dealing with confusing words?

3 Which words in English are confusing for speakers of your language?

1 **a** 2.24 Listen to someone describing how two popular products were developed. Write true (T) or false (F).

1 Clarence Birdseye was the first person to put food in salt water to freeze it. ☐

2 The equipment for his experiments was cheap. ☐

3 Birdseye sold the first modern freezer for $22 million. ☐

4 Chester Carlson's job was to invent a machine to make copies. ☐

5 Carlson found his work difficult because of his own health problems. ☐

6 The first commercial photocopier was made over 20 years after Carlson had first invented the machine. ☐

b Listen again to check.

2 Work in pairs and discuss the questions.

1 Why do you think it took so long for the photocopier to get funding?

2 Would you describe frozen food as an 'original' idea?

3 Can you think of any other popular products that are based on earlier inventions?

3 **a** Work in pairs. You are planning a new business venture and need to persuade the rest of the class to invest in your idea. Choose one of the following ideas (or come up with one of your own) and plan how you are going to 'sell' it to the rest of the class.

A new product
You have invented a jacket that can change colour and _____. Made of the latest hi-tech material, and with a range of ten colours, the jacket takes five seconds to change colour. It also has special _____. ...

A new service
Doitforyou.com offers to help you with _____. Users pay a fixed monthly fee and can use the service as often as they wish. Additional benefits include _____. ...

A new course
You are setting up a new course which teaches people how to _____. What is special about the course is that everyone who participates _____. ...

A new film
It is 2100. The world has become _____. Only one person can save the planet because he/she has the key to the secret _____. The problem is that there is a terrible _____ who doesn't want the world to be saved. ...

b Write the name of the product, service, course or film and a short summary of the main ideas behind it, its main benefits, etc.

c Take turns to present your proposals to the rest of the class. Ask and answer questions about each proposal.

d Which proposals are the most interesting? Which would you invest in?

Dependent prepositions

Sometimes verbs are followed by a preposition:
*ask **for**, contribute **to**, range **from** ... (**to** ...), suffer **from***

The verb and preposition can be separated by the object: *remind someone **of**, distinguish someone **from***

Sometimes, nouns are followed by prepositions. These are sometimes described as collocations:
*relationship **with**, insurance **against**, in the fields **of***

Sometimes, adjectives are followed by a preposition:
*bad **at**, similar **to**, famous **for**, concerned **about***

Sometimes, prepositions can begin common phrases:
***in** advance, **out** of order, **at** the time, **on** one occasion*

Discourse markers

Discourse is a piece of language that is longer and more complex than a sentence. We use discourse markers to organise our speech or writing and make clear the relationship between what we have said and what we will say. We also use discourse markers to show our attitude to the subject. The use of discourse markers depends on the function of our speech (e.g. persuading, agreeing, etc.). Some common discourse markers are as follows.

focusing on the main topic: *regarding, as regards, as far as ... is concerned, as for*

returning to the main point (what was said before didn't matter): *anyway, anyhow, at any rate*

returning to a previous line of discussion: *as I was saying, anyway, what I was going to say was ...*

introducing a strong opinion or criticism: *all the same, and yet, still, on the other hand*

Unreal past

wish/if only

We use *wish/if only* to describe unreal or imaginary situations. These are often regrets.

Wish/if only + past forms describe an imaginary present or future: ***If only I was** stronger.*

Wish/if only + Past Perfect describes the imaginary past: *I **wish I had bought** that CD.*

Wish + object + *would* is used to complain:
*I **wish** you **would** be quiet!*

We cannot use this construction about ourselves. The subject and object must be different.

NOT: ~~I wish I would be more intelligent.~~

it's time/it's high time/it's about time

We use *it's time*, etc. + past forms to say something should be happening now, but it isn't. It is often used for criticising someone/something:
***It's high time** you **stopped** acting like a child.*

would rather/would sooner

We use *would rather/would sooner* + Past Simple to describe preferences: *I'd **sooner** she **gave** me the cash.*

If the person who expresses the preference and the subject are the same, we use *would rather/would sooner* + infinitive without *to*:
*I'd **rather dance** the tango than the foxtrot.*

We often use *would rather/would sooner* to refuse permission:
*I'd **rather** you **didn't** smoke in my flat.*

what if/suppose/supposing

We use *what if/suppose* + past forms to ask about an imaginary situation in the present or future:
***Suppose** you **asked** the bank for a loan?*

We use *what if/suppose* + Past Perfect to ask about an imaginary situation in the past:
***What if** we **had arrived** earlier?*

We use *what if/suppose* + Present Simple to ask about a situation that we think is probable:
***What if** your plan **doesn't work**?*

Key vocabulary

Describing art

abstract striking avant-garde tranquil colourful plain traditional monochrome disturbing figurative dull stunning
I'm a big fan of his stuff
It's not my kind of thing at all
It's really not my taste
I'm really into her work
It's not my cup of tea
He's one of my all-time favourites
I've always admired her work
I can't relate to this type of thing

Vision

evocative intriguing quirky clichéd breathtaking novel overused stereotype bring to mind unconventional break new ground
pique (someone's) curiosity
make (someone) sit up and take notice

Commonly confused words

classic/classical opportunity/possibility
in the end/at the end fit into/suit vacation/vacancy propaganda/advertising sensible/sensitive
at the moment/actually friendly/sympathetic
assist/attend reunion/meeting prove/test

 Listen to the explanations and vocabulary.
ACTIVEBOOK

see Writing bank page 163

1 Match sentence beginnings 1–8 to sentence endings a–h.

1 Doris Lessing won the Nobel Prize for literature in recognition
2 Stephen Pinker, a well-known academic, is a master in the fields
3 Many people have drawn inspiration from
4 Kurosawa was one of the greatest film directors
5 Leonardo's abilities ranged from
6 Thomas Edison succeeded in
7 Madonna's constantly changing image is characteristic of
8 US pilot Amelia Earhart devoted her life to

a her ability to repackage herself for different generations.
b of her contribution to the novel.
c the life of Helen Keller.
d of all time.
e flying.
f painting to designing weapons.
g registering 1,093 patents for new inventions.
h of both cognitive science and linguistics.

2 Complete the dialogue with words/phrases from the box.

> more or less   as regards   be honest   in fact
> as far as my work is concerned   kind

A: Rachel, how are you feeling now you've won the Turner Prize?
B: Absolutely delighted. To (1) _____ , I never expected to win. I ... er ... (2) _____ of knew I had a chance, but it was a great surprise.
A: How will this affect you?
B: (3) _____ , it won't affect me at all. I already have three exhibitions planned. (4) _____ the money, it'll mean I can focus on my work.
A: We hear you'll be making videos, rather than painting. Is this true?
B: That's (5) _____ true. I'll be making videos, but I'll still paint. (6) _____ , my next exhibition will be mainly paintings.
A: Thank you, Rachel. We look forward to it.

3 Choose the correct words in *italics*.

1 What if we *are leaving/left/would have left* really early? Would we arrive on time?
2 I would rather *know/to know/knowing* the truth now than later.
3 I wish I *will/can/could* dance better.
4 It's high time we *had gone/went/go*.

5 He wishes he *had got up/got up/was getting up* earlier yesterday.
6 Supposing you *are running/run/have run* into trouble, what will you do?
7 It's about time they *learn/learned/had learned* to act like adults.
8 We'd sooner you *didn't bring/hadn't brought/ wouldn't bring* your dog yesterday.

4 Complete the sentences with words/phrases similar in meaning to the words in brackets.

1 It was a disaster – a really a_____ performance! (poor)
2 The show is quite funny. The characters are really o_____ t_____ t_____ . (exaggerated)
3 He does have interesting ideas, but his style makes it a rather h_____ read. (hard work)
4 The decor hasn't changed since the 1980s, so it's not very c_____ . (modern/up-to-date)
5 Michelangelo's 'David' is without a doubt his f_____ p_____ . (best work)
6 The i_____ special effects were what made the film such a success. (unbelievable)

5 Complete the text with words/phrases from the box below. Some words are not needed.

> classic/classical   opportunity/possibility
> in the end/at the end   fit into/suit
> vacation/vacancy   propaganda/advertising
> sensible/sensitive   at the moment/actually
> friendly/sympathetic   assisted/attended
> reunion/meeting   proved/tested

I managed to catch Brett Sankey, director of Another World, before he took off on (1) _____ . While the film's (2) _____ focuses on Darwar, the (3) _____ hero, the film is (4) _____ about the rights of native peoples. Sankey is (5) _____ to the indigenous people's cause, but what he really loves is the (6) _____ to work with actors.

'All the (7) _____ films have great performances at their heart. Another World doesn't really (8) _____ any genre – it's a love story, a thriller and a comedy. But it does have great acting,' he says. 'When I (9) _____ an early (10) _____ with the producers, I stressed that the performances would be vital. Anyway, (11) _____ I got what I wanted. We (12) _____ the film with audiences and they loved it.'

Lead-in

1 Look at the photos. How do you think the people are feeling? Why?

2 **a** Check you understand the meaning of the underlined idioms. Which could apply to the people in the photos?

1 She was <u>at her wits' end</u> with worry.
2 He failed his exam, so he's a bit <u>down in the dumps</u>.
3 They saw the same car at nearly half the price, so now they are <u>kicking themselves</u>.
4 She is very <u>pleased with herself</u> for getting through the interview.
5 I've been running around all day – I'm <u>buzzing with energy</u>.
6 I'm <u>in two minds</u> about whether to accept the invitation.
7 Try not to get so <u>wound up</u> – it's only a game!
8 They are moving to the Caribbean, and they're <u>over the moon</u> about it.

b Match sentences a–h with sentences 1–8 from exercise 2a.

a It's like a <u>dream come true</u>.
b She deserves <u>a pat on the back</u>.
c Just <u>chill out</u>!
d We should try to <u>cheer him up</u>.
e But they <u>can't do anything about it</u> now.
f We went out to <u>take her mind off the problem</u>.
g I just can't <u>make my mind up</u>.
h When I finish work I need somewhere to <u>relax and wind down</u>.

3 Work in pairs. Choose some of the idioms from exercise 2a and exercise 2b and describe a time you felt this way.

I was very pleased with myself when I got my new job ...

Listening

1 Work in pairs and discuss the questions.

1 Do you think your outlook can affect what happens to you in life? How?

2 Do you think some people are luckier than others?

3 Would you call yourself optimistic?

2 **a** 🔊 2.25 Listen to the interview and choose the correct words in *italics*.

1 'Lucky' and 'unlucky' people have a *similar/different* psychology.

2 'Lucky' people have positive expectations, which are often *realistic/unrealistic*.

3 Positive thinking can *help improve/be a big problem for* business.

4 'Lucky' and 'unlucky' people are genetically *the same/different*.

5 *Extroverts/Introverts* use body language to get people to respond to them.

6 Children who *receive praise/pray regularly* do better at school.

b What do the speakers say about each statement from exercise 2a?

3 Listen again. What do the speakers say about the topics below?

1 Rhode Island

2 1993

3 being robust and resilient

4 having boundless optimism

5 failed business ventures

6 developing drive and focus

7 sales figures

8 a particular colour

9 gifted children

4 Work in pairs and discuss the questions.

1 Do you agree with what Wiseman says about luck and positive thinking?

2 Do you think motivational business training can improve business?

3 What does the American high-school experiment tell us about education?

4 Do you consider yourself lucky or unlucky?

Grammar | modals (and verbs with similar meanings)

5 Look at the way the underlined words are used in sentences 1–12. Match them to uses a–l in the Active grammar box.

1 ... some people <u>might</u> seem luckier than others?

2 ... the differences between them <u>must</u> be related to their psychology.

3 ... it <u>will</u> come as no great surprise that ...

4 They <u>won't</u> give up.

5 They didn't <u>need to</u> win.

6 You <u>can't</u> win the lottery if you don't enter ...

7 ... others <u>are bound to</u> go from one failed venture to another.

8 ... <u>can</u> I ask you, are some people just born unlucky?

9 You <u>might</u> do better if you have a more positive outlook.

10 Lucky people <u>are likely to</u> create opportunities ...

11 ... he <u>is supposed to</u> speak only to people wearing that colour.

12 You <u>must</u> keep your winning ticket to verify the claim.

Active grammar

will

a) for predictions:
Do you think the government will win the election?

b) for willingness/unwillingness:
I'll get that for you. He won't pay the bills.

might

c) to talk about possibility:
Majda might phone later.

d) to make suggestions (polite):
You might try asking your brother.

must/can't

e) for obligation:
You must be at the office by 8 a.m.
You can't leave before 5 p.m.

f) for deduction:
There must be some kind of problem.
That can't be the manager – he's far too young.

can

g) for permission: *Can we leave our bags here?*

h) for possibility/impossibility:
We can't all fit in one car.

(be) supposed to

i) to talk about what you have to do according to the rules/regulations:
We are supposed to be at the presentation.

(be) bound to

j) for future prediction of certainty:
She's bound to give the secret away.

(be) likely to

k) for probability: *You're not likely to pass.*

ought to/need to/should

l) for obligation/duty/necessity:
Do you think we ought to let them know we are here?
Do we need to book a table?
You really should contact the office.

see Reference page 145

6 Work in pairs. Discuss the differences in meaning (if any) between the words in *italics*.

1 You *might try catching/needn't catch/won't catch* the bus home.
2 I think I *can/must be able to/'m not supposed to* smoke in here.
3 He *ought/'s supposed/'s likely to* meet us at the theatre.
4 She *can't/must/'s bound* to be older than him.
5 We *didn't need to get/needn't have got/were supposed to get* good marks to get into university.
6 The price of oil *is bound to/is supposed to/must* go down soon.
7 *Do you need to/Are you likely to/Will you* change some money for your trip?

7 Rewrite the sentences (1–6) with the words in brackets so that they mean the same.

1 This is definitely not the right direction.
This ... (can't)
2 Do you think she'll pass the exam?
Is ... (likely)
3 Surely there's a mistake on this bill.
There ... (must)
4 I'm sure he'll cheer up soon.
He ... (bound)
5 I thought we had to register at the front desk.
Aren't ... (supposed)
6 It's time for you to make up your mind.
You ... (ought)

Pronunciation |

connected speech

8 **a** 🔊 2.26 Listen to rewritten sentences 4–6 from exercise 7 and answer the questions.

1 What consonant is before *to*?
2 What happens to these consonant sounds in connected speech?

b 🔊 2.27 Listen and repeat the phrases below.

1 *bound to → he's bound to → he's bound to know*
2 *supposed to → she's supposed to → she's supposed to go*
3 *ought to → you ought to → you ought to see it*

Speaking

9 Work in pairs. Discuss the topics below.

1 three things you should/ought to/are supposed to do this week
2 what you think your best friend is likely to be doing right now
3 how you think teachers can best motivate or encourage their students
4 how you think people's working lives will change in the future

Vocabulary | outlook/attitude

10 **a** Read and complete the questionnaire from Richard Wiseman's book, *The Luck Factor*. Check you understand the <u>underlined</u> phrases.

HOW LUCKY ARE YOU?

How strongly do you agree/disagree with the statements? Use the scale below.

> 1 strongly disagree   2 disagree
> 3 uncertain   4 agree   5 strongly agree

1 I sometimes chat to strangers when queuing in a supermarket or bank. ☐

2 I do not **have a tendency to worry** or feel anxious about life. ☐

3 I am **open to new experiences**, such as trying new types of food or drinks. ☐

4 I often act on my **gut feelings** and **hunches**. ☐

5 I have tried some techniques to boost my **intuition**, such as meditation or just going to a quiet place. ☐

6 I nearly always expect good things to happen to me in the future. ☐

7 I tend to try **to get what I want from life**, even if the **chances of success seem slim**. ☐

8 I expect most people that I meet to be pleasant, friendly and helpful. ☐

9 I tend to **look on the bright side** of whatever happens to me. ☐

10 I believe that even negative events will **work out well** for me **in the long run**. ☐

11 I don't tend to **dwell on things** that haven't worked out well for me in the past. ☐

12 I try to learn from mistakes I have made in the past. ☐

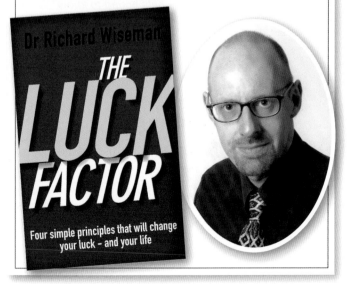

Dr. Richard Wiseman
THE LUCK FACTOR
Four simple principles that will change your luck – and your life

b Read the results of the questionnaire on page 151.

c Work in small groups and compare your answers. Do you agree with the rating?

11 **a** Complete the article below with one word in each gap.

However unlucky you have been in life, there is always a chance that things will work (1) _____ well in the (2) _____ run. Take the story of Ted Williams. Williams was a homeless man living on the streets of Columbus, Ohio, US. His chances of success in life seemed (3) _____ .

While begging on street corners, he held up a sign saying he had the 'gift' of a golden voice. Passersby (4) _____ a tendency to ignore the homeless, but a videographer called Doral Chenoweth saw Williams and, going with a gut (5) _____ , asked Williams to prove his talent on film. In his beautiful bass voice, Williams began imitating a radio announcer, and Chenoweth put the clip on YouTube. Eight million hits later, Williams was a star. He received job offers from numerous radio stations, was interviewed on the 'Today' show, and was even offered a house by a basketball team. Williams has had a difficult life, but he doesn't dwell (6) _____ the drawbacks and he is able to look on the bright (7) _____ of life, and marvel at how one stroke of luck has given him an amazing opportunity.

b Work in pairs. Do you know any other stories of someone getting a lucky break and finding fame/success?

Speaking

12 **a** Complete the sentences about yourself.

1 The luckiest break I ever had was …
2 I was lucky to meet … because …
3 If I'd had more luck, I could have …
4 I was lucky enough to get the chance to …
5 I do/don't believe in luck because …

b Work in small groups. Take turns to talk about your sentences.

Grammar modals of deduction (present and past)

Can do make guesses about imaginary situations

Listening

1 Look at the photos. Work with a partner and discuss the questions.

1 What would it be like to be there?

2 What problems might you associate with the pictures?

2 🔊 2.28 Listen to three people discussing similar situations. How did they feel?

3 Listen again and answer the questions.

1 Why is it easier for people to get to Machu Picchu these days?

2 When Machu Picchu was discovered by modern explorers, how was it different from now?

3 What difficulties with the first flight does the speaker mention?

4 What doubts did the pilot have?

5 What emotions does the speaker think Gagarin had?

4 Work in pairs. Think of someone who has achieved something amazing. What did they achieve? How do you think they felt?

Grammar | modals of deduction (present and past)

5 Complete the tasks in the Active grammar box.

Active grammar

1 Look at the modals of deduction below and read audioscript 2.28 on page 175. Can you find any examples?

must be/must have been

might see/might have seen

can't have/can't have had

couldn't take/couldn't have taken

could play/could have played

may live/may have lived

2 Which three modal verbs above have similar meanings?

3 Which verb forms mean that something is not possible?

4 Which verb form means we are sure about something (in the positive)?

5 How is the meaning of *must (be)* and *must have (been)* different?

We can also use:

will be to make a guess about the present when we are almost sure that something is true because of habit or deduction.

That'll be John on the phone. He always calls at 6.30.

will have been to make a guess about the past when we are almost sure that something happened.

That noise will have been the water heater. It always makes a noise in the morning.

see Reference page 145

6 Work in pairs. Discuss the difference in meaning (if any) between the modal verbs in *italics*.

1 She *will/must* have felt very upset.

2 He *can't/shouldn't* be happy about his exam result. He *normally does much/could have done* better.

3 You *couldn't/can't* have stayed awake all night. You never do that!

4 He *might be/could have been* hungry: that would explain him crying.

5 They *may/might* have found the gold.

6 That noise *must/might* have been the wind.

7 Joanne *couldn't/might not* have been successful without you.

8 The boss *must/will* have told you about the Saturday meeting.

Speaking

7 **a** Look at the photos on page 153. Work in pairs and discuss what you think is happening/has happened and why.

b Read the story behind each photo on page 150. How similar were your ideas?

Reading

8 Read the introduction to a book review and discuss what you think 'some of the biggest highs' and 'some of the worst lows' might be.

> *Esquire* magazine interviewed 61 people who had experienced some of the biggest highs and the worst lows known to humanity. The result is a book called *Esquire Presents: What it Feels Like.*

9 Work in pairs. Read the rest of the review. Write true (T) or false (F). Give reasons.

1 According to the review, the book was published so that ordinary people could read about extraordinary experiences. ☐

2 The book is mainly about famous people's achievements. ☐

3 Buzz Aldrin talks about certain regrets he has. ☐

4 According to the review, Craig Strobeck's experiences are worse than Max Dearing's. ☐

5 Geoffrey Petkovich is probably a fun-loving person. ☐

6 The book is a serious, academic text. ☐

7 A.J. Jacobs researched and wrote the stories in *Esquire Presents: What it Feels Like.* ☐

8 The man who hurt his thumb with a hammer doesn't care because he is physically very tough. ☐

10 Work in pairs. What motivates people to do the things described in the review? What is the book's 'message'? Would you like to read it?

So what does it feel like ...?

As we watch James Bond jump out of a plane, shoot 28 bad guys in five seconds flat, mix a perfect cocktail and get the girl, most of us know that real life just isn't like this. We're never going to win the Nobel Prize, walk on the moon, win the lottery or get attacked by grizzly bears. And that's why *Esquire* magazine decided to find out what these things really feel like.

Thanks to Buzz Aldrin, we can share the thrill of walking on the moon. He describes, 'powdery dust ... the sky velvety black ... surreal', and his feelings of responsibility: 'If we made a mistake, we would regret it for quite a while.' Aldrin's account gives us just the right blend of emotion and cold, hard fact. Aldrin's story is, of course, extremely well-known. One of the strengths of *Esquire Presents: What it Feels Like* is that it also covers normal, unexceptional people who find themselves in exceptional circumstances.

Max Dearing tells us what it feels like to be struck by lightning: 'I was absolutely frozen, just as cold as I've ever been in my entire life, but then part of me was incredibly hot, too. I saw these red flashing lights, and I kept thinking, 'It's a fire truck! A fire truck!' as if I were a little kid. Then there was the most incredible noise I'd ever heard.'

If Dearing's experience is shocking (literally and metaphorically) because of its sudden life-changing violence, Craig Strobeck's story is altogether more terrifying because it affects every minute of his life. Strobeck describes what it feels like to have an obsessive-compulsive disorder. He has to take two-and-a-half-hour showers. He runs out of hot water but doesn't stop. He cleans every inch of his body a thousand times, and sometimes he gets back in the shower because one area just doesn't feel clean enough.

Possibly the strangest experience described in the book, though, is that of Geoffrey Petkovich. He went over Niagara Falls, one of the world's largest waterfalls, in a barrel. He did it 'for a bit of fun', though it was a rather bumpy ride. With him in the barrel were two cans of beer, a packet of cigarettes and two hours' worth of oxygen in tanks, just in case the barrel sank.

Petkovich's story is an example of the book's humorous tone, but its editor, A.J. Jacobs, thinks *Esquire Presents: What it Feels Like* has a serious message. 'The guy who was buried under 50 feet of snow in an avalanche says that nowadays he can hit his thumb with a hammer and it doesn't bother him. He's just happy to be here.' The same is true for most of the people in this fascinating book.

Vocabulary | strong feelings

11 Work in small groups. Write the underlined adjectives in sentences 1–16 in the table.

1 You've just been offered the best job in the world. You must be absolutely <u>thrilled</u>!

2 One thing that makes me <u>furious</u> is when people drop rubbish in the street.

3 I was <u>taken aback</u> when they asked me to be the team captain. I hadn't expected it at all.

4 She was <u>ecstatic</u> when she finally passed her driving test.

5 I feel completely <u>indifferent</u> about technology. I just don't care one way or the other.

6 They split up after ten years together and now they're both <u>miserable</u>.

7 I'm feeling rather <u>chuffed</u> because I managed to beat Nikolai at chess!

8 I know Maths isn't your favourite subject, but do you have to look so <u>uninterested</u>?

9 She was <u>terrified</u> when she saw the spider.

10 I was absolutely <u>flabbergasted</u> when they told me I'd won the lottery.

11 When she was voted Best Actress, she was <u>dumbstruck</u>. She just couldn't believe it!

12 He was absolutely <u>outraged</u> by your terrible behaviour.

13 I will be <u>delighted</u> to attend your party.

14 When the TV repair man didn't show up again I was <u>livid</u>. I'd taken the day off work.

15 Stuck in the middle of the avalanche, they were <u>petrified</u>. They fully expected to die.

16 We were a bit <u>upset</u> that you didn't remember our wedding anniversary.

happy	unhappy	neither happy nor unhappy
scared	surprised	angry

12 Look at the table in exercise 11 and answer the questions.

1 Which word meaning 'happy' is informal and weaker than the other?

2 Which word meaning 'unhappy' usually describes a feeling we have for just a short time?

3 Which expression meaning 'surprised' is the most formal?

4 Which word meaning 'angry' also means 'shocked because of some injustice'?

13 Work in pairs. How would you feel in situations 1–6 below? Why? Try to use adjectives you haven't used before.

1 You were chosen by NASA to go to the moon.

2 You found a large, unfriendly looking snake in your living room.

3 You were caught in the middle of a storm while wearing your beach clothes.

4 You were abducted by aliens who gave you a free massage.

5 You found a large box, full of treasure under your floor.

6 You saw a tiger wandering around your local supermarket.

14 Read the Lifelong learning box and follow the instructions.

Personalise and memorise

❗ Write new vocabulary in a personalised sentence about you, your family or your hobbies, etc. This will help you to remember the words.

1 Write full sentences to answer questions a–c.
   a) When was the last time you felt chuffed about something?
   b) What makes you livid?
   c) What are you petrified of?

2 Choose four more adjectives from exercise 11 and write personalised sentences.

Lifelong learning

Listening

1 Work in pairs. Which of the situations from the box do you remember from your childhood? How did they make you feel?

> moving house   starting/changing school
> playing/inventing games   making friends
> summer holidays   staying with grandparents
> birth of a brother/sister   spending time alone
> looking after other children   doing sport
> arguing with friends/family   doing exams

2 **a** ● 2.29 Listen to four people describing childhood memories. Which topics from exercise 1 does each speaker mention?

b Work in pairs. Discuss whether any of the stories you heard remind you of your own experiences.

3 Listen again and answer the questions.

1 Did speaker 1 find it easy to get on with the other children? Why/Why not?

2 How has his experience shaped his character?

3 Where did speaker 2 use to run?

4 What was bad about the experience?

5 Is she keen on sports now?

6 What smells, sensations and colours does speaker 3 mention?

7 What was different about the breakfasts she used to have on holiday?

8 How did speaker 4 use to get into the woods?

9 How did playing in the woods make him feel? How does he describe that time?

Reading

4 **a** Look at the picture. Work in pairs and discuss the questions.

1 Where do you think the story is set?

2 What do you think it is about?

3 How do you think the girl is feeling?

b Read the story. How similar were your ideas?

5 Work in pairs and discuss the questions.

1 What is the significance of the following words/ideas in the story?

> bread   steps   fields   toys   mirror   sack
> mattresses   baseball bat

2 What do you think life is going to be like in the house on Holloway Street?

Holloway Street

At suppertime, the red-brick walls of our house would glow like embers. It was a hot house. In July and August you could have fried an egg on the roof. Mother would swoon in the kitchen as she baked bread, the curtains shut to keep out the heat.

When sunset came, I'd sit at the top of our steps and watch the world go by – factory workers heading home caked in grease, lost trucks rumbling down the road, cats sliding in and out of windows.

Everything about this world, this street, was alien to me. We'd moved to the city so my father wouldn't become a cripple. He'd worked in the fields so long his back was bent like a boomerang, and now the farmers didn't want him and he didn't want them. With six kids in tow – me the eldest – he roamed the district trying to sell children's toys for a company in Pittsburgh. To do that job, you needed a twinkle in your eye and a tongue full of honey. He had neither. With his old man's stoop, and his hungry belly, he looked nothing like any salesman I ever knew. But he wouldn't give up. They'd taught him a script which he'd memorised, a sales pitch full of patter and rhyme, and he practised it every morning in front of the rusting mirror, like an actor delivering lines. Then he would go out into the world with his sack of goods, a lugubrious Father Christmas in a cheap suit.

The house was our fifth in two years. The landlord had kicked us out of the one before that, for missing a payment. I'd watched my father beg the man to let us stay, but the landlord wouldn't listen. He just flicked his cigarette and walked away. That's when we came to Holloway Street.

At night, the rats would shoot through the darkness, their tiny feet scraping under the floorboards beneath me, Jessie, Lou, Bella, Jim and Willie. We'd lie heaped and snoring on three mattresses laid side by side. My father said we would all have our own rooms one day, but I didn't believe it. Every night I'd lie awake, listening out for the bellow of the summer thunder. All around us were our possessions – raggedy clothes, comic books, the wooden baseball bat that Jessie had taken from a trashcan two summers before, all the detritus of our little lives. And in the corridor, the poisoned apple sent to test us: a bag of toys we couldn't touch.

Grammar | uses of *would*

6 Match the example sentences (1–7) in the Active grammar box to the different uses of *would* (a–g).

> ### Active grammar
>
> 1 *I'd sit at the top of our steps and watch the world go by.*
> 2 *The landlord **wouldn't** listen.*
> 3 *My father said we **would** all have our own rooms one day.*
> 4 *We'd moved to the city so that my father **wouldn't** become a cripple.*
> 5 *We'd have moved to a different area if we'd been able to afford it.*
> 6 ***Would** you shut the window, please?*
> 7 *I wish they **wouldn't** make so much noise at night.*
>
> a) polite request
> b) recurring situation in the past
> c) past purpose/reason (often used after *so that*)
> d) imagined situation in the past or a possibility in the past that didn't happen
> e) strong desire for something (annoying) to change
> f) a reported past intention/expectation
> g) refusal

see Reference page 145

7 Complete the sentences with *would* or *wouldn't*.

1 Hello, you like to follow me? I'll show you to your room.
2 I have much more time to do my work if you looked after the kids a little more often.
3 When we were alone at home, we always cook for ourselves.
4 He never help me with my homework.
5 If only he answer the phone, I could explain what happened.
6 She have loved to see her grandchildren grow up.
7 We hid the parcel in the cupboard so that she notice it.
8 Her parents pay for her to go to university as they didn't believe in education for girls.

8 **a** Complete the sentences.

1 When I was ten years old, I thought … *I would grow up to be a doctor.*
2 Would you mind if I … ?
3 At school, my friends and I would …
4 I wish people wouldn't always …
5 If I was younger, I'd …
6 I told (name) that I'd …
7 When I was a child, my parents wouldn't …

b Work in small groups and compare your ideas.

Reading and speaking

9 **a** Read the stories (1–5) and think of a title for each one.

b Work in pairs. Compare your titles. Which do you like best?

10 Think of different ways to complete the phrases in the How to... box. Compare your ideas with the original examples from the extracts.

How to... talk about memories/experiences

Introducing the story	*One memory that (1) ____ in my mind ...*
	I have a (2) ____ recollection of ...
	I'll (3) ____ remember ...
	One of my (4) ____ memories is of ...
Background	*We always/usually/(5) ____ spent ...*
	We were always (6) ____ ...
	My parents kept (7) ____ me ...
	On Sundays, we (8) ____ often ...
	I had never .../I thought I'd ...
Specific event	*One time/But (9) ____ night*
	On this occasion ...
	I felt .../I was (10) ____ to death.
	However, ...
	The problem was that ...
Reflecting	*Looking back, ...*
	I just remember ...
	It reminds me of ...
	It's (11) ____ to believe
	I can hardly believe ...

11 **a** Choose two or three memories/experiences to talk about. You can talk about any experiences you like or choose from the topics below.

- a song/story from your childhood
- a journey you went on
- a game you played
- a holiday you remember
- a time when you experienced freedom
- an important discovery you made

b Write a few notes and try to use language from the How to... box.

c Work in small groups. Take turns to talk about your memories/experiences.

Stories from Childhood

We asked you to send in stories about some of your earliest childhood memories.

1 _____

I have a vivid recollection of walking to school when I was about ten years old and living in Southall, West London. Every morning I would meet my childhood sweetheart at the corner of the street and carry her satchel all the way to the girls' school gate. In the afternoon, I would wait for her outside the same gate at 3.45 p.m. and we would walk home together singing, 'You were made for me' by Freddie and the Dreamers.

2 _____

I'll always remember my granddad bringing a newly born black sheep up to the house one time. He let me hold him without completely letting go because the little ball of curls was wriggling like an eel. I was five years old and had never seen a black sheep. His skull was hard as a rock. Later my granddad told me I was like that little black sheep … hard-headed and very special.

3 _____

My earliest memory is of my dad carrying me on his shoulders. On Sundays, we would often go for an afternoon walk, and when I got tired he would carry me. I felt I could see the entire world. And I could … in my three-year-old world, at least.

4 _____

One memory that sticks in my mind is of me and my brother when we were younger. We generally spent most of our time fighting. We were always chasing each other around the house hitting each other with golf clubs, throwing things. But one night we were staying at my aunt's house, and I was particularly sad about something. I just remember crying into my brother's arms as we were going to bed. I can't even remember now what I was so sad about, but the important thing is that I have this memory of knowing he was there for me, and being comforted by him. Looking back, it's hard to believe what happened that night.

5 _____

One of my earliest memories was of being scared to death because I thought that I'd been abandoned in the hospital ward. I had my tonsils removed aged two and a half, and had to stay overnight by myself. My parents kept telling me that they'd come to take me home tomorrow morning when the sun shines. The problem was that the next morning, it was raining!

1 a Look at the underlined phrases with *under* in the story below. What do they mean?

> We were working <u>under pressure</u>, so we were <u>under a lot of stress</u>. The boss needed to work overtime, but his wife wouldn't allow it: he was completely <u>under her thumb</u>. Eventually, the business <u>went under</u>.

b Choose the correct rule in *italics*.

Expressions with the particle *under* tend to be used with *positive and pleasant/negative and unpleasant* situations.

2 a Look at the meanings that particles sometimes have when used with phrasal verbs. Then complete sentences 1–6 with the particles.

back	return
on	continue
off	travel to another place
around	do a pointless activity
up	complete something/have no more to do
down	(1) put something onto paper (2) reduce (speed, number, etc.)
out	(1) distribute something among people (2) lose ability to function

1 Bill tried to write _____ everything Tania said, but because she was speaking too fast, he asked her to slow _____.
2 Lisa finally came _____ after several years away from home.
3 Sam decided to carry _____ until she'd finished.
4 Tom and Jo ran _____ together to get married! They set _____ at 6 a.m.
5 Don is always lounging _____. He's so lazy!
6 The last customer drank _____ and left. Majid counted _____ the money, locked _____ the café and went home.

b Work in pairs. What do you think the phrasal verbs from exercise 2a mean?

3 Choose the correct words *in italics*.

1 The river dried *up/on/back* completely, so there was no water in the village.
2 I decided to cut *around/down/off* on fatty food and I lost 10 kilos as a result.
3 The blood went to my head and I passed *up/on/out*. I regained consciousness a few minutes later.
4 When the police officer tried to interview him, he clammed *on/up/around*; he didn't say a word.
5 Can you hold *up/on/around* for a few more minutes? We're getting a signal.
6 I applied for the job but they never wrote *up/down/back*.
7 We couldn't get tickets, so we just hung *up/off/around* on the street for hours. It was so boring!
8 The task was difficult, but she soldiered *on/around/off* and eventually finished.
9 Absolutely exhausted, I crashed *up/out/around* on the sofa and slept all night.
10 We had no idea where the party was, so we drove *around/up/down* for an hour and eventually went home.

4 Work in pairs. What do you think the phrasal verbs from exercise 3 mean?

'Dry up' means there was no more water. It probably hadn't rained for a long time.

5 Work in pairs and discuss the questions.

1 Have you (or has someone you know) ever done any of the things from the box below?
2 When might you do each thing?

> clam up   soldier on   pass out
> drive around   hang around
> cut down on something
> pack up all your possessions

10 Communication

1 Read the dictionary definitions. Work with a partner. When was the last time you moaned about something, raved about something or took a stand on something?

> **rave** /reɪv/ v [I] **1 rave about/over sth** to talk in an excited way about something because you think it is very good

> **moan** /məʊn/ v **1** [I] *informal* to complain about something in an annoying way

> **take a stand** v [I] to state publicly a strong opinion about an important issue

2 🔊 2.30 Listen to three speakers and answer the questions.

1 What does each speaker talk about?
2 Are they moaning, raving about something or taking a stand?
3 What are their opinions?

3 a Complete the How to... box with the expressions below.

- *It should be banned completely.*
- *I couldn't believe my eyes!*
- *It was sensational!*

How to... express strong feelings

Saying something is good	*... the most amazing ...* *It was the most fascinating ...* (1) _____
Saying something is surprising (could be good or bad)	*You would not believe it!* *I've never seen anything like it ...* (2) _____
Saying something is bad	*It's just ridiculous* *It's not really acceptable* (3) _____

b Listen again and tick the expressions from the How to... box that the speakers use.

4 a Think of an issue that you feel strongly about. It can be something you love or something you dislike or something you think needs to be changed. Use the photos if you need help with ideas.

b Prepare to moan, rave or take a stand about the issue. Think about the points you want to make and write notes.

5 Work in small groups. Take turns to talk about your issue. As you are listening to other students, write down their topic and one question to ask when they have finished.

Modals (and verbs with similar meanings)

will

willingness/unwillingness: *He **won't speak** to me.*

predictions: *They**'ll be** here in a minute.*

may/might

possibility: *We **might need** an umbrella.*

suggestions: *We **might as well just pay** the bill.*

must/can't

deduction: *They **must be** hungry by now.*

obligation: *You **mustn't talk** to him like that.*

can

permission: ***Can I use** the telephone?*

possibility/impossibility: *This **can't be** the right place!*

is supposed to

obligation: *You **were supposed to be** here early.*

(be) bound to

prediction of certainty: *He**'s bound to get** the job.*

(be) likely to

probability: *Children living in rural areas **are likely to move** to the city as adults.*

ought to/need to/should

advice: *You **should see** a doctor.*

recommendation: *You **ought to see** the castle.*

obligation: *Guests **should not smoke** in the hotel.*

uncertainty: ***Should** we **lock** both the doors?*

expectation: *They **should be** here by now.*

should with thinking verbs, to make them less direct:
*I **shouldn't think** the meeting **will take** long.*

need behaves like a normal verb: ***Do** you **need to speak** to the doctor?*

don't have to

lack of obligation: *We **don't have to be** there until 2.30 p.m.*

can + be

criticism: *He **can be** so annoying!*

Modals of deduction (present and past)

must, might, may, can, could, will + past participle can be used when making a guess based on evidence.

must have (+ past participle)

certainty: *The crash **must have been** terrifying.*

might have (+ past participle)

possibility: *I **might have left** my keys in the car.*

can't have/couldn't have (+ past participle)

impossibility: *He **can't have finished** already!*
*They **couldn't have come** this far.*

could have/may have (+ past participle)

possibility: *We **could have been** left there for ages. There **may have been** a good reason for the delay, but we were angry nevertheless.*

will be/will have (+ past participle)

when we are fairly certain that something is true or has happened: *That will be Susan. She**'ll have left** work early.*

Uses of *would*

polite request: ***Would** you help me get the files?*

recurring situation in the past:
*She **would** always have a bag of sweets in her pocket.*

past purpose/reason (often used after *so that*):
*We took a taxi so (that) we **wouldn't** be late.*

imagined situation in the past:
*I**'d** love to know what happened!*

strong desire for something:
*I wish he **would** make more of an effort!*

a reported past intention/expectation:
*They asked if we **would** like anything to drink.*

refusal: *He **wouldn't** let go of my bag.*

Key vocabulary

Feelings/emotions

at her wits' end   down in the dumps
kicking themselves   pleased with herself
buzzing with energy   in two minds   wound up
over the moon

Outlook/attitude

have a tendency to worry   be open to new experiences
gut feelings   hunches   intuition
to get what I want from life   look on the bright side
dwell on things   chances of success seem slim
work out well in the long run

Strong feelings

thrilled   furious   taken aback   ecstatic
indifferent   miserable   chuffed   uninterested
terrified   flabbergasted   dumbstruck   outraged
delighted   livid   petrified   upset

Phrasal verbs and particles

under pressure   go under   under (someone's) thumb
hand out   wear out   count up   lock up   set off
come back   carry on   lounge around   slow down

ACTIVEBOOK   Listen to the explanations and vocabulary.

see Writing bank page 164

1 Rewrite each sentence with the words in brackets, so that the meaning stays the same.

1 It won't be a surprise if the manager is angry about the situation. (likely)

2 I'm sure they'll phone us this morning. (bound)

3 The interview is at 10.30, but they asked me to be there half an hour before. (supposed)

4 There must be another way out of the building. (can't)

5 Maybe we'll have time for a quick drink before the meeting. (might)

6 They are refusing to pay the invoice until the dispute has been resolved. (won't)

7 Do you want us to wait for you outside the conference hall? (should)

8 It's better if he brings his own laptop. (ought)

2 Complete each sentence with a suitable past modal verb.

The mud was up to five metres deep in places.

It _must have been_ impossible to drive through.

1 There is no reason for her not to come. She _____ understood your instructions.

2 You should have seen their reaction! They _____ been happier.

3 We were lucky to get out alive. We _____ killed.

4 They didn't come home until the early hours of the morning. The party _____ good.

5 She could see my face. She _____ realised who I was.

6 They'd had such a difficult journey. They _____ relieved when they arrived.

7 It's not a very good score. There's no doubt Evans _____ disappointed with that.

3 Find mistakes in five of the sentences and correct them.

1 If I'd have known, I'd have called you earlier.

2 I wish she won't always tell me what to do.

3 I wouldn't change it for all the world.

4 We left the keys in the office so you will see them when you got there.

5 I'd sit on my grandfather's knee and put tobacco in his pipe.

6 Wouldn't it be easier if we went home first?

7 I told Marcella that we meet her outside the cinema.

8 My parents wouldn't never have dreamed of sending me to private school.

4 Complete the text with words from the box.

> worked   end   pleased   terrified   tendency
> minds   moon   calm   aback   delighted
> upset

When I was about ten years old, I remember my father coming in to the room, looking terribly (1) _____ with himself, to tell us that we were going to have another brother or sister. It was unexpected, so we were both taken (2) _____ , but I was (3) _____ . My brother, on the other hand, was rather in two (4) _____ . He was younger than me, and I don't think he was too impressed with the idea. He has a (5) _____ to worry about things, and I think he was (6) _____ by the fact that he might not be the centre of attention all the time. When the big day came, unfortunately there were problems, and my mother had to stay in hospital. We weren't allowed to visit, and we were all at our wits' (7) _____ with worry. We tried to (8) _____ each other down, but basically we were all (9) _____ that something awful would happen. It all (10) _____ out well in the end though, and when I was finally able to see my little sister, I was over the (11) _____ . She was so tiny, and special. And we all love her to bits.

5 Complete the sentences with a particle.

_I'm afraid we've been _under_ a lot of pressure at work recently._

1 I can't understand how he can just lounge _____ all day, doing nothing.

2 It's no good thinking about her all the time. Try to snap _____ of it!

3 Look _____ the bright side. At least we're being paid for doing this.

4 I can't wait for John to come _____ . He was such fun to work with.

5 The marketing department are always messing _____ with the brochure.

6 She just got into her car and drove _____ . I couldn't believe it!

7 Could you keep _____ trying until you get hold of someone?

8 Drink _____ ! It's time to go.

9 I'm just noting _____ a few telephone numbers.

10 I've brought along a couple of samples for us to share _____ .

Lesson 1.3 | Ex. 2, page 14

Carlos Acosta ★ a Cuban dream

Dressed anonymously in black trousers and roll-neck, Carlos Acosta sits awkwardly in a red armchair in the interview room of the Royal Opera House. As we shake hands he winks, not confidently, but shyly. But when he starts to speak, although he talks softly, the aura of power seems to grow ...

Carlos Acosta was born in Cuba in 1973. After an incident-filled childhood featuring brushes with crime, he reluctantly took up dancing, at his father's insistence, at the age of ten. His early years were full of ambivalence towards dance as he trained at the National Ballet School of Cuba. Unusually for a great male dancer, his teacher was a woman, Ramona de Saa, who persevered with him. Her training bore fruit and in January 1990 Acosta won the Gold Medal at the Prix de Lausanne. In November 1990 he won the Grand Prix and Gold Medal at the Paris ballet competition. They were to be the first of many competitions and prizes where Acosta attained the highest honours.

Asked about which award meant most to him, he answers unhesitatingly that it was the Prix de Lausanne, his first competition. 'I was the 127th competitor, the last one, entered at the last moment. My greatest hope was to reach the final. I never dreamed of winning. There were a lot of talented people in the competition who I admired.' This was the first time that Acosta realised just how talented he was in world terms. 'I knew that I had something special because in Cuba I would skip class for two months and I was still at the same level as everyone else when I returned, something my teacher commented on many times.' The Lausanne win was tinged with sadness because he couldn't share it with his parents. They were in Cuba and his only means of communication was by letter. 'My family is not of the art world. I tried to explain the importance of the Prix de Lausanne. They were pleased but they didn't really understand.'

It is a poignant irony that Acosta's greatest triumphs as a dancer have still been unwitnessed by his mother and father. Without his father's influence the young Carlos might have been lost to the world of ballet, and might even have been killed in the dangerous milieu of street gangs. 'At the age of ten I was mixing with people who were stealing, and the chances were that I would become a delinquent. My father thought that I might end up shooting somebody. With his eyes on the future he realised that there would be trouble. We lived in a suburb of Havana where it could be pretty rough. I wasn't in a gang. We didn't do drugs. But we didn't go to school either.' Astonishingly, Carlos' father decided to enrol him in the National Ballet School.

'My father had always liked ballet but in his youth, as a black man, he could not practise it. He thought it would be good for me as a career. It would have been nice of him to ask me what I wanted to do' ... (he pulls a comic face) ... 'but thank God he made the right decision. My father was always a strong hand. When the school threw me out, he went there to speak for me. He could have said that he was tired of running around after me and just given up. He could have taken me out of the ballet and put me in a regular school but he just kept pushing me. I did not like the idea of ballet. At the beginning, I didn't even know what it was! Then there was what my friends would say, because there was prejudice that ballet was not for boys. It was embarrassing. I would always rejoin the school with black eyes after fist-fights with boys who teased me. I was treated like the neighbourhood clown. But I was curious about dancing. I was always very physical and did a lot of sport, especially football. But we are all born to do one thing and you can't go against destiny.'

Lesson 9.3 | Ex. 4a, page 126
Student A

The Bigger Picture

A picture is worth a thousand words – but only if it's good.

Introduction

Imagine this: late afternoon, the sun sinking slowly into the western sky, giant dunes of the Namibian desert looming on the horizon; the sand begins to burn a deep orange. The scene evokes such an emotion – all you know is that you wish you could capture the image forever. So you take a picture.

Unfortunately, on returning home, you find that the photo is blurred at the edges and your finger takes up half the frame. 'If only I could take good pictures!' you cry. 'I wish I had a decent camera!' Actually, it's not about the camera. If you really want a good photographic record of your trip, it's high time you learnt a few basics.

1 Composition

Suppose you see a beautiful landscape stretching in front of you for miles. What do you do? Don't try to fit it all in. Pick one interesting part and focus on it. Look for natural lines that draw the viewer in and give your picture depth: a river starting in the foreground and disappearing into the distance.

2 Light

If travelling, the best time of day for a photo is either early morning or late afternoon. At these times, the light is soft, giving subjects a warm glow. Keep the sun behind you and avoid midday light, which can be very harsh. If you're shooting at night, keep your subjects no farther than 3 metres (8–10 feet) away; even the strongest flash can't illuminate more space.

3 Focus

What if you want a close-up of a person or animal? What do you focus on? The eyes. The best travel photography is about people in their environment as much as stunning landscapes, and people's eyes tell stories. Get as close as possible and fill the frame. There should be nothing in the picture which doesn't relate to the subject. Also, look for symmetrical subjects; it doesn't have to be a mirror image, just well-balanced.

4 Look and learn

Keep your eyes open; be aware of your surroundings. Before travelling, spend some time looking through big coffee-table picture books and magazines to see how the professionals do it. Watch for different uses of light, angle, line and texture. And don't be afraid to experiment: change the angle, get on your knees, climb onto a chair, find a balcony with a view.

5 Be considerate

In many cultures, the people would sooner you asked before photographing them. Take time to get to know them. Learn a few words of the language so that you can be polite. They are more likely to smile if you have addressed them in their language.

Lesson 8.3 | Ex. 5a, page 113
Student A

You friend works too hard. He has a tough job and spends all his time working. He looks ill and he isn't much fun to be with. You want to help him, but you are worried he will reject your advice.

Communication 7 | Ex. 4a, page 102
Student A

You want to start a hippy commune for a maximum of 50 people. The hippies will farm the land, growing all their own food and living in harmony with nature. Throughout the year, there will be music festivals, as well as regular yoga, tai chi and lessons for children.

Lesson 2.3 | Ex. 2a, page 28
Student B

Cape Town

The first thing I can tell you about Thabo, my South African guide, is that he is the world's worst driver. From the airport to the heart of the city, he does 100 km per hour, swerving around
5 lorries, motorbikes and taxi-vans crammed with people. The second thing is that he knows everybody and everything about Cape Town. This is good, because I am trying to complete Mission Impossible: see Cape Town in just three days.

10 On the first day, Thabo takes me to the posh areas: suburbs with unpronounceable names – Tamboerskloof and Oranjezicht – from where you can watch the sun go down on Africa. The views are stunning. 'This is all very pretty,' I tell him
15 that evening, 'but show me a community. Show me something the tourists never see.' So the next day, we go off the beaten track to Cape Flats, the run-down township where the buildings are made of cardboard and corrugated iron. It is the poorest
20 part of the city and it is truly vast – nearly a million people live here, side by side. Skinny dogs slide out of the way as Thabo zooms along roads of mud and rotting rubbish. Some people wave, others stare. Children run barefoot by the car.

25 Later that night we walk around the bustling Victoria and Alfred Waterfront, Cape Town's most fashionable area. The contrast from the township could not be greater. As we stroll, the smells of cooking drift up from the kitchens – Asian,
30 French, Italian and of course the wild animals of South Africa that end up on your plate. The bars and restaurants are packed, and I soon find out why. Cape Town is a paradise for gourmets, seafood-lovers and people like me, who just like
35 eating. We go into a charming little bistro, and Thabo tells me I can't leave Cape Town without trying some Cape seafood, so I do. It's delicious.

On my final morning, we spend a tranquil hour sitting outside a café. I gaze at Table Mountain,
40 which forms the backdrop to the city, while Thabo shouts greetings to everyone that passes by. Then we are driving again, experiencing the diverse landscape – sandy beaches, mountain slopes and green valleys unspoilt by tourism. It's
45 a great way to say goodbye to a place I've known only too briefly. I promise myself, and Thabo, that I'll be back.

Lesson 3.3 | Ex. 9a, page 44
Student A

An artist has been displaying his paintings in an art gallery. He asks the gallery owner if anyone has bought his work.

'I have good news and bad news,' says the gallery owner. 'The good news is that a man asked if your work would be worth more after your death. I told him it would and he bought all ten of your painting.'

'That's wonderful,' says the artist. 'What's the bad news?'

'The man was your doctor ...'

Lesson 7.3 | Ex. 5b, page 99
All the sentences are true, except:

2 = eight offspring at a time

4 = 17 days

5 = 22 hours per day

Communication 5 | Ex. 4a, page 74
Group B

You represent the management. You want:

• to build a new café with better food. The workers want a gym and swimming pool. You think the café is more important. You can't build both.

• to arrange buses for employees to come to work, but the employees should buy a subsidised (cheaper) ticket every day.

• to install some modern art in the reception area. This is to impress visitors.

The workers also want a free telephone in the factory. You are worried about the cost of phone bills.

Which issues are very important, or not so important?

Decide how you will argue for what you want.

Communication activities

Lesson 4.3 | Ex. 13a, page 58
Student A

The British press has nicknamed him 'mini Monet'. Buyers from all over the world want his work. He has been hailed as a once-in-a-generation artistic prodigy. Meet Kieron Williamson, an eight-year-old with the world in his hands.

It all began when five-year-old Kieron, on a family holiday in Cornwall, UK, asked his parents for pencils and paper. He amazed them by producing an outstanding picture of boats in a harbour. 'We don't know where it comes from,' his mother said later. 'But when your child has got such a gift and a talent, you have to support him.' Kieron soon moved onto depictions of the local landscape in Holt, UK, where they live.

His parents showed his sketches to a local artist, Carol Pennington, who was immediately impressed. She arranged for him to spend an hour a day at her studio, and he blossomed. Soon he was exhibiting his work at local galleries. One exhibition of 33 watercolours sold out in 27 minutes for £150,000.

The work itself has been described as neo-Impressionism: landscapes in pastel colours, huge skies, winding streams. What marks out Kieron's his work is his extraordinary sense of composition, and his mastery of the basics of perspective and colour. He says cows are the easiest things to paint, because 'you don't have to worry about doing so much detail. Horses are harder because you have to get the legs right'.

Despite his gift, Kieron is a normal little boy. He attends school, plays in the football team, and watches TV. He advises aspiring painters: 'Never give up. Try and keep your buildings straight. And don't do a plain blue sky.'

Lesson 8.3 | Ex. 5a, page 113
Student B

You go to the gym with a friend, but he spends the whole time chatting, not exercising. You don't want to go with him any more, but you are afraid of hurting his feelings.

Communication 7 | Ex. 4a, page 102
Student B

You want to build a luxury hotel with a golf course. The town needs somewhere for rich tourists to stay. The hotel could also serve as a conference centre. This will bring lots of money and jobs to the local economy, and encourage tourist shops, tour guides, new bars and restaurants, etc.

Communication 5 | Ex. 4a, page 74
Group A

You belong to the workers group. You want:
- to build a gym and swimming pool for workers to use at lunch or after work.
- free buses to and from work.
- a free phone in the factory for workers to call home.
- to redecorate the workers' changing rooms.

Which issues are very important, or not so important?

Decide how you will argue for what you want.

Lesson 10.2 | Ex. 7b, page 137

Photo 1
Polo player Peter Koscinsky feels the pain after falling off his horse. It happened when he was attacking the ball and collided with an opposing team player. To make matters worse, the umpire awarded a free goal to the other side, which meant his team lost.

Photo 2
Stuntman Todd Carter does his stuff for a forthcoming film about tornadoes. The car, which is made of a very light metal and has no engine, was lifted into the tree by a crane, with Carter in it!

Photo 3
Chimpsky is on a beach, being filmed for a soft drink ad. Apparently, the three-year-old chimpanzee enjoyed the drink so much that he finished four bottles and had to be excused for numerous bathroom breaks.

Photo 4
Comic actress Myra Barking, 74, is best-known for her impressions of the Queen. A technophile, Barking says she stays in touch with her 11 grandchildren by texting them every day. Here, she sends a photo from Buckingham Palace!

Lesson 10.1 | Ex. 10b, page 136

HOW LUCKY ARE YOU?

Rate yourself

Statements 1–3

A combined total of twelve or more is high, whereas a score of eight or less is low. Lucky people will score highly because they are more likely to create, notice and act upon chance opportunities.

Statements 4–5

A score of eight or above for these statements is high, whereas a score of two–four or below is low. Unlucky people score low because they tend not to rely on gut feelings, hunches and intuition. In contrast, lucky people listen to their intuition and take steps to develop their intuitive feelings.

Statements 6–8

A total of up to nine points for these three statements is low; a score of twelve or more is high. Lucky people score well in this section because they are certain that the future is going to be wonderful for them, and their expectations have the power to create that future.

Statements 9–12

A total of up to ten points is low; seventeen or more is high. Lucky people score much higher on these statements than other people because they use psychological techniques – often without realising it – to turn misfortune they encounter to their advantage.

Lesson 3.3 | Ex. 9a, page 44

Student B

The Queen is on a trip abroad when she decides that she wants to drive. The chauffeur gets into the back of the car and the Queen gets into the front and starts driving. She goes too fast and a police officer stops the car. One minute later, the police officer calls headquarters.

'I can't make an arrest,' he says. 'This person is too important.'

'Who is it?' asks the police chief. 'The mayor?'

'No. Someone more important.'

'The governor?'

'More important.'

'The President?'

'No. More important.'

'Who can possibly be more important than the President?' asks the Chief.

'I don't know, Chief, but he has the Queen as his chauffeur.'

Vocabulary 7 | Ex. 3, page 101

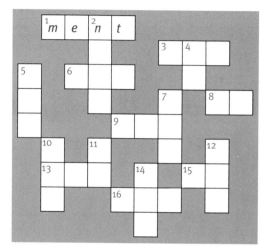

Which word fits the definitions? Only write the suffixes from words 1–16 in the puzzle. You are given the first letter of the word in brackets.

1 a clash of opinions between two people (a)
   argument
2 the opposite of a sad state (everyone wants to achieve this) (h)
3 a choice you can make in a particular situation (o)
4 a person whose work is published (a)
5 a catcher of fish (male) (f)
6 to choose one particular area or subject to focus on/become an expert in (s)
7 give off heat (r)
8 ability to speak for a long time, easily (it's the goal of most students) (f)
9 someone who has gone to live permanently in another country (i)
10 to represent/mean something (s)
11 relating to *me* only (so it's none of your business!) (p)
12 not the same (d)
13 be appreciative when someone has helped you (g)
14 a person who plays a six-stringed instrument (g)
15 to make something broader (w)
16 from Denmark (D)

Lesson 9.3 | Ex. 4a, page 126
Student B

On Being a Travel Writer

Introduction

Moving out of the shade of the high palm trees, you stroll for one last time along the sand dunes, allowing the transparent water to brush over your feet. You head for the bar, taking in the breathtaking view, sip slowly on a cocktail, go to your beachfront hotel suite and write six hundred words. You email it the following morning to the travel magazine, before checking out with the immortal line, 'Put the bill on my company's expense account.'

'Ah, if only I was a travel writer!' you say. 'I wish I could live like that!' Unfortunately, being a travel writer is no picnic.

1 Write on

The way to become a better writer is to write regularly. Some people say they don't have time. This isn't true. You have to make time. Start by keeping a journal every day. It doesn't matter what time of day you write it as long as you do it. Use it to record sights, sounds, smells, tastes. If you've always wanted to write, it's about time you started – no excuses.

2 Travel with your senses

Suppose you could either have a week on a beach, or a week exploring a hot, dangerous jungle. Which would you choose? Travel writers would rather go to the jungle. Don't be a tourist; be a traveller. Keep your eyes and ears open for unusual or evocative details. Professional travel writers don't just see the normal things (the clichéd pretty sunset); they spot things that most tourists don't see (the sound of a bat's wings, the way a boat leans in the wind). Learn from them. And interact with the local culture: talk to people, try the food, haggle in the markets. You can't write well about something unless you really understand it.

3 Look for a story

Like journalists, travel writers look for intriguing stories, not only descriptions. Find something quirky or unusual that has happened and ask why it happened and what the consequences were. Why did it pique your interest? Did it make you sit up and take notice? Does it have a beginning, a middle and an ending? Alternatively, find a novel angle that breaks new ground. Thousands upon thousands of people have written about the Grand Canyon, but what if you could interview someone who lived in it, or parachuted into it, or got lost in it ...?

4 No cash but a strong stomach

Only a tiny minority of travel writers get paid to do it, and it's rarely enough money to live on. You need a combination of talent, luck and perseverance. Oh, and a strong stomach. Who knows what you'll have to eat in the name of research?

Lesson 8.3 | Ex. 5a, page 113
Student C

Your friend is an Internet addict. She spends up to seven hours a day surfing the net. You want to help her, but you are worried that she will be offended.

Communication 7 | Ex. 4a, page 102
Student C

You want to create a wildlife sanctuary. You believe there needs to be a place where wild animals are protected. You are happy for paying customers to come and view the wildlife, but don't want too many tourists to spoil the atmosphere. You will bring in a lot of wildlife especially for the sanctuary.

Lesson 2.3 | Ex. 2a, page 28
Student C

Corsica

'Day in, day out, they're always watching: the shepherd on the hillside, the road workers resting under the shade of a tree, the old man on the bench in front of his house, his wife airing the
5 sheets at the window, the boules player next to the war memorial. They hardly move their heads but they see everything. It's a survival instinct moulded out of two thousand years of dangers coming from across the sea.'

10 The stereotypical Corsican community is introverted, family-based, dignified and shy. The truth behind the stereotype is that Corsicans love Corsica so much that they don't want the outside world to ruin it. Tradition is important;
15 Corsica is one of the last McDonald's-free zones in Europe. It is also simply stunning; the ancient Greeks called it 'Kalliste', meaning 'the most beautiful one'.

The island is famed for its diverse landscape.
20 You can find magnificent mountains, long stretches of Mediterranean coastline, and thick forest almost side by side, as well as charming villages, perfect for long, slow days in the sun. The island belongs to France but it has an
25 atmosphere all of its own.

A good place to start is Ajaccio. In this charming town, you can sit outside the cafés and watch fishermen mending their nets, or stroll in the bustling market which sells delicious seafood and
30 Corsican specialities: macchia honey and brocciu cheese. Old run-down houses stand proud on the side of the hill, overlooking modern yachts and wooden boats. Stroll along the streets and you will notice something interesting as you gaze at
35 the monuments, the street signs and restaurant names: the town stands in the vast shadow of its greatest son, Napoleon Bonaparte. His influence is everywhere, and in the Musée Napoléonien you can see his baptism certificate and his death mask.

40 Although Napoleon is at the heart of Corsican history, it is Corsica's natural beauty that you'll remember. Fishermen, surfers, sailors and hikers all find everything they need here. And for the less energetic, there is always the pleasure of a wander
45 along some of Europe's most tranquil scenery. Despite the tourists, the island is unspoilt. You won't find any packed nightclubs here, but there are plenty of cosy bars off the beaten track, where you can taste the atmosphere of Europe's own
50 natural paradise.

Lesson 10.2 | Ex. 7a, page 137

Lesson 3.3 | Ex. 9a, page 44
Student C

A woman goes to a doctor, complaining of pain.

'Where does it hurt?' asks the doctor.

'Everywhere,' says the woman.

'Could you be more specific?'

So the woman touches her knee with her finger.

'Ow!' she says. Then she touches her nose. 'Ow!'

Then she touches her back. 'Ow!' Finally, she touches her cheek. 'Ow!'

The doctor tells her to sit down, takes one look at her, and says, 'You have a broken finger.'

Communication activities

Lesson 4.3 | Ex. 13a, page 58
Student B

Nathan Chan has music in his genes. His mother, a classical pianist, and his father, a violinist, took him to concerts when he was a baby. By the age of two, Nathan had begun 'air-conducting'. As seen on many amusing YouTube clips, the little boy would wave his arms around while watching music videos, even splashing water on his face to represent the conductors' sweat. In fact, his mimicry was so accurate and perfectly timed with the rising and falling cadences of the music that it caught the attention of Sara Jobin, assistant conductor at the San Francisco Opera. At the age of three, Chan was invited to conduct the San Jose Chamber Orchestra. That day, they played the works of the most famous musical prodigy of them all: Wolfgang Amadeus Mozart.

A year later, Chan conducted the Palo Alto Philharmonic Orchestra. Then when he was five, his parents decided it was time for him to learn an instrument. He wanted to play the double bass, but as the instrument was about three times bigger than him, he began playing the cello instead.

Since then, Chan has forged a reputation as an outstanding cellist. He has won numerous prizes, played with some of the world's greatest orchestras, recorded CDs, and appeared on several TV programmes about musical prodigies. At the same time, he has managed to maintain a balanced life, attending school, playing badminton and table tennis, and, like teenagers everywhere, enjoying computer games.

Lesson 5.2 | Ex. 2, page 67
Student B

Rags to riches

Sixteen-year-old Zhou Xiaoguang hauled a 50kg bag of trinkets over her shoulder and ascended the steps of the night train. Too poor to pay for a seat, she crouched on the floor for three days and nights, assailed by the stench of the nearby toilets and unable to lie down for lack of room. There she tried – and usually failed – to sell her goods to assorted travellers. It was a humiliating experience, but not the first humiliation she had faced. As a schoolgirl, she was constantly being removed from class because her parents couldn't pay the school fees. Her reluctant entrance into the retail industry was borne of the need to help feed her little brother and five sisters.

Fast forward three decades and multi-millionaire Xiaoguang sits in her own office in Yiwu, Zhejiang Province, China, head of the world's biggest fashion and costume jewellery company. Neoglory, which she founded in the mid-1990s, has nearly 1,000 stores in China alone, employs over 6,000 people, and has a sales force in 70 countries. She has diversified into property holdings, fine wine and other investments, but jewellery is her main business. How did she go from rags to riches?

Her story is a tale of hard work and determination. In the early days, Neoglory was a low-cost manufacturer of cheap bracelets, rings and necklaces. It might have stayed that way if Xiaoguang had not seen the potential of the industry. Gradually she built up the brand by employing professional designers to give the jewellery its own distinct appeal, so that by the mid-2000s, Neoglory was using over 300 designers to produce more than 100 new designs per day. Of her beginnings in the business, she says that she wishes she had not needed 'to become a vendor at such a young age'. But she also acknowledges that if she hadn't experienced those difficult times, she would not have become the extraordinary businessperson that she is today. She still travels all over the world looking for ideas on design, research and investment. It's a safe bet that she doesn't use the night train.

1 | A leaflet or brochure

Can do write a promotional leaflet

1 Read the leaflet and answer the questions.

1 What is the leaflet advertising?
2 When and where can you study?
3 How old is the company?
4 Who are the teachers?

2 **a** Which of the following <u>doesn't</u> a leaflet usually do?

a advertise a place, event, product or service
b provide information about 'what', 'where' and 'when'
c give the company's background in brief
d explain how to get more information
e discuss the latest trends in the field

b Read the leaflet again. Which parts of the leaflet match the points in exercise 2a?

3 Read the How to... box and find more examples in the leaflet.

How to... write a promotional leaflet/promote something

Use a clear layout with subheadings for the key points	*Language and Culture courses*
Write clearly and concisely and use lists	*LinguaLife offers language and culture courses all over Europe.*
Use positive language	*leading provider highest quality*
Include a slogan	*Courses that change your life!*
Include recommendations/ testimonials	*The market leader in language courses*
Give reasons why the product/service/event is special	*We have been delivering programmes ... for over 20 years.*
Include contact details	*Tel: 0207 7816653*

4 **a** Think of a course or event for the public – it can be real or imaginary. Make notes about the 'what', 'where' and 'when'. Then write a leaflet for the course or event, with language from the How to... box.

b Work in pairs. Take turns to read each other's leaflets. Does the leaflet make you interested in the course or event? Why/Why not?

LinguaLife

Courses that change your life!

About us

LinguaLife is the leading provider of language and culture courses in Europe. We have been delivering programmes of the highest quality for over 20 years. Based in London, UK, we have branches in 18 major cities in Europe.

Language and Culture courses

LinguaLife offers language and culture courses all over Europe. You can learn Italian language and culture in Rome, Spanish language and culture in Madrid, Russian language and culture in Moscow, and many more.

Courses include: language lessons for all levels of proficiency from Basic to Advanced; lectures on art, architecture, literature and customs; cooking demonstrations; field trips to museums and places of historical interest; concerts and theatre performances.

Dates

Courses begin on the first Monday of each month.

Staff

Our outstanding staff consists of a group of dedicated teachers, lecturers and historians, all of whom are accredited, with an average of 15 years' experience in the classroom.

Prices

For a full list of our prices, please visit our website LinguaLifeLondon.com.

What they say about us

"*The market leader in language courses*" Education Weekly Inc.
"*An excellent service to students all over Europe*" Learning Solutions magazine
"*Simply the best value for money in language and culture courses*" NGD Journal

Contact

Tel: 0207 7816653 **or email:** languageculture@LL.org
Website: LinguaLifeLondon.com

1 Read the emails and answer the questions.

1 Why is Demetri Leopoulos writing? Who is he?

2 What two things does he need from Ms. Foong?

3 What information does Ms. Foong provide in the body of the email? What does she send in an attachment?

4 What is Ms. Foong's official position in her company?

2 Match informal expressions 1–6 to formal expressions in the emails.

1 I'm happy to tell you
2 We want you to come to
3 Can you tell us ...?
4 to go in the ...
5 We'd love to come
6 you asked for

3 Complete the How to... box with words from the box. Which phrases are not included in the emails?

> take   grateful   accept   pleased   find

How to... write a formal email

Giving good/ bad news	I am (1) _____ to inform you that ... I regret to inform you that ...
Inviting	We would like to invite you to ... You are formally invited to ...
Responding to an invitation	We are happy to (2) _____ your kind invitation. I am afraid I am unable to attend.
Making a request	We would be (3) _____ if you could ... Would you (also) be able to ...
Responding to a request	Please (4) _____ attached the document you requested. We would be happy to (send the document that you requested). I am afraid we are unable to (forward the document that you requested).
Including additional information	The event will (5) _____ place ... The venue is located ...

4 **a** Write an email inviting your partner to a formal occasion. It could be a dinner party, a conference, etc. Include an additional request (to make a speech, bring or send something) and additional information (how to get there or where to stay). Use language from the How to... box.

b Exchange emails with your partner.

c Write your response.

d Exchange emails with your partner and read their reply. Which formal expressions have they used?

Dear Ms Foong,

I am pleased to inform you that your company has been shortlisted for Website of the Year by WIA. We would like to invite you to attend the awards ceremony. The event will take place at Turpiric House, 136 Curtain Road, London EC2A 3AR on 4 August at 7 p.m. The venue is located a short taxi ride from Old Street tube station. This year the evening will consist of a formal dinner and entertainment before the official ceremony.

We would be grateful if you could let us know by 4 July how many of your team will be attending. WIA can host up to four people from each shortlisted company. Would you also be able to send a 150-word history of your company for inclusion in the programme?

We look forward to hearing from you.

Yours sincerely,

Demetri Leopoulos

Head of Judging Panel

Web Innovations Awards

Dear Mr Leopoulos,

Thank you for this great news. We are happy to accept your kind invitation. We will bring four members of our team to the awards ceremony: myself, Aisha Holder, Praveen Shastri and Kathleen Smith.

Please find attached the document you requested. If there is anything else you need from us, please don't hesitate to ask.

We look forward to seeing you on 4 August.

Regards,

Sze Foong, M.A.
CEO, magnumlove.com

3 | A story

Can do | write a detailed narrative

1943: The Man from the Sky

1 Look at the photo and the title of the story. Where do you think the story is set? What might happen?

2 Read the story and answer the questions.

1 How old do you think the narrator is?

2 Who do you think 'the man from the sky' is? Where might he really be from?

3 What can we guess about the narrator's character from his actions?

3 Complete the How to... box with the words/ sentences from the box below.

> lush grass   "Back to the sky"
> spewing orange flames
> His hands were the size of Yorkshire hams

How to... write fiction with style

Use metaphors (describing something by referring to it as something different)	*He was a giant.* *Darkness began to fall.*
Use similes (comparisons that often use *like* or *as* + adjective + *as*)	*He had a jaw like a bucket.*
Use personification (describing an inanimate object as if it were human)	*the plane's outstretched arms*
Use adjectives	*dazed cows*
Use dialogue	*"I need water," he said.*
Use a variety of sentence lengths	*I looked around. From the hill you could see fields and cows and clumps of trees and the box-like buildings of the farm.*

4 **a** Prepare to write a short story. Choose one of the titles below or write a story you already know. Make an outline of the story.

- A Family Tale
- A Dream Come True
- The Secret
- 24 Hours

b Write your story. Include the techniques in the How to... box.

c Work in small groups. Take turns to read each other's stories.

I would never forget him: the smell of his burned-out plane, the colour of his eyes, the way the apple disappeared in his hand. Pilots, along with everything else, seem smaller these days.

A trail of black smoke cut through the clouds. The plane was burning as it dropped. We saw it land roughly and bounce over Mowbray Hill. Then we chased it, me, Ronald, Arthur and Sue, haring across the green fields while the dazed cows barely turned their heads. Arthur, six years old and the youngest of us, tripped in the lush grass, but we kept going.

There, over the hill, the plane had stopped, spewing orange flames, its outstretched arms askew. Suddenly, from out of the wreckage, a man was running towards us. We scattered, but he followed me and, limping, soon caught up.

"Hello," he called after me.

I stopped and turned. He was a giant. His hands were the size of Yorkshire hams and he had a jaw like the bucket we used for milking cows. There were goggles on top of his head attached to a leather cap that matched his jacket. And beneath the cap, from the murk of his face blackened with soot and grime, his eyes shone, the same blue as the sky he came from.

"I need water," he said.

He had a strange accent, one that I had never heard before.

"I'll get some."

"Wait."

He took me by the arm. I saw that his trousers were wet with blood.

"What's your name?"

"John," I said.

He pulled off the cap and wiped his brow with the back of his hand.

"John, don't tell anyone I'm here. OK?"

"OK. We have a barn. Come with me."

We walked across the field, then across the cobbled stones. No one saw us. I pointed out a bed of straw in the barn and he lay down. I brought him water and he drank it in one gulp. I went back and brought him more and stole a hunk of bread and cheese and an apple from the pantry, which he ate in silence. As darkness began to fall, I said I had to go but I would bring him breakfast the following day.

I told no one about the man. There was no one to tell because my mother had gone to bed and my father and brothers had joined some of the other villagers wandering the fields with guns and pitchforks. They had congregated around the parched and blackened plane and, from there, gone in different directions, in pairs, some with lanterns, to search the gloom for the missing pilot.

I lay awake most of the night, thinking about the man from the sky. In the morning, I brought bread and milk to the barn, but he was gone. There was an indentation where he had slept, and a stain of dark blood on the straw. First I waited. Then I walked every inch of the farm, clambering over the locked gates. I went back to Mowbray Hill and skirted the remains of his wrecked plane. Suddenly I heard a voice.

"Where is he?"

It was six-year-old Arthur climbing over the hill.

"Gone," I replied.

"Gone where?"

I looked around. From the hill you could see fields and cows and clumps of trees and the box-like buildings of the farm.

"Back to the sky," I said, and tore off a hunk of the bread in my hand.

Progress in our classrooms

If you could transport yourself back 100 years to a classroom in a British school, you would see the teacher standing at a raised blackboard, a piece of chalk in hand. He or she is lecturing and writing down large swathes of information, which the children faithfully copy onto a piece of slate. Later the children go home and memorise this information. The next day they come back to school and do it all over again. They rarely talk in class except to answer the teacher's questions, barely move a muscle, and never work in groups.

The first half of the 20th century saw the opening up of numerous new fields of understanding, among them psychology and anthropology, which led to more progressive methods in education. Educators realised that children do not necessarily learn best by copying and memorising. The development of 'hands-on' experiential learning meant that children would benefit not just from reading about how a butterfly flaps its wings but from actually seeing one; not just from reading engineering texts but from watching a bridge being built; not just from learning the rules of foreign languages but from actually trying to use them.

In time, other developments occurred. The desks were unbolted from the floor so students could move around and work in groups. Collaborative learning was born. Blackboards changed colour. They were now whiteboards, and chalk went out of fashion, much to the delight of teachers: they would no longer go home wearing clothes covered in white smudges.

Gradually, new technologies such as the cassette recorder, the video and the computer made their way into classrooms. Then, at the beginning of the 21st century, smartboards arrived. These provide access to the Internet, save everything the class has written on them, and allow users to do all sorts of things such as drag images and words around the screen. Then a hand-held device called a clicker arrived, allowing each student to answer questions in private, their answers seen only by the teacher.

So, what if we could transport ourselves 100 years into the future? What would we find in classrooms? There have been many predictions, some based on ideas that come straight out of science-fiction (brain implants, knowledge pills). Others sound less far-fetched. A few select language schools in Korea are already experimenting with robots that can teach languages. And one day smart classrooms that can track the brain movements of individual students and send messages to teachers may also become reality.

1 Look at the photo and the title of the article. What type of progress do you think it will discuss?

2 Read the article and answer the questions.

1 According to the writer, how did children learn in British classrooms 100 years ago?
2 What 21st-century technologies are mentioned?
3 What innovations does the writer think might one day become normal in children's classrooms?

3 Read the advice in the How to... box. Add more examples from the article.

How to... develop a writing style for articles

Begin by capturing the reader's attention	*If you could transport yourself back one hundred years to a classroom in a British school, you would see the teacher standing at a raised blackboard ...*
Use the present tense for an effect of immediacy	*Later the children go home and memorise this information.*
Use the active voice for more powerful sentences	*The first half of the 20th century saw the opening up of numerous new fields of understanding*
Use lists of three (for rhythm and flow) when giving examples	*They rarely talk in class ..., barely move a muscle, and never work in groups.* *... new technologies such as the cassette recorder, the video, and the computer ...*
Avoid repetition by using pronouns and reference words	*... children would benefit not just from reading about how a butterfly flaps **its** wings but from actually seeing **one*** *There have been many predictions, **some** based on ideas that come straight out of science-fiction ... **Others** sound less far-fetched.*
Use questions to involve the reader	*So, what if we could transport ourselves 100 years into the future?*
Close the article by echoing the beginning	*If you could transport yourself back 100 years ...*

4 a Think about how your profession, hobby or field of study has progressed in the past and might progress in the future. Plan an article for non-experts in your field.

b Now write your article.

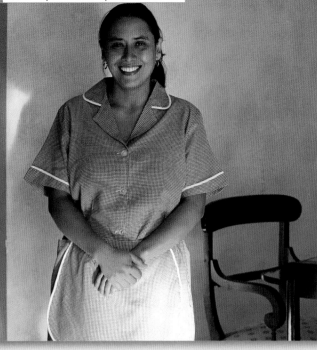

Democratic Companies: The Next Step

The people who make our shoes never wear them. Workers in sweatshops would need to save up for a year to afford a pair of $150 trainers. Imagine, then, a world in which workers maintained control of the product. Instead of seeing the results of their labour packaged and sent away to the wealthy West, the shoes would be in their hands or, rather, on their feet. The key question is this: would the world's economic system collapse if the workers became the owners?

The answer, if we look at numerous examples, is no. Worker-owned companies consistently outperform traditionally run businesses. The reason is simple: worker-owners care more. Working for themselves and for each other in small dedicated teams, they feel a sense of responsibility to their colleagues. They identify with the company and they invest more of themselves in it. One example of this is women's cooperative 'We Can Do It!' The New York house-cleaning company is owned by the immigrants who work for it, and they have an equal vote in all decisions. What's more, the company is thriving.

Perhaps the biggest argument for worker-owned companies is that they are a talent magnet. Bright, creative people want to work as equals with other bright, creative people. Generally, they are not motivated by power, but rather by achievement. And, as we all know, happy employees work more effectively than those sulking in the shadows of giant top-down organisations.

Some might say worker-ownership is a recipe for chaos. For instance, wouldn't many employees do less for the company while living off the hard work of others? Again the answer is no. The fact is that peer pressure ensures that everyone pulls their weight. Those who, at first, don't understand this generally learn it quickly or get kicked out.

So, business owners, what can you do? The first thing is to ditch the big office. Then flatten the hierarchy. Then tell everyone they are working as equals in pay, status and responsibility. Then watch your company grow.

1 Read the persuasive essay. Do you agree with the writer?

2 Look at one possible structure for an opinion essay. Does the example follow this structure?

1 **introduction:** announces the topic (problem), prepares the reader for the argument (solution)

2 **body (a):** gives context and evidence (anecdotes, statistics, quotes, etc.)

3 **body (b):** gives additional arguments

4 **body (c):** acknowledges opposing views and points out weaknesses in them

5 **conclusion:** ends with a call to action

3 **a** Read the How to... box. Tick the expressions used in the essay.

How to... write persuasively

State your position	*I will here argue that ..., the key question is ..., in essence, ... the fact is ...*
give examples or use lists to illustrate a point	*for example, ...; one example of this is ...*
anticipate counter-arguments	*some might say... , the counter-argument is..., it has been argued that ... (but ...)*
use hedging devices (cautious language to sound less direct)	*perhaps, it can be argued, apparently, tend to, may/ might/could, generally*

b Add the phrases from the box below to the How to... box.

> arguably,   for instance, ...
> the main point is that ...   to a certain extent,
> a common misconception is ...
> the fundamental issue is ...
> it has been put forward that ... (but ...)

4 **a** Prepare to write a persuasive essay on an aspect of work or student life. Decide on a problem that has affected you, and think of a possible solution (see below for ideas). Think about how you will persuade others to agree. Make notes.

The cost of higher education → it should be paid for by the government.

The work environment is noisy and uncomfortable → employees should be allowed to work from home three days a week.

b Now write your essay.

Can do | write about your personal history

I was born in London, but I grew up in Taunton, which is a small town with not much to do, so my two sisters and I had to improvise and invent a lot of games. This is probably one reason why I was good at making things. As a child, I always enjoyed designing objects to put in rooms, and my teachers encouraged me to develop my artistic abilities. I also found that I had a particular aptitude for maths.

At the age of 16 I decided to leave school and do an apprenticeship in a design company. I worked for Bilosh Design Solutions for two years, mainly doing clerical work in the office, but also observing some of the projects. During this time, I learned a lot, especially from Judith Baker, who was my line manager. She was quite inspiring in that she taught me how to solve problems by looking at things in a different way. From her I learned how to access my creativity when I needed to 'think out of the box'.

In 2006 I felt I needed a new challenge so I decided to enrol on a cartoon animation course. My application was successful and I spent a very enjoyable month working on film animation. It was at this time that I realised my true vocation was designing graphics for advertisements and commercial films. For this reason I have applied for a degree course in graphic design. I really hope to develop my skills so that I will be able to work in this field for the foreseeable future.

Cheryl Hodgson

1 Read the autobiographical statement. What is its purpose (a, b or c)?

a The writer is applying for a job at a design company.

b The writer is explaining how she became a graphic designer.

c The writer is trying to enrol on a course of study.

2 Tick (✓) the expressions in the How to... box that the writer used in her autobiographical statement.

How to... describe life experiences

Referring to life stages	*as a child ...*
	at the age of ...
	during this time,
	I spent a month/year ...
	it was at this time that ...
	... for the foreseeable future
Referring to stages in your career path	*do an apprenticeship*
	apply for a course
	enrol on a course
	(find/realise) my true vocation (is)
	work in this field
Referring to achievements	*(my) application was successful*
	won an award for ...
	led a team
Referring to skills/abilities	*had an aptitude for*
	develop my skills
	become confident in

3 **a** Read the advert for a scholarship to study the subject of your choice at a university in Australia. Think about what you would choose to study.

Piaget Educational Consultants is offering a scholarship award to study a subject of your choice for one year at a university in Australia. The winner will be given lodging, tuition and $7,500 spending money. To apply, send an autobiographical statement of 250–300 words describing your background, hobbies and interests, and experience in your chosen field. Send your statement to Piaget Educational Consultants, PO Box 52680, Perth, Australia by May 5.

b Make notes about any achievements, skills, and events from your life/career that are relevant to the application.

c Write an autobiographical statement to apply for the scholarship.

Can do | write an advertisement

1

Black Jake, 16ft fibreglass speedboat for sale for €10,400. The boat has a VRO 50 outboard that is as good as new. The boat was repainted recently and the seat coverings are immaculate. Also included in the price is a spare fuel tank, two oars, anchor, two life jackets and a winter cover. If you have any questions or wish to view the boat, please call 28716547.

2

16-piece porcelain tea cup and saucer set made in England and dating from the 1930s Art Deco period. This exquisite tea set is decorated with flowers in several colours (see picture). Every piece is in excellent condition with no cracks or chips. There is slight fading on the patterns of the saucers. Bidding starts at $50. Call 8973639 for a closer look.

3

7-inch portable DVD player (Ramashay Model DVR30) comes with headphones and remote control. Battery life is 3 hours and the player has a built-in speaker. There is some wear and tear on the DVD player with a 2-inch scratch on the cover, but everything is in good working order. The box is rather tatty but I will package in a separate container. Email me on tgsmithson@yahoo.com if you have questions.

1 Read the online advertisements. Would you or anyone you know be interested in buying these things?

2 What are the general features of online adverts? Write true (T) or false (F).

Online advertisements ...

1 ... are dense with information; they say a lot in few words. ☐

2 ... give details about size, age, etc. ☐

3 ... describe the condition of the piece for sale. ☐

4 ... say where and for how much the seller originally bought the item. ☐

5 ... compare the items on sale to items you can buy in shops. ☐

6 ... include contact details. ☐

3 Read the How to... box. Add examples from advert 3.

How to... write a web advertisement

Give concise details about size, age, etc.	*Black Jake 16ft fibreglass speedboat* *16-piece porcelain tea cup and saucer set* *dating from the 1930s*
Describe condition (positive)	*repainted recently ... as good as new* *the seat coverings are immaculate* *This exquisite tea set ...* *Every piece is in excellent condition with no cracks or chips.*
Describe condition (negative)	*slight fading* *some wear and tear*

4 **a** Choose an object to sell (furniture, toys, clothes, vehicles, etc.) and write an advertisement for it. Use the How to... box to help you.

b Work in small groups. Take turns to show your adverts. Ask and answer questions about the items and try to find something to buy.

8 | Cause and effect essay

1 Read the essay. Which title fits best?

   a Insomnia – Reasons and Consequences

   b How Stress Affects Your Sleep

   c Five Ideas for a Better Sleep

2 Read the essay again and answer the questions.

   1 Where is the topic stated?

   2 How many paragraphs deal with the causes of insomnia?

   3 How many paragraphs discuss the consequences?

   4 Are the first sentences of each paragraph (topic sentences) usually long or short?

   5 What information already mentioned in the body of the essay does the conclusion refer back to?

3 Read the How to... box and tick (✓) the expressions used in the essay.

How to... organise information in an essay

Stating the facts	*it has been estimated that ...* *recent research points to the fact that ...* *many people report that they ...*
Ordering information	*This paper will first examine ...* *We will then ...* *The primary cause of insomnia is ...* *First and foremost,* *The second ...*
Adding information	*Another aspect to take into consideration is ...* *In addition to this, ...* *A further effect is ...*
Referring to previous information	*With respect to ...* *Regarding ...* *Concerning ...*

4 **a** Prepare to write an essay. Choose one of the topics below and make notes on causes and effects.

> stress   new technology   unhealthy lifestyles
> pollution   unemployment

stress

causes: work and money problems, major life changes, conflicts with family and partner

effects: poor sleep, moodiness, eating too much or too little, feeling isolated

   b Write your cause and effect essay.

It has been estimated that around 90% of adults in the developed world have, at some time in their life, suffered from a period of insomnia of at least one week. Other recent research points to the fact that women are nearly twice as likely as men to have it. This paper will first examine some of the most common causes of insomnia. We will then take a brief look at some of the consequences of the illness.

The primary cause of insomnia is lifestyle. Lifestyle greatly affects the way we sleep. People who smoke or drink alcohol and coffee (or other drinks with caffeine) close to bedtime are more vulnerable to insomnia. Another aspect to take into consideration is physical activity. People who exercise are more likely to sleep soundly than those who do no physical exercise. In addition to this, those who work in highly stressful jobs, under a lot of pressure, often have trouble 'switching off' and relaxing, and this affects the quality and quantity of their sleep.

The second cause is environment. With respect to our home environment, bedrooms should be quiet, dark and cool. Furthermore, they should not be used as an office or a place of work. Instead, the bedroom should be a retreat from our daily activities. While many people report that they get used to living in noisy neighbourhoods, for others silence is essential for a good night's sleep.

The third cause of insomnia is health. Both physical and mental health can affect the way we sleep. Pain, illness and an unhealthy diet can all cause insomnia. Regarding mental health, any stressful situation causing emotions such as fear, panic and nervousness may stop us sleeping.

So, what are the effects of insomnia? Many insomniacs report feeling drowsy during the day. This prevents them from learning, recalling information and concentrating to their full capacity. One potentially dangerous side effect of this may occur when we are handling machinery. A large number of car accidents take place because of the effects of insomnia.

A further effect is irritability. Insomniacs may experience mood swings during which they feel angry for no reason, while long-term lack of sleep may lead to depression. For this reason, the people who are living with the insomniac need to be aware of the effects.

Overall, insomnia takes a great toll on people from all walks of life. While there have been many suggested remedies, the best advice seems to be 'live a healthy lifestyle'. Although this cannot guarantee a good night's sleep, in most cases troublesome bouts of insomnia disappear within a few days.

1 Read the proposal and answer the questions.

1 What project is being proposed?

2 What benefits does the project have?

2 Which of the following do you think apply to proposals?

Proposals should ...

a be easy for the reader to understand

b use only short sentences

c contain separate sections with a line between each section

d use subheadings that name the section

e use a formal, impersonal tone

f be comprehensive (include all the necessary information)

g sound enthusiastic and positive

3 Complete the How to... box with language from the proposal.

How to... write a clear proposal

Use clear headings	(1) _____ of the project Goals and (2) _____ Competitors Costs Schedule Conclusion
Use a formal tone	The costs ... will be (3) _____ by ... (Entries) ... will be accepted from January to May. Furthermore, there are many (4) _____ for spin-offs
Use positive language	This will ensure maximum exposure. We (5) _____ it will be very popular

4 **a** Prepare to write a proposal. Think of an idea for a product or service that you would like to propose. Make notes on what to include in the proposal.

b Write the proposal with language from the How to... box.

My vision: my world

Description of the project

'My vision: my world' is an annual photo competition. Open to anyone – professionals and amateurs – the competition will be for the best photo of a place in the city. Fifty shortlisted photos will be shown in an exhibition at the Harper Rhone Art Gallery, and the winner will receive a new IKAM camera.

Goals and objectives

'My vision: my world' will help people to look at their local environment with fresh eyes, and give them an incentive to preserve that environment. It will also be an outlet for creativity and artistic vision in the city.

Competitors

In our area, there are no competitions similar to 'My vision: my world'. There are various national photography competitions, but very few of these have a local theme.

Costs

The judging panel will work on a voluntary basis, looking through the photos at a designated date in May. The costs of mounting the exhibition will be borne by the gallery. IKAM Inc. has agreed to sponsor the competition in return for their logo appearing on the programme.

Schedule

Entries for 'My vision: my world' will be accepted from January to May. At the end of May the judges will choose a shortlist of 50 photos. These will be exhibited in June, one of the busiest times of year for the gallery. This will ensure maximum exposure for the work on display. During the exhibition the public will vote for their favourite photo, and the winner will be announced in July.

Conclusion

'My vision: my world' is an exciting new project. We believe it will be very popular among local people and visitors to the city. Furthermore, there are many opportunities for spin-offs such as book projects, a web site, and talks by local photographers.

1 Look at the photo. What feelings do you associate with it?

2 Read the anecdote and answer the questions.

1 Why was the writer expecting a sad Christmas?

2 What did his big sister do to make it a happy Christmas?

3 What lesson did the writer learn?

3 Complete the How to... box with the sentences from the box below.

> Little did we know what was about to happen.
> Never again would I ...
> We had been living there since 1988.
> I was over the moon!

How to... write about a personal experience

Give background information	When I was eight, my father lost his job.
Arouse the reader's curiosity	Instead, it turned out to be one of the best.
Describe emotions	Positive: We were thrilled.
	Negative: I went to bed that night with a heavy heart.
	Surprise: to our surprise ... I couldn't believe my eyes
Add a personal reflection	it taught me a valuable lesson
	I'll always remember ...

4 **a** Prepare to write a story. Think about an experience from your childhood or your teenage years. What happened? How did you feel? Why was it so important to you?

b Write your anecdote.

Lost and found at Christmas

When I was eight, my father lost his job. For a year after this, we were extremely poor. We had to sell a lot of our furniture, jewellery and books to make ends meet.

It was Christmas Eve of that year. A friend had kindly donated a Christmas tree, but there were no presents under it because we simply didn't have the money to buy them. I went to bed that night with a heavy heart. I was expecting it to be the worst Christmas of my life. Instead, it turned out to be the best.

When we woke up the following morning, we saw, to our surprise, a pile of wrapped presents under the tree. There were two for everybody - my parents, my sisters and me. As was traditional in those days, we ate our lunch and then began opening the presents. My younger sister went first. She tore off the paper and almost jumped with surprise. It was a doll that she had 'misplaced' months ago! Then I opened the first of mine. I couldn't believe my eyes. It was a scarf that I'd 'lost' at school. My mother received a pair of stockings that had gone missing from her closet months before. And my father got a fountain pen that he'd 'mislaid' at the local library. Every time we opened a parcel, we got a tremendous surprise: things that we thought we had lost forever suddenly reappeared in our lives. We were thrilled.

It turned out to be the doing of my older sister, Martha. For months she'd been 'removing' things and storing them in a hiding place in her room. On Christmas Eve, while the rest of us were asleep, she'd wrapped them, sneaked down the stairs, and put them under the tree. It was a wonderful day, and it taught me a valuable lesson. The best thing about Christmas is the people you share it with, not the things you receive.

The following year my father was hired by an insurance company. It was a relief to us all. We were able to replace a lot of the things we had sold, and we always had proper Christmas presents from that time onwards. But I'll always remember the 'lost and found' Christmas gifts with pleasure.

Pronunciation bank

English phonemes

Consonants

p	b	t	d	k	g	tʃ	dʒ
park	bath	tie	die	cat	give	church	judge
f	v	θ	ð	s	z	ʃ	ʒ
few	visit	throw	they	sell	zoo	fresh	measure
h	m	n	ŋ	l	r	j	w
hot	mine	not	sing	lot	road	yellow	warm

Vowels and diphthongs

iː	ɪ	e	æ	ɑː	ɒ	ɔː	ʊ	uː	ʌ
feet	fit	bed	bad	bath	bottle	bought	book	boot	but
ɜː	ə	eɪ	əʊ	aɪ	aʊ	ɔɪ	ɪə	eə	ʊə
bird	brother	grey	gold	by	brown	boy	here	hair	tour

Sound–spelling correspondences

Sound	Spelling	Examples
/ɪ/	i	this listen
	y	gym typical
	ui	build guitar
	e	pretty
/iː/	ee	green sleep
	ie	niece believe
	ea	read teacher
	e	these complete
	ey	key money
	ei	receipt receive
	i	police
/æ/	a	can pasta
/ɑː/	a	can't dance*
	ar	scarf bargain
	al	half
	au	aunt laugh
	ea	heart
/ʌ/	u	fun husband
	o	some mother
	ou	cousin double
/ɒ/	o	hot pocket
	a	watch want

Sound	Spelling	Examples
/ɔː/	or	short sport
	ou	your bought
	au	daughter taught
	al	small always
	aw	draw jigsaw
	ar	warden warm
	oo	floor indoor
/aɪ/	i	like time
	y	dry cycle
	ie	fries tie
	igh	light high
	ei	height
	ey	eyes
	uy	buy
/eɪ/	a	lake hate
	ai	wait train
	ay	play say
	ey	they grey
	ei	eight weight
	ea	break
/əʊ/	o	home open
	ow	show own
	oa	coat road
	ol	cold told

Weak forms

Word	Strong form	Weak form
a, an	/æ/, /æn/	/ə/, /ən/
at	/æt/	/ət/
and	/ænd/	/ən/
are	/ɑː/	/ə/ (or /ər/ before vowels)
been	/biːn/	/bɪn/
can	/kæn/	/kən/
do	/duː/	/də/
does	/dʌz/	/dəz/
has	/hæz/	/həz/, /əz/
have	/hæv/	/həv/, /əv/
than	/ðæn/	/ðən/
them	/ðem/	/ðəm/
to	/tuː/	/tə/ (before consonants)
was	/wɒz/	/wəz/

* In American English the sound in words like *can't* and *dance* is the shorter /æ/ sound, like *can* and *man*.

Pronunciation bank

Stress

Stressed and unstressed words (units 1 and 4)

We usually stress the words which carry the main meaning of a sentence. These are content words (usually nouns and verbs). We are less likely to stress other words which are less essential to the meaning (for example, auxiliary verbs and prepositions).

The <u>President</u> <u>arrived</u> in Turkey today.

After the <u>game</u>, the <u>manager</u> <u>blasted</u> his <u>players</u> for their <u>attitude</u>.

When we use inversion, we usually stress the adverbial phrase. We do not usually stress auxiliary verbs or pronouns.

<u>No way</u> would I do that!

<u>Rarely</u> do I come late.

Emphasis (units 5 and 9)

We can add emphasis to sentences by adding certain words (*own*, *very*, *actually*, etc.). These words are usually stressed. When we emphasise, our intonation usually rises.

I <u>actually</u> have my <u>own</u> car.

We can also add auxiliary verbs (*do*, *did*, etc.) for emphasis, which are also stressed.

You're wrong. I <u>did</u> see her cheating!

When we use cleft sentences, we usually emphasise different parts of the sentence.

It's <u>David</u> that I'm <u>talking</u> to, not <u>Ben</u>.

Emphasis using *however*, *whatever*, etc. (unit 6)

When we use *however*, *whatever*, etc. we stress the second syllable of the word.

I'll be here for you what<u>ev</u>er happens.

Stress shift on long adjectives (unit 6)

Adjectives that end in *-ic* (*romantic*, *acrobatic*, *pathetic*, etc.) tend to have the stress on the syllable before the letters *-ic*.

id<u>io</u>tic, ec<u>sta</u>tic, ac<u>a</u>demic, po<u>e</u>tic, patri<u>o</u>tic, enthusi<u>a</u>stic, photo<u>gen</u>ic

Adjectives that end in *-tional* or *-sional* (*professional*, *international*, etc.) tend to have the stress on the syllable before the letters *-tional* or *-sional*.

<u>fic</u>tional, sen<u>sa</u>tional, ir<u>ra</u>tional, confron<u>ta</u>tional, tra<u>di</u>tional, con<u>ven</u>tional

Fronting (unit 8)

We often use fronting phrases (*the trouble is …, the question is …, the thing is …*) to emphasise the importance of what we are going to say. These phrases usually affect the stress patterns of the sentence.

The <u>trouble</u> is, the <u>company</u> is <u>running</u> out of <u>money</u>.

The <u>question</u> is, <u>can</u> you <u>finish</u> your <u>studies</u> by <u>May</u>.

Connected speech

Connected speech (unit 10)

There are several features of pronunciation which occur in fast connected speech:

1 Elision: this is when a sound disappears.

See you next Saturday. (The /t/ in *next* disappears. Next is pronounced /neks/)

We hoped for sunshine. (The /d/ in *hoped* disappears.)

2 Assimilation: this is when sounds are changed because of the sounds that follow them.

What a good boy! (The /d/ in *good* sounds like /b/.)

It was a bad call. (The /d/ in *bad* sounds like /g/.)

That guy's funny. (The second /t/ in *that* sounds like /k/.)

3 Linking: this is when we pronounce a consonant (e.g. /r/, /w/ and /j/) at the end of a word to link it to the following word. We pronounce it of it comes between two vowel sounds.

The car disappeared. (The /r/ in *car* is not pronounced.)

The car is mine. (The /r/ in *car* is pronounced.)

Are you on the train? (There is a /w/ sound between *you* and *on*.)

I asked. (There is a /j/ sound between *I* and *asked*.)

Speech units (unit 3)

When we talk for a long time, we usually divide our speech into logical parts. Between each part, we pause slightly to make it easier for the listener to follow what we're saying. The pauses have a similar function to punctuation and often occur: at the end of a sentence; between clauses linked by and, but or because; and before and after a phrase which adds extra information.

Now John told me // and I don't know if it's true // that Mary broke up with Steve, // which would amaze me. // Those two // if I'm not mistaken // are completely in love!

Contractions (units 3 and 5)

When two words make a common verb form (e.g. *I am*, *do not*, *would have*), we often contract the words so that they are pronounced as one word (*I'm*, *don't*, *would've*).

<u>He's</u> always saying he <u>would've</u> been the best if <u>he'd</u> had the chance.

auxiliary verb *have* (unit 4)

Auxiliary verbs, modal verbs, prepositions and articles are often pronounced with a weak form.

Where have you been?
      /həv/

to (unit 7)

The word *to* is usually pronounced as a weak form.

I need to leave at quarter to two in order to get to the meeting.
           /tə/   /tə/   /tə/ /tə/

as (unit 7)

The word *as* is usually pronounced as a weak form.

That car is as big as a bus.
              /əz/   /əz/

Audioscripts

Track 1.02

M=Mark, I=Interviewer

I: Mark, you speak seven languages.

M: That's right.

I: Can you tell us a little about your level of fluency and proficiency in the languages?

M: Well, Russian is probably my best language. I speak it pretty well because I spent a lot of time in the country, but it's a little rusty. I have quite a good ear, which is a good thing and a bad thing because my accent suggests that I know more than I really do! The other languages are mainly Latin-based: Spanish, Portuguese, Italian, but also French and Polish.

I: You learned the languages through a combination of techniques.

M: That's right. In different ways, like going to classes, travel, private study ...

I: Did you use any special techniques? Any magic secrets?

M: Magic secrets, no! But I did do some interesting things, like memory training. I watched films in their original language and at some point I tried sticking lists of words around the house. But I think, with me, it was more a case of being motivated, and the biggest motivator was a love of languages and pleasure in communicating with people from other countries.

I: Would you say it's easier to learn new languages if you already know languages in that family? For example, you speak Spanish and French, so maybe it was fairly easy to pick up Portuguese.

M: I wouldn't say it was easy, but yeah, I would definitely say it's a help, although occasionally it gets confusing. You might be speaking in one language and suddenly a word from another language slips out, causing complete confusion.

I: Is there any little word of encouragement you could offer those poor souls who are trying to master a language?

M: Er ... that's a tricky one. What I would say is that knowing how to read and write a language doesn't mean you can speak it. You really have to get out there and try to speak at every opportunity. Take risks. Don't be afraid to look stupid, because that's the only way you're going to learn. And you know, everyone has to start somewhere. As a young man, I went to France after years of studying French and, to my complete embarrassment, I couldn't speak the language or understand anything. All I could do was order breakfast in my hotel!

Track 1.03

P=Presenter

P: To continue our series on famous firsts ... If you ask a Brazilian who first flew an aeroplane, she'll tell you it was Alberto Santos Dumont. Ask an American and he'll answer the Wright brothers. In 1906, Santos Dumont was widely believed to have flown the first plane that was heavier than air. Others say that the Americans Wilbur and Orville Wright first flew in 1903. The truth is, we don't really know who flew first, but Santos Dumont was certainly a colourful character. He's said to be the first person to have owned a flying machine for personal use. He kept his balloon tied up outside his Paris flat and regularly flew to restaurants! Our second question ... It's commonly assumed that Alexander Graham Bell invented the telephone, but now we're not so sure. Many people believe that Antonio Meucci, an Italian immigrant, got there first. And in 2003, files were discovered which suggest that a 26-year-old German science teacher, Philipp Reis, had invented the phone 15 years before Bell.

Now, who was the first to the North Pole? In 1908, Dr Frederick Cook said he'd done it, but it's commonly believed that he lied, and that a man called Robert Peary made it first. There are others who claim that neither of them reached the North Pole. The light bulb. It's widely asserted that Edison invented it, but we don't really know for sure. Edison based a lot of his inventions on other people's ideas. Also, he worked with a team, and he never shared the credit.

Moving on to our football question, it's widely assumed that South America's football glory belongs to Brazil and Argentina ... but it was Uruguay that hosted and won the first World Cup in 1930. They beat Argentina 4–2 in the final in front of 93,000 people in Montevideo. The cheering of the crowd is said to have been the loudest noise ever heard in Uruguay.

Talking of sport, it is often thought that rugby and sheep are the main claims to fame for New Zealand. Not many people know that in 1893, New Zealand became the first country to allow women to vote. Now, talking of empowering women, one woman who has empowered herself is Ellen MacArthur. MacArthur is sometimes wrongly assumed to be the first woman to sail around the world. She wasn't. She was the fastest but not the first. That honour goes to another Englishwoman, Naomi James, who did it in 1979. Apparently, she got so seasick that soon afterwards she gave up sailing altogether. And our final question. The Ancient Olympic Games were of course first held in Greece. They were quite different from the Games today. Instead of money, the winners received a crown of leaves. They were also said to be allowed to put their statue up on Olympus.

Track 1.04

N=Newsreader

N: The headlines this lunchtime are ...

A conservation institute in the United States has produced wild kittens by cross-breeding cloned adult cats. It is believed to be the first time that clones of wild animals have been bred. Researchers at the Audubon Centre for Research of Endangered Species say that the development holds enormous potential for the preservation of endangered species.

An American millionaire has succeeded in his long-held ambition to circumnavigate the world in a balloon. Fifty-eight-year-old Steve Fossett had already made five attempts on the record, but was frequently beaten back by the weather. In 1997 he was forced to land in Russia, in 1998 it was Australia, and in 2001 he found himself crash-landing on a cattle ranch in Brazil.

And finally, the story of a man who has entered the record books as the world's most renowned eater of burgers. It is estimated that Don Gorske has eaten over 15,000 Big Macs, and he even proposed to his girlfriend Mary in the car park of a McDonald's. In 15 years, he says, he has missed a Big Mac on only seven occasions, including the death of his mother, a snowstorm and a 600-mile drive without a McDonald's in sight.

Track 1.06

1

When I was at school, a friend of mine was injured in an accident while playing rugby. He was paralysed and needed to spend the rest of his life in a wheelchair. Together with some friends we decided to organise a sponsored bike ride to raise money for his family, and other people in a similar situation. So we set up a charity called 'One Step Ahead' and arranged to cycle from Scotland to Gibraltar. I'd never done anything like that before, so it was a fantastic learning experience. I'd always thought it would be great to cycle across a whole country, but this exceeded my expectations. There were about 20 or 30 of us on bikes, and the rest of the crew in vans with all the equipment, and camping gear. It was very tough cycling, especially in Spain where we had to battle against the heat. But we had a fantastic time, and at the end, when we arrived, there was a huge party for us, and the media came and took photos. We were even on the news! We felt we'd accomplished something quite important, and we raised lots of money for people with spinal injury too.

2

I've been doing volunteer work here in the rain forest, in Brazil, for a while now. Next week I'll have been here for three months, helping to teach English to the young children in the village. It's been an amazing experience, because I'd never even left Europe before, so you can imagine how different things are here. When I arrived, I really didn't know what to expect. It was a real culture shock, and I was here on my own for the first couple of months. Now my girlfriend has come out to join me, and things are a bit easier. I've been living with a small tribe of people right out in the forest, and I'd never done any teaching before either, so the whole thing has been quite a challenge, and I've learnt a lot. But some of the children are speaking quite good English with me now, and a few of them are starting to write little stories too, so I feel it's been quite an achievement.

3

I've run a marathon. In fact, I'm planning to run it again this year. I did it last year for the first time and it was great. It felt like a major achievement. I had to train really hard, getting up early in the morning to run before going to work. And as the distances got longer I had to get up earlier and earlier. And it was incredibly hard because I'd never done any training like that before. I've always run, but just for myself, to relax and to keep fit, but this was a chance to be more competitive, and really push myself to the limit. It is a fantastic run, because London is a beautiful city, and there's such a good atmosphere as you go along the route, with people cheering you on. My parents even came over from New Zealand to see me arrive at the finish. I couldn't move for about a week afterwards last time, but I was glad I'd done it and I'm looking forward to the next one.

Audioscripts

Track 1.08
E=Expert

E: If you ticked mainly 'a', then you seem to be very comfortable as you are and you're not too keen on new challenges. I think you need to make an effort to get off the sofa. Go on! Take a risk – it might have a positive effect!

Now, if your answers were mainly 'b', it means you love a challenge and you take advantage of your opportunities. You seem willing to have a go at anything and everything. So, good luck, but be careful! Those of you who ticked mainly 'c', well, you obviously make a habit of checking everything before committing yourself. You are super-cautious. Well, you may live a long, safe life, but a bit of a challenge from time to time won't do you any harm!

Track 1.09
1

I'm from South Africa. I spent two and a half years, actually more like two years, living in Vancouver, Canada. Er … my wife and I were trying to set up our own business there as packagers in the publishing industry. Unfortunately, things were not going very well economically. Canada wasn't in a depression, but it was just not a very good time to try and start your own business in publishing. What did I like about Vancouver? Well, Vancouver is one of the most beautiful cities in the world. In fact, Vancouver is regularly named as the best place in the world to live. Stunningly beautiful because of mountains, sea, forests and natural beauty and for me, combined with a large city. Vancouver is a city where you can walk to the beach. Vancouver is a city where the beaches are right in the city and you can go to the beach for your lunch break. You can take a bus and go skiing in the mountains 40 minutes later. Canadian food, of course, is not at the top of the world's list of good food, but Vancouver has got a very large Chinese population, Indian population, and of course as the rest of Canada, people from all over the world, so you can eat extraordinarily good food in Vancouver. Erm … the only food that people might consider uniquely Vancouverite is what they would call 'fusion' cuisine, which is food prepared by chefs that mix their diverse background from Asia or Europe and integrate it with the local foods and in fact you can have a very good meal that way. My best memories about Canada? Well, the open spaces, the vastness and the friendly people as well.

2

I'm from Belfast originally, but over the past ten years I've been living, erm, I've lived in Spain, Austria, France and other parts of the UK. Erm, I lived in Austria for a year when I was about 22, 23. It was a gap year from university. Er, I was studying German so I wanted to spend a year there. I was a teaching assistant there. I worked in a school four days a week, so it was really great because it meant I had long weekends. Erm, I usually went travelling with my friends at the weekends. Erm, we went to Slovenia, Prague, Italy, Germany and the best thing was I pretended I was 15 so that I could get some rail discount. I got half-price train tickets which was excellent. Erm, the other great things about living there was obviously skiing and ice skating on lakes, which you can't do in Northern Ireland. Erm, obviously the scenery is beautiful. The people were lovely. The thing I didn't really like was the food,

because I'm vegetarian and in Austria they tend to eat a lot of meat, but apart from that everything else was great. Erm, I think my favourite memories of Austria are the scenery, being able to go off into the mountain after school every afternoon, and go skiing or swimming in the lakes in the summer, and I'd definitely like to go back one day.

3

When I lived in Japan, actually in Tokyo, for about two years – this was about two years ago now – erm, it was, as you can imagine, a completely crazy experience for me, coming from Oxford which is a very, you know, small, provincial, very quiet kind of town. Er, I was living in Tokyo because I was working as an English-language teacher for a really tiny language school run by this lovely, lovely old lady erm, in a suburb of Tokyo. Erm, I thoroughly enjoyed Tokyo. It was such an interesting experience. It was like being, you know, dropped in the middle of a lifestyle that was completely different to my own. Erm, even going to the supermarket was a massive adventure because of course I couldn't read anything because the writing system's so different, so I'd sort of pick up a tin and think, 'Ooh that looks interesting, I'll take that take that home and, you know, I'll see what comes out' and got a few surprises of course, a few unidentifiable foods that I'd never seen before, but that's always a good thing. Erm … I think my favourite memories of the country would have to be the people. Because I was teaching English, I knew a lot of Japanese people as students, as colleagues in the school and so on, and I just found them so lovely. They were friendly, funny, really interested in what a foreigner like me was doing in Tokyo and very keen to, you know, share experiences of travelling abroad and to … to tell me all about the social customs in Japan and things like that. So it was a, it was a really rewarding experience, absolutely great.

Track 1.10
W=Woman, M=Man

M: It's made such a big difference to me. I mean, communication is miles easier than it was before. Do you remember the days when we had to go through all that hassle of writing letters?

W: Sure, I'd agree with that. But I'd still say that face-to-face communication is better. Sending an email is nowhere near as personal and meaningful as a conversation.

M: Well, it depends, doesn't it?

W: On what?

M: OK, an email is nothing like as good as seeing someone you love, or your friends or something, but I can tell you this much: rather than going to see my clients every day, or nattering on the phone, I'm much better off sending them an email. It saves time.

W: Yeah, I see what you're getting at, but I just think, the more we use email, the more we need it. It's like an addiction, with people checking their emails every five minutes even in meetings.

M: Fair enough. But I'd still rather have it than not.

W: And, well, the internet in general, there's so much rubbish on there. Do you use it to do research?

M: All the time. I think it's OK. Maybe it's not quite as good as looking in books. Well, it's not as reliable, though it's considerably faster.

W: I'd say that looking up something on the internet is marginally less reliable than shouting out of the window, 'Does anybody know the answer to this?' It's not regulated, is it? Anyone can publish anything on the internet and it may or may not be true.

M: Much the best thing about the internet is that it lets you do things more cheaply than before, like buying holidays, buying stuff on ebay.

W: I've never used eBay.

M: Or Amazon. You can get loads of cheap books.

W: Yeah, but I'd sooner go to a second-hand bookshop. I'm not into the idea of giving my bank details over the internet. No way.

M: There're lots of security measures these days …

Track 1.11
1

Erm, I'm a member of an old boys' club, erm, which is basically when when you leave school you keep in touch with your old friends and every five or ten years you have a reunion and you get together and party and remember the old days, erm … some good, some bad, obviously. Erm, we also get involved in quite a few charity events in the area where I'm from, erm … and recently we actually did some charity events to save the school that I was at, which was going to be closed. So that was something we did specially. I did it, I didn't join straight after school. Erm, I went abroad for a few years, and I found out about it through a website, er, called Friends Reunited, where you can find where your old friends are and your old school is. That was great. We probably only meet once every two years as a group. Erm, we have a big party and get to meet all the people that we remember, and some of the teachers as well, er, which is fun. What's really interesting about the group is that we've now all known each other for about 20 years, and it's so interesting to meet people every two years and see how they've changed. I'm sure that if I met some of those people in the street now after 20 years, I wouldn't recognise them, and in, in a bad sort of way, I suppose, it's, you like to measure yourself against your friends, where they've got to and how have you done in comparison. Erm, If there's something I don't like, it's that, er … it's very difficult to keep in touch when you are not meeting so regularly. Erm, and you do rely on other people to run the club and sometimes people aren't as involved as they should be, sometimes you don't hear anything for a year or two, so it is quite difficult to do. But I will definitely stick with it, because it is great to meet people and remember some of the good days.

2

Well, I'm a member of a … of a kind of society, I suppose. It's a ballroom-dancing club. Erm, it's kind of lessons, but it's also social as well. There's about … oh I suppose … it must be about 30 people in the club, and I think I'm quite unusual because I think I'm the youngest there. Erm, I go with a friend of mine, who's … who's my partner in the dancing. Erm, it's great fun, really great fun. It's kind of fun being the youngest there as well because everyone else is retired and they think we're very cool and exotic for being young. Erm, I joined about I suppose six months ago now, erm, because I just fancied giving ballroom dancing a go. I've never been terribly coordinated as a dancer and I'm not very good with choreography, but it's been absolutely great. I mean, there's quite a lot of beginners in the class so you never really feel like you know you're stuck out in the middle of all these wonderful advanced dancers. Erm, we meet once a week and sometimes we meet in a school hall, in a local suburb near to where I live. Erm, we meet in the evenings after work and sometimes it can be quite hard to get yourself out of the house again ready to do some exercise and some dancing, but it's fantastic fun. So far we've been learning … erm … the Waltz, the Foxtrot, erm … and some Latin dances like, erm, the jive and the tango. It's great fun.

Track 1.12

E=Expert

E: In 1957 a news programme called Panorama broadcast a story about spaghetti trees in Switzerland. While the reporter told the story, Swiss farmers in the background were picking spaghetti from trees. Following this, thousands of people called the show, asking how to grow spaghetti trees.

In 1998 large numbers of Americans went to Burger King asking for a new type of burger. The food company had published an ad in USA Today announcing the new 'left-handed Whopper', a burger designed for left-handed people. The following day, Burger King admitted that they had been joking all along.

Swedish technician Kjell Stensson had been working on the development of colour TV for many years when he announced in 1962 that everyone could now convert their black-and-white TV sets into colour. The procedure was simple: you had to put a nylon stocking over the TV screen. Stensson demonstrated and fooled thousands.

Pretending that it had been developing the product for some time, a British supermarket announced in 2002 that it had invented a whistling carrot. Using genetic engineering, the carrot grew with holes in it, and, when cooked, it would start whistling.

Track 1.13

1 I'd seen it before.
2 I'd prefer to go home.
3 She'd lost the opportunity.
4 Would you like to dance?
5 I didn't set the alarm.
6 What would you cook?
7 I'd have done the same.
8 Had she been there?

Track 1.14

1

My favourite fictional character has to be Philip Marlowe, the detective created by Raymond Chandler. The most famous book and movie in which he appears is, of course, *The Big Sleep*, with erm … Humphrey Bogart playing Philip Marlowe. Once you've seen Humphrey Bogart, of course it's very difficult to imagine Philip Marlowe as being anybody else other than Humphrey Bogart, because like Humphrey Bogart, Philip Marlowe is tall, good-looking, tough, very smart and a smooth talker. I suppose those are also the characteristics that I do like about Philip Marlowe. The thing about Philip Marlowe is … like … unlike most modern characters, he doesn't always say the right thing, although he always has a clever retort and he doesn't

always win. Philip Marlowe is not always on top of the situation. Philip Marlowe sounds like a real guy with real problems who's very clever, very tough and likes to get to the bottom of the problem. Erm, the sort of problems that he has to overcome, of course, as a detective in Los Angeles is generally solving murder crimes, but he's often not so much interested in who did it as to why or how. By the end of the story, you care much about, you care as much about the erm … victim as perhaps the murderer or Philip Marlowe himself. This is actually one reason why you can re-read and re-read the Raymond Chandler novels with Philip Marlowe in them, because it's not what happens in the story, it's how Philip Marlowe deals with the problems, that matters.

2

I think my favourite fictional character has to be, erm, the lead character, the heroine if you like, of, erm, Jane Austen's *Pride and Prejudice*. She's absolutely, I think, one of the best-drawn characters in, in English literature. She is of course Elizabeth Bennett. Erm, she's the heroine, she's she's sparky, she's lively, she's feisty, and when you think that this is a book that's set in the 1800s, it's really quite remarkable that you've got such a modern woman as the heroine. I mean she's, she's lippy, she talks back to all these men who are older than her and in more authority than her. Fantastic! I think it's, erm, character traits that I'd really quite like to have myself. Erm, I imagine her, and I think I'm quite influenced here by the films and so on that have been made of *Pride and Prejudice*, as being quite tall with a very lively, mobile face and possibly dark hair, as well. Erm … memorable things that she does: well, the thing that I really like about her, erm, from the story of *Pride and Prejudice* is the way that she takes control of her own life in a period of history when women really had very little power and very little control over what happened to them in the marriage market, and I think it's great that she, erm, sort of comes to a self-realisation through the events of the novel and decides to do the right thing and go for the guy that she really loves, and of course she meets lots of problems along the way: people who think she's socially unacceptable or people who, erm, have very prejudiced views about class and society and of course she succeeds and she wins the day, wins her guy in the end.

3

I think my favourite fictional character was er, the old man from *The Old Man and the Sea* by Ernest Hemingway. Er, I still have quite a strong visual image of this man. The whole story takes place in a boat off the coast of Cuba, with, with just this one character, mostly. I imagine him to be quite old. He was a lifelong fisherman. He had quite a tough life, so I imagine he had these really big strong hands that were … were cut and bruised from hauling in nets his whole life every, every night out, out in the sea. I imagine him with a little bit of grey hair, er, just old and wise, somebody who had been a fisherman his whole life, took a lot of pride in it and tried to do it as, as best he could, and he was down on his luck in the story. He hadn't caught anything for quite a long time, erm, but he still dragged himself out every night and cast his nets and hoped for, hoped that he would catch something.

In a way, he sort of reminds me of my dad, somebody who had limited opportunities in life, but found a job that he could do and did

it to the best of his ability, even though there was very little glamour attached to it, and I think this in a way the fisherman was like him. He was a fisherman and he took pride in that, and did the best job he could.

Track 1.15

W=Woman

W: Groucho Marx didn't want to be a comedian at first. He loved reading and singing, and he wanted to become a doctor. But his mother had other ideas. She got the boys to start a group called the Six Mascots. During a radio show they started making jokes, and this is when they decided to become a comedy act. Their popularity grew quickly. But in 1926 the boys' mother died, and the Great Depression began. In the 1930s a man called Irving Thalberg helped the Marx Brothers to get on television. They made their most famous films, the last of which was called *A Day At the Races*. After this, Groucho became a radio host and he also made more movies, but without his brothers. In the 70s he toured with a live one-man show, but by now in his 90s he was getting weaker, and he died in 1977 on the same day as Elvis Presley.

Track 1.17

N=Newsreader

N: Resistance to antibiotics is on the increase. Research out today shows an increase in the number and strength of superbugs, resistant to normal antibiotics. Analysis of particularly resistant strains, kept in laboratory test tubes, shows that in the last 12 months …

A new virus, developed by hackers in South-East Asia has been crashing computer networks around the globe. The virus penetrates standard firewalls to affect computer software and eventually data stored in the microchip. Experts have warned that …

A breakthrough in genetic engineering technology means that human cloning can now enable scientists to re-build damaged organs in children. Cells taken from skin tissue are used to provide the necessary genes, which are then implanted …

The on-going budget crisis has been cited as the reason for the latest delay to the space mission. The new shuttle, Discover XVIII, which was originally due to launch last Thursday, is set to orbit Mars, scanning the surface for evidence of early life forms …

Track 1.18

I=Interviewer, S=Stan Lee

I: Legendary veteran comic writer Stan Lee co-created Spider-Man and the Fantastic Four, amongst others. We asked him how he thought of Spider-Man and this was his response:

S: When trying to create a superhero, the first thing you have to think of, or at least the first thing I have to think of, is a super power. What super power would be different, that people hadn't seen before? I had already done the Hulk, who was the strongest character on Earth; I had done a group called the Fantastic Four: one of them could fly, one was invisible, and one's body could stretch and I was trying to think, 'What else can I do?' And

Audioscripts

I've told this story so often that for all I know it might even be true! But I was sitting and watching a fly crawling on the wall, and I thought, 'Gee – that would be great – what if a character could crawl on walls like an insect?' So I had my super power, but then I needed a name. So I thought, 'Insect-man' ... that didn't sound good. 'Crawling-man?' And I went on and on. 'Mosquito-man?' And then somehow I said 'Spider-Man' and it just sounded dramatic and mysterious to me. So that was my name.

I: When asked why he made Spider-man a scientist, he replied:

S: I had always resented the fact that in most superhero stories, or actually in most comic books, the hero is some sort of a rugged, muscular outdoorsman, a sportsman, an adventurer. And anybody who was literate or scholarly ... they were ... he was always considered to be somewhat of a nerd. And I thought, 'My gosh, people don't have enough respect for intelligence.' So again, in trying to be different, and in trying to be realistic, I thought I would make my teenage hero a scholarship student, extra-bright; he was studying science. And just to show that there's no reason why a hero couldn't also be a kid who likes science and is good in school and is smart ... and that was the thinking behind it.

I: When asked if he was at all scientific, he replied:

S: I'm not much of a scientist. I love reading science-fiction but when it comes to actual science, I'm ... I'm a dummy. But I like to make things seem scientific!

I: Our final question asked if Stan Lee thought there would ever be real superheroes.

S: I believe that they will be able, through cloning, through genetics, they will be able to find a way to abolish most diseases. They will be able ... they will have to, see? Once these wars are finished with, if they ever are, we're going to want to go to the planets. They're going to want to go to Mars. Now it's such a long trip, and it will be so hard to get back again, they're going to have to make human beings able to adapt to Mars, adapt themselves. Or is it adopt? I never ... I always get those two mixed up! But at any rate, I believe that they will find a way to make people able to live in the atmosphere of Mars, through altering them genetically. Because of genetics, I think we can do virtually anything.

Track 1.21
Dialogue 1
K=Kevin, L=Lizzie
K: Hello?
L: Hi, Kevin. It's Lizzie.
K: Oh hi, Lizzie. How are you?
L: Yeah, great. You?
K: Yeah, fine.
L: I guess you're busy as usual this Saturday?
K: Erm ... sort of.
L: Yeah?
K: Well, I'm playing cricket.
L: Oh, I didn't know you played cricket.
K: I don't really. Well, once in a blue moon.
L: So that's all day Saturday?
K: Yeah, that'll be ... yeah ... more or less all day.
L: What are you up to in the evening?

K: Well, I might be free. Let me think. Mm, maybe about eight-ish. What have you got lined up?
L: Erm, we're thinking of going to Clancy's ...
K: Oh yeah? I used to go there from time to time when I was a student. Do you want me to pick you up?
L: Erm, or should I drive?
K: I don't mind driving. Do you want me to?
L: In a way, it's easier if I take my car. Yeah, don't worry. I think I'll drive ...

Dialogue 2
L=Lauren, A=Andy
L: Lauren James.
A: Hi, sweetheart.
L: Oh hi, darling.
A: Still working?
L: Yep.
A: Bit of a hard day?
L: Kind of. Nothing major ... just various bits and pieces.
A: Right.
L: Filling in forms, replying to emails, that kind of thing.
A: Uhuh.
L: Going over the accounts again, checking petty cash, etcetera etcetera. Actually, there were loads of mistakes.
A: Oh really?
L: Yep. But I'm nearly finished.
A: So, do you want me to get something ready?
L: Yeah, I'm a bit peckish actually.
A: Pasta maybe? Or we've got chicken in the fridge.
L: Chicken sounds good. Erm, I'll be home in an hour or so.
A: OK, I'll put the chicken in the oven ...

Track 1.22
1 How many phone calls do you make per day?
2 How many times do you check your emails per week?
3 How many close friends do you have?
4 How frequently do you write letters?
5 What do you do in the evening?
6 How long do you spend studying English at home?

Track 1.23
1 Not since Mozart has there been a greater genius.
2 Only after the age of three did she begin to show her gift.
3 Nowhere do the rules say you can't teach advanced subjects to children.
4 Only later did we understand the truth about our gifted child.
5 Not only was he able to write poetry when he was five years old, he also played the violin well.
6 No sooner had we given her a paintbrush than she produced a masterpiece.

Track 1.24
I=Interviewer, W=Woman
I: Can you tell us a little bit about the case and what made it so special?
W: The case concerned a pair of twins called John and Michael. They were, I suppose in their late teens, but they were absolutely tiny and they wore thick glasses. They used to get laughed at at school because, in a conventional sense, they weren't very bright or social.
I: They were outsiders.
W: Well, that's right. Outsiders. But they had an amazing gift. You could name any date in the past or future 40,000 years and they would be able to tell you what day of the week it was.

I: So I could say, for example, 5th June 1376 and they could tell me it was Sunday or whatever ...
W: That's right.
I: Or 10th July 2099, and ...
W: And they would say 'Monday!' But that wasn't all. During one interview, the psychologist dropped a box of matches on the floor and the twins immediately called out 'one hundred and eleven'. The psychologist counted the matches and there were exactly 111.
I: And the twins hadn't counted them?
W: No. There was no time. As soon as the matches hit the floor, they knew there were 111. Now another thing the twins could do was remember extremely long sequences of numbers. You could say a number of up to 300 digits, and they were able to repeat it back to you perfectly.
I: So they basically have an extraordinary ability with numbers.
W: Not only with numbers. They have another talent, which is that you can name any day of their lives since they were about four years old, and they are able to tell you what the weather was like, what they did, and other events in the wider world. They can remember absolutely everything about that day.
I: Just any ordinary day?
W: Any and every ordinary day.
I: Obviously the twins, John and Michael, were studied at length by various psychologists, educators ...
W: Yes, they were.
I: What progress did these people make in coming up with explanations of their ability?
W: I think the main thing is that we realise that John and Michael's ability is actually a visual one as well as mathematical. If you ask them how they do it, they say they can 'see' the answers. When the box of matches fell, they 'saw' 111. It wasn't a calculation. Similarly, they can 'see' themselves as five-year-olds. Somehow they have an ability to record incredible numbers of things in the mind. Of course, we have no idea how it works, but it would be very interesting to learn ...

Track 1.25
1
Great discoveries of our time ... well, in the last 100 years or so, I guess medical advances, like the use of X-rays in diagnosis, or the discovery of penicillin by Fleming. I mean, he made that discovery almost by mistake, and it changed modern medicine completely. Or perhaps the elucidation of DNA by Watson and Crick in the 50s. That paved the way for the whole area of genetics and genetic engineering ...
2
I would say that sending man to the moon was one of the greatest scientific achievements, learning about space. The man who invented the liquid-fuelled rocket, Robert Goddard, was fascinated by the idea of sending a rocket into space, and he spent years researching his ideas, until he developed the first rocket, called Nell. It was 10-feet-tall, and he fired it from his aunt's farm in the US. At first nothing happened, but when the fuel finally ignited, the rocket was launched. It only reached a disappointing 14 metres into the air though and scientists were sceptical of its success. When the newspapers got hold of the story they wrote the headlines 'Moon rocket

misses target by 238,799 miles.' But later, engineers in Germany and America used his ideas, and the film footage of Nell, to develop military and space-exploring rockets. The *New York Times* had to write Goddard a public apology …

3
Computers, it has to be. Information technology and the internet. The whole way in which information is distributed and kept nowadays. It's just been revolutionised by information technology. And things have happened so quickly. I mean, the first computer was built in 1948, I think. And was so big it took up a whole room! If you think about the latest designs now, and the capacity, it's just amazing. And it has made the world a smaller place, because it is so easy now to get information about anywhere in the world. There are no secrets …

4
I don't think we should underestimate the importance of domestic appliances, like the washing machine, dishwasher, all your electrical goods. And processes like freeze-drying food. These time-saving discoveries have allowed a whole new freedom to women, who previously had to spend their whole lives in the kitchen. It's meant that they could go out to work, and that has had a huge impact on society. Or perhaps it should be the advances in travel, with the bicycle, then the car and the aeroplane. The world must have been a very different place when the fastest way to get anywhere was on a horse!

Track 1.27
P=Presenter

1 **Business partners. Why not go with friends and family?**
P: While we're on the subject of choosing business partners, I cringe whenever I hear that two old friends or family members are planning to start a business together as fifty–fifty partners. It isn't that doing business with friends and family is a bad idea – many very successful businesses are family-owned. It's just that being someone's friend or relative is one of the worst reasons I can think of for making that someone your business partner. One of the problems is that once someone becomes your business partner, there is generally only one way to get rid of them (legally, of course) if things don't work out. You must buy them out for the fair value of their interest in the business. And that can be an expensive proposition.

2 **What type of person makes a good business partner?**
P: There are a few ways to determine if someone has what it takes to be your business partner, however. Firstly, you need to decide, are you a visionary, or an operations person? Successful partnerships combine those two kinds of people. A visionary is a strategic, 'big picture' thinker who understands the business model, the market and the overall business plan. An operations person is someone who rolls up their sleeves, wades up to their hip boots in the details and executes the strategy that the visionary comes up with. You are either one or the other – it is almost impossible to be both. Once you have determined if you are a 'visionary' or an 'operations person', look for your opposite number. That way your business is more likely to strike the right balance between strategy and tactics.

3 **What skills does the company need?**
P: Do you have all the skills you need on board to make the business work? Perhaps you are an inventor who is excellent at product design but clueless about selling. Perhaps you have a strong marketing background but need someone to help you crunch the numbers and make sure your products or services can be delivered within budget. Your partners should complement your set of business skills, not duplicate them. Keep in mind that you can acquire someone's skills without making them a partner. If a particular skill, such as contract negotiation or bookkeeping, is not critical to the success of your business, you may be better off hiring a lawyer, accountant or consultant to do it for you and keeping ownership of your business.

4 **Will communication be a problem?**
P: Can you communicate directly and honestly with this person, without pulling any punches? Communication between partners can often get rough; disagreements and arguments break out all the time. It is difficult to criticise someone harshly, yet sometimes you must be cruel with your business partners in order to do the right thing for your business. Your business may well suffer if you consistently hold back important information for fear of offending your partner or jeopardising the underlying friendship or emotional bond between you. Sometimes the most successful business partnerships are those where the partners do not socialise outside the office.

5 **The long-term. Will your partner stay through good times and bad times?**
P: And lastly, is your business partner willing to hang around for the long haul? This is the critical test of a business partner. Many people are happy to help out with a business during its start-up phase, only to lose interest later on when something more attractive (like a job offer from a big corporation) comes along, a life-changing event (like the birth of a new child) occurs, or the going is getting tougher and the business isn't as much 'fun' as it used to be. If you are not sure if someone is committed to the long-term success of your business, make them an employee or independent contractor, with perhaps an 'option' to acquire an interest in your business at a date two or three years down the road … provided, of course, they are still working for you at that time and you continue to be satisfied with their performance.

Track 1.29
I=Interviewer, W=Will

I: 98 percent of staff working at Piranha recruitment say they laugh a lot with their team. As many as 95 percent say that they are excited about where the company is going. So what have they all got to smile about? Last month this small London-based company won a prestigious award for being one of the best small companies in the UK to work for. With us today is Will Becks, the company director. Will, first of all, tell us a little bit more about the company and what you do.
W: Good morning. Well, Piranha is more than just a normal recruitment agency. The difference is that we actually train and then place graduates in sales jobs. That means we have a lot of young people working for us, so it's a bit like a continuation of university, but with a salary. We're only a small company, with as few as 60 employees, but there's a good atmosphere in the office. There's a great deal of energy.
I: Yes, your employees have said that there is a fun atmosphere, with outgoing, like-minded people. You have regular parties, an annual skiing holiday, a present for the most-appreciated employee of the month, and plenty of other benefits too. I'm not much of an expert on these things. Why such an emphasis on staff incentives?
W: Well, our staff are young and highly qualified. They are good at what they do, and they believe in it. We have trained sales people going into companies to try and place graduates. Quite a few of them get offered the jobs themselves. If we didn't look after our staff, they would quickly get poached by other companies. So the incentives need to be good to keep people.
I: So how are your salaries?
W: Salaries are good and there are monthly, performance-related cash bonuses. Staff also set their own targets for the coming year, and for the most part they have a say in their incentives too. Our accountant has just got the new Audi A3. He chose it, and he's delighted.
I: And how about the atmosphere in the office. How do you influence that?
W: We have a company bar, where we offer free breakfasts, and cappuccino all day long. People spend an awful lot of time in there discussing ideas over coffee, but it's very productive.
I: The vast majority of your staff say that they admire their managers, and feel that they can actively contribute to the future success of the company. How did you achieve this?
W: Well, one of the things is that we help them with finding somewhere nice to live. Rent is very expensive in London, and as lots of our employees are fresh out of university, with a lot of debts, they don't have a huge budget for accommodation. So, we've bought some properties, and quite a few staff rent them from us at reasonable rates. It makes a real difference. It means that working for the company becomes a lifestyle choice. They are involved personally. Also, we like to give people a say in the company. We have monthly meetings to discuss big issues, when we all sit around and talk about things. Initially, only a handful of people would come to the meetings. So we decided to offer free food, sandwiches and pizza, so now everyone comes, and everyone has something to say.

Track 1.31
K=Keith, B=Bridget

K: Well, I'd replace these chairs for a start. No wonder I've got backache.
B: Oh come on, we can do better than that. How about blowing it all on an all-expenses-paid jaunt to the West Indies or something?
K: Erm … would you really want to go on holiday with the rest of the staff?
B: Well, no, but … erm …
K: I think it should go on day-to-day things that'll make a difference in the long term, like renovating the office.

B: God, how boring.

K: Or maybe ... what d'you mean boring?!

B: Well, it's loads of money – let's have some fun! The company could get a house by the sea that the employees could use whenever they were on holiday.

K: Yeah, but that would only be useful once every few years for each person. I mean it wouldn't make the least bit of difference really. My main priority would be to do something practical with the money ...

Track 2.01

E=Expert

E: The Great Pyramid is arguably the most accomplished engineering feat of the Ancient World. Built to house the body of the dead pharaoh, the base of the Great Pyramid in Egypt is 230 metres squared, large enough to cover ten football fields. According to the Greek historian Herodotus, it took 400,000 men 20 years to construct this great monument. They used 2.3 million blocks of stone, some of which weighed as much as 50 tonnes!

'La Tour Eiffel' in Paris was built in 1889 to commemorate the 100th anniversary of the French Revolution. The Industrial Revolution in Europe had brought about a new trend – the use of metal in construction. The tower, built from a lattice made from very pure iron, is light and able to withstand high wind pressures. For 40 years from the time that it was built, it stood as the tallest tower in the world, and still today it is the tallest building in Paris.

The Sydney Harbour Bridge is one of Australia's best known, and most photographed landmarks. It is the world's largest (but not the longest) steel arch bridge with the top of the bridge standing 134 metres above the harbour. Fondly known by the Australians as the 'coathanger', Sydney Harbour Bridge celebrated its 70th birthday in 2002, with its official opening in March 1932. Nowadays, a group of 12 people leave every ten minutes to climb to the top of the bridge and admire spectacular views of the city, and out to the Tasman Sea.

The Pentagon, covering 13.8 hectares, is thought to be the largest office building in the world. It takes a person 15 to 20 minutes to walk around the building once. It was built in five concentric rings, in record time during the Second World War, in order to relocate employees of the War Department from the 17 buildings they occupied within Washington D.C.

Built between 1406 and 1420 during the Ming dynasty, The Forbidden City, also called the Purple Forbidden City, or Gugong Museum in Chinese, is located in the centre of Beijing, PRC. Occupying a rectangular area of more than 720,000 square meters, the Forbidden City was the imperial home of 24 emperors of the Ming (1368–1644) and Qing (1644–1911) dynasties. It is one of the largest and best-preserved palace complexes in the world, with over a million rare and valuable objects in the Museum.

Opening on 31st December, 1999, the Millennium Dome was built to celebrate the new millennium. The massive dome is over one kilometre round and 50 metres high at its centre. It covers 20 acres of ground floor space. How big is that? Well, imagine the Eiffel Tower lying on its side. It could easily fit inside the Dome. With its 100 metre steel masts and translucent roof, the Dome was meant to paint a portrait of the nation. Unfortunately, the project became one of the most controversial in Britain, due to its enormous cost, and doubts about how to best utilise the space after 2000.

Hassan II Mosque, in Casablanca, Morocco, was built for the 60th birthday of former Moroccan king Hassan II. It is the largest religious monument in the world after Mecca. It has space for 25,000 worshippers inside and another 80,000 outside. The 210-metre minaret is the tallest in the world and is visible day and night for miles around. The mosque includes a number of modern touches: it was built to withstand earthquakes and has a heated floor, electric doors, a sliding roof, and lasers which shine at night from the top of the minaret toward Mecca.

Track 2.02

J=Jodie, I=Interviewer

J: I think, with technology, it was Microsoft that started it.

I: 'It' being the use of teenagers ...

J: Using teenagers really to find out what's in and what isn't, what the market wants next. Around the year 2000, they started observing these kids to find out what they were doing with technology.

I: And this was an American thing?

J: It was ... well, no, actually they went all over the place observing these kids: from street markets in Seattle to skating rinks in London, bars in Tokyo, anywhere they thought trends might kick off.

I: So the idea was to watch these children, or teenagers, and learn what they wanted to do with their mobile phones, with software ...

J: That's right. Because it's teenagers that really drive technology. Kids have no fear of technology. They experiment and they automatically home in on the new. One thing that became clear is that teenagers want technology they can carry around. Anything bigger than a few inches is out. That's why there was the development of these tiny mobile phones that could be attached to your arm, that type of thing. Text messaging caught on because kids wanted to pass notes to each other during class. The lights that you find on IBM's ThinkPad keyboard are there because IBM noticed that kids take notes in the dark during lectures.

I: So all of these things came about because of the needs of kids.

J: That's right.

I: And what's coming up on the horizon? Is there any big new development that has been led by teenagers?

J: Well, the next big area is collaborative computing, where you have groups of people working together online. This is really going to take off in the next few years, because it has massive potential for working environments in the sense that you may be able to work simultaneously on a project with someone who's on the other side of the world, moving data around together.

I: So is it just technology with these kids?

J: You mean where teenagers are leading the market?

I: Yes.

J: Not at all. I mean, fashion has been youth-led for years and years, but in particular, trainers. Now, if you want to keep up with the latest style of trainers, who do you ask? You don't ask anyone over 20, that's for sure. And I think it was Converse trainers who used to do lots of their market research on the streets, on the basketball courts of New York, anywhere you find teenagers. They may still do this, I don't know.

I: And, what, they just talk to these kids?

J: Talk to them, watch what they are wearing, the colours, the style, and maybe bring in a prototype, ask the kids if they'd wear these. If not, why not?

Track 2.03

A=Alison, J=Jim, M=Mark, L=Leah

Dialogue 1

A: It depends on the age.

J: Uh huh.

A: 'Cos when they're young teenagers, no I don't think so.

J: What kind of limits would you put on, say, a 15-year-old?

A: Depends. There are some places that are not for teenagers but still they want to go to these places. I wouldn't let my 15-year-old go to a bar.

Dialogue 2

A: Teenagers? I don't think so.

J: Really? Why not?

A: Because they ... they can't ... er, well, they still can't evaluate what they're seeing and how much time they're spending. They could be doing other things.

J: It's not that good for them either, is it, their eyes. And sort of, it's a bit passive, can be a bit passive.

Dialogue 3

M: Oh, definitely, yeah. They're our friends.

L: Me too. If parents can choose who they hang out with, then we should too.

M: What's the difference?

L: Exactly. It's not like we're stupid and can't judge someone's character.

Dialogue 4

L: I think if it's a school day the next day, then it makes sense to have some kind of limit.

M: Yeah, but who sets the limit? If you know you're gonna be OK on six hours' sleep or something ...

L: Yeah, you should discuss it, but if you're going to be exhausted in the morning then that's not really ...

M: I'm saying it's not up to the parents to dictate it. We know how to switch off the lights, don't we?

Track 2.06

1

Looking after rabbits is really easy. The first thing you need to do, before you even get the rabbits, is to plan where they're going to be and make sure that you buy, erm, a hutch that's the right size for your rabbits, so that they're comfortable, and make sure that your hutch is going to be in a position where they're not exposed to anything. So you need to plan well. Once you've got your rabbits, erm, basically you feed them twice a day. Erm, you have to make sure they like the food they're given. It can be a bit tricky because they're a bit picky about what they eat, rabbits, so you need to make sure you give them the right thing. You have to clean them out once a week or more, er, so you need, er, fresh straw and hay. It's best to get it from a farmer because it's cheaper. Erm

... and you need to have them vaccinated against myxomatosis because they can come in contact with wild rabbits and then they can get ill. Erm, apart from that, that's it really.

2

It seems pretty straightforward, but actually there are lots of things that can go wrong when you choose a dog. A lot of people, for example, just go for the, erm … the cutest dog they can find, which is understandable, but not the right way to go about it. The first thing you've got to do is er, to ask yourself a number of questions. Will you have enough time to walk the dog and give her attention? Can you afford a dog? I mean, people often forget that it isn't just food; you also have to pay a vet if the dog gets sick. Do you have enough space in the house? So, once you've answered these questions, the next thing is to think about what type of dog. If you buy a puppy, you need to consider how big and active it will be once it's grown up, and this depends on the breed. But, different breeds have different characteristics. If you have quite an active lifestyle it's OK to get a chihuahua or a doberman, but if you spend most of your time at home watching TV, get a less active dog, like a Saint Bernard. The key thing is to do your research before you buy. Talk to other dog owners and vets and maybe look in the library.

Track 2.09

D=David

D: The first thing I noticed when I entered the bureaucrat's office was that it was bright white, like a doctor's surgery or the cell of a madman. There were a few filing cabinets next to the desk and a huge photo of the king staring at us from the wall. The air was thick and a fan droned weakly, whirring overhead as a gang of flies zig-zagged across the air.
The bureaucrat behind his desk looked up to greet me.
'How can I help you?' he said. I told him I needed a visa for my trip to the Danakil Depression, and he asked me if I'd ever been in a desert. 'I've been in many,' I replied. He shifted in his chair and said, 'The Danakil Depression is the world's hottest place. It's not a tourist site. There's nothing there but hot air and salt.' I told him I knew that, and that's why I wanted to go there. 'Typical British,' he said. 'Obsessed by the weather.'
He asked me what I'd do if I got lost, and I told him I wouldn't. 'And what about the three s's?' he said. 'What three s's?' 'Snakes, spiders and scorpions. What if you get bitten?' 'I won't.' He stared at me again, glanced at my passport, and with a resounding thump, stamped it. 'One visa,' he said. 'This will get you into Danakil, but it won't get you out.'

Track 2.10

D=David

D: Going to the Danakil Depression means walking into hell on Earth. The land is sunk 100 metres below sea level and the place is a furnace. The air shakes, warped by the sun. Even the wind brings no relief from the heat. Almost everything around you is dead: stumps of trees, cracked earth, the occasional white glow of animal bones.
Along the way we saw a group of bandits on camels, brandishing their weapons. They waved and went on riding. Salt statues loomed out of the spectacular landscape, three metres high, vibrant colours and shapes from another world. An active volcano was hunched on the horizon, biding its time. We stopped to visit a ghost town, with its abandoned shacks stripped bare by the wind and the nomads and the scavenging animals. This was Danakil, where an American company had tried to set up a business in the 60s and been defeated by the heat. The ruined buildings made of salt blocks were now crumbling away, and there were metal tracks in the ground where they had tried to build a railway but which now led nowhere.
For three days my shirt was drenched and my mouth parched. Even covered up against the sun, my skin baked and burned, and there seemed no escape from the cauldron of heat. They tell you to drink 12 litres of water a day, to remember to drink even when you're not thirsty, but it's never enough.
When we finally arrived at our destination I felt empty, as if everything had been a mistake. I didn't regret going to Danakil, but the land was so inhospitable that permanent settlement seemed impossible, and it felt wrong being there, as if we were trespassing on a place nature had intended only for itself.

Track 2.11

1 A monkey costs as little as that?
2 It's as big as an elephant.
3 We're as happy as can be.

Track 2.12

Example

A: You've got bad eyesight haven't you?
B: I'm as blind as a bat.
1 You're free now, aren't you?
2 You're strong, aren't you?
3 You're quiet, aren't you?

Track 2.13

R=Rachel, G=Graham

R: Well, it's a piece of land that's about 50 square kilometres, so there's really quite a lot you could do with it, but I mean I don't really know, I don't really have any expertise in managing the land. I don't know about you, Graham, but have you got any ideas what we could do with it?
G: Well, when I see 50 square kilometres of land, I think money. I think …
R: Ha, that's typical!
G: Well, yeah. I think, you know, a hotel will be great here. I think there's enough room for it, and as it's in the middle of, you know, this kind of wonderful environmental area that we could really sell it.
R: Yeah, but the problem with the hotel is that you, I mean, the land's got this, these really lovely environmental features, you've got these lovely hilly bits and there's all these lovely trees, and you know it's quite a little forest down there. Perhaps it would be nicer to do something that's kind of more sympathetic with the environment, you know, like erm, you could leave it, we could leave it wild and just let the animals roam free, or you could have like a more organised animal sanctuary, erm, to really, you know, get the most out of, of the features of the land. There's a lot of wildlife.
G: What would we get out of that?

R: It's good for the environment, Graham. I mean, it's doing something good, and giving something back to, to the Earth, and making sure that they, you know, these sort of, erm, animal species are left to, to live in their own environment.
G: Mm. OK. Perhaps not a hotel then, but I think we could think of, you know, a commercial use that would fit in more with the environment. What about some kind of health resort, maybe?
R: Well, that's quite a nice idea because there's, you know, there's so much land and, you know, people could go walking in the hills, and we could do nature trails through the forest. Erm, we could even have like a little organic garden or, you know, provide food that's really fresh and healthy because it's … the land's really good for growing vegetables and things like that and it's a great climate in this area, so you know, maybe that's a nice idea, we could have an organic health spa. What do you think?
G: Hm … yeah, that's a nice idea.

Track 2.14

1

That's a good question. Erm, I think I'd like some kind of gadget that means I don't have to clean the house. Like a machine or a robot that tidies everything away. Does the washing up, the ironing. Either that or get a maid.

2

A time machine. Not so I could go back and see earlier civilisations and dinosaurs (I mean, who cares about dinosaurs?) but so I could go back this morning and hit that guy who took my parking space.

3

Ooh, that's a difficult question. I'd have to think about it. Well, I wouldn't mind a weather machine, with me in control, of course. So when my friends go on holiday, I could make it rain every day and they'd stop telling me how beautiful the weather was.

4

That's tricky. How about a pill that you can substitute for food, so no one would need to starve? And so I wouldn't have to cook.

5

Let me see. You could have a pill that makes you extremely intelligent. You'd take it just before every exam or whenever the computer breaks down.

6

Well, I'd like to invent a special device that could take you to other places but only in your mind. Like a hat or glasses that give you all the sensations of being there. Then I'd use these glasses to go straight to a beach in Hawaii and spend the week there instead of in the office with all these other idiots.

7

I'd invent a clock that extends hours of the day when you need it. Like every morning when I'm lying in bed and have to get up.

Track 2.15

T=Thomas, E=Elise

T: I was on a business trip in Rome a few years ago. I'd been having dinner with a client all evening, and afterwards I discovered that the Internet connection in my hotel wasn't working. So there I was at midnight, wandering around one of the most beautiful cities in the world, and I was tearing my hair out trying to get Internet access. Anyway, I went back

Audioscripts

to the hotel, lay down on my bed and thought, do I really have to live like this? Are those emails really so important? And it just seemed as if my life in the fast lane meant I was missing out on other, more important things. So anyway I started to reappraise my life. The world is one stressed-out place. When I go to cities now, I see everyone rushing around with their mobile phones and everyone's scared they're going to miss something. You know, just before we die, no one ever says, 'Ooh, I wish I'd spent more time working in the office.' Rome was a wake-up call for me. After leaving my job, I moved to the coast. I sell surfing gear now. It doesn't make much cash, but then money isn't the be-all and end-all. To be honest, I just go with the flow and try to enjoy every day. I'm happier than ever before because I think living by the sea gives you a certain perspective on life. The waves will be rolling in every morning long after we're gone. And it makes you realise all that rushing around isn't going to make any difference.

E: I've been working in an investment company for about four years. It's a very competitive business, of course, and you have to know about every fluctuation in the market even as it's happening. So I live a very fast-paced, high-pressure lifestyle. Basically, we work around the clock. A lot of my job is done on the move, so I carry my office around with me: laptop, phone, Blackberry. I suppose you could call these my weapons of war! I don't live a particularly healthy lifestyle: I grab a sandwich when I can and drink far too much coffee. But it's not going to be like this forever. Most people in my profession burn out after three and a half years. In fact, the statistics are getting worse – I think it's under three years now. So by the time I'm 40, 45, I'll be slowing down a bit. If I get some kind of golden opportunity in another field I might change career earlier, but I don't have itchy feet. I like what I do. And I don't think I'll ever live on a farm in the middle of nowhere with my slippers on, growing vegetables. I'd hate that. I enjoy the buzz too much.

Track 2.17
M=Man, W=Woman
Dialogue 1
M: This stupid thing keeps getting jammed.
W: What, again?
M: I can't get it to make any copies.
W: It happened to me yesterday. Give it a good kick. Is that better?
M: Well, I feel better, yeah, but it's still not working.
Dialogue 2
W: See? It's always coming up with the same message.
M: You have performed an illegal operation. Ooh, naughty.
W: See? I don't know how to make it shut down normally.
M: Have you tried dropping it onto the floor?
W: What?
M: Or shouting at it? That works sometimes.
W: You're not funny.
Dialogue 3
M: I'm having problems switching it on.
W: Oh really?
M: This thing seems to be stuck. It won't go round.
W: Oh yes.

M: Which means I can't get any air in here. And it's so hot.
W: Right in the middle of summer as well. You can always open the windows.
M: Oh! Yeah, thanks.

Track 2.18
I=Interviewer, E=Expert
I: What can you tell us about what happens when geniuses relax?
E: Without a doubt, we can be sure that great scientists don't always make their discoveries in the lab. Archimedes's famous 'Eureka' moment came while he was having a bath. Physicist Richard Feynman saw a plate flying through the air in a college cafeteria, and was inspired to calculate electron orbits. He later won the Nobel Prize. And Alexander Fleming was making mould for his hobby, microbe painting, when he accidentally came across *Penicillium notatum*, later known as penicillin.
I: So what does this tell us?
E: Well, we're looking into the psychology of high achievers. A recent study by Robert Root-Bernstein compared the hobbies of 134 Nobel-prize winning chemists to those of other scientists. He found that the Nobel prize winners were accomplished outside the lab. Over half were artistic and almost all had a long-lasting hobby: chess or insect collecting. Twenty-five percent of the Nobel-prize winners played a musical instrument and 18 percent drew or painted regularly. Of the normal scientists, under one percent had a hobby.
I: Fascinating. So should we conclude then, that only a creative person can be a genius?
E: Well, I think that's debatable. Perhaps it's true up to a point, but I don't think it's as clear-cut as that. What we do know is that to a certain extent, creative thinking can help people to solve problems, even scientific ones. That if you are thinking about a problem all the time, often the answer eludes you. But it may come in an inspiration when you are least expecting it – perhaps when you're asleep, or thinking about other things, doing a hobby, for example. It's not 100 percent certain, but it seems that the mind has the ability to make connections from one part of your life to another, so that actually stepping back from a problem can often provide the answer. And people who are good at making these connections, people who pursue creative hobbies and interests, often excel in their particular fields.

Track 2.19
A=Abby, B=Becs, C=Chris
Dialogue 1
A: What do you think of this one?
B: Erm ... it's OK. To be honest, it's not really my taste. I'm not really into this style of portrait. And it sort of looks like a photo to me.
C: Yeah, you have to get up really close to it to see that it's a painting.
A: What do you think of it?
C: I really like it, actually.
A: Me too.
C: I like the colours, and the expression on her face is kind of intense.
A: It's a bit enigmatic, isn't it? You don't really know what she's thinking. And the details too. You can almost see the pores of her skin. Don't you think?

B: Well, as I was saying, it really does look like a photo – the detail is amazing, so as far as the skill is concerned, and the technique, I think it's great, but to tell you the truth, I still wouldn't want it hanging on my bedroom wall.
Dialogue 2
A: I love this one.
C: He's just got such an interesting face, hasn't he? He looks like one of those hippy poets from the 70s.
A: With that big beard.
C: With that big beard and the shirt.
B: Is it Hawaiian, that shirt?
C: And the medallion.
A: Oh yeah, I didn't notice that.
C: As a matter of fact, I prefer this one to the other one. At any rate, I think it's more interesting visually.
A: How about this one for your bedroom wall?
B: Nope. 'Fraid not. Mind you, I'd put it in the bathroom.
Dialogue 3
B: I think this one's great.
C: It's kind of menacing isn't it?
B: For me, what's interesting is that they are in a group, almost like a gang with this uniform.
C: The jeans and white T-shirts.
B: Exactly, except for the guy sitting in the middle. Now he's the only one sitting and looking directly at us, sort of challenging us, so maybe he's the boss.
A: Well, what I noticed is that, as you said, they're in a group, but somehow they look isolated. They're all facing in different directions and they don't seem to relate to each other at all.
C: And I wonder why it's called 'La Familia'. They obviously aren't a family in any traditional sense. At any rate, they don't look like a family, so it's kind of intriguing. I think this one should win, actually.
A: Me too.

Track 2.20
A=Abby, C=Chris
C: So which one won in the end?
A: Which do you think?
C: Well, as I said before, my favourite is 'La Familia', but ...
A: That one didn't win.
C: Oh really?
A: The winner was 'Giulietta Coates', the one that looks like a photo.
C: Right. Well, I think it's really good too, but it isn't my favourite.

Track 2.24
E=Expert
E: Clarence Birdseye was a taxidermist from New York. On a visit to the Arctic he saw how the native people preserved their food by putting it in barrels of sea water, which froze quickly. This way, the food maintained its freshness for later. So in 1923 he bought a $7 electric fan, some ice, and some buckets of salt water and experimented by putting food in them. Birdseye's experiments worked, and he went on to become the pioneer of frozen foods in the Western world. In 1929 he sold the patent for $22 million and in 1930, frozen food went on sale for the first time in the United States.

As a young man, Chester Carlson's job involved making multiple copies of patent documents by hand. Writing everything down was difficult for Carlson because he was short-sighted and had arthritis, so in 1938 he invented a machine to make copies. He tried to get funding for his idea from all sorts of well-known companies, including IBM and General Electric, but they turned him down. Eventually, the company that became Xerox bought his idea, and the first photocopier was manufactured in 1959. Now there's hardly an office in the world that doesn't contain his invention.

Track 2.25

I=Interviewer, R=Richard

I: In June 1980, Maureen Wilcox became one of the US lottery's biggest losers. She bought tickets for the Rhode Island and Massachusetts draws and chose winning numbers for both. But her Massachusetts numbers would have won the Rhode Island lottery, and vice-versa. Meanwhile, lawyer John Woods was one of many to narrowly miss death in the Twin Towers on September 11. Not that unusual, except that he also escaped the 1993 bombing there, and the Lockerbie plane crash in a similar way.

So, are some of us just born lucky? Is there a scientific reason why some people might seem luckier than others? With us today in the studio is Professor Richard Wiseman, who has studied 'lucky' and 'unlucky' people, and thinks that the differences between them must be related to their psychology. So, Richard, how are these two groups different?

R: Lucky people are more open to opportunity, and trust their hunches. They tend to be optimistic and expect good fortune. And when things go wrong, they are robust and resilient. They won't give up. We did some research, to see if people who thought they were lucky, actually won the lottery more often, and things like that. Well, it comes as no great surprise that they didn't actually win more often.

I: No? Right.

R: But there was something interesting happening. The lucky people had much higher expectations of winning. They didn't need to win. Their optimism was still boundless. And this is important. It's what psychologists call a positive delusion. Although it's a delusion, it's actually good for you because it keeps you trying. You can't win the lottery if you don't enter, and in many areas of life, having positive expectations makes a favourable outcome more likely.

I: Is that really the case? What areas of life are you talking about?

R: In business, for example, some people seem to have the knack for making a business work, while others are bound to go from one failed venture to another. We showed in our research that you can improve your business success by learning how to be 'lucky'. Let me explain. We teamed up with a management firm, and for five months, employees took part in a specially devised programme of lectures, questionnaires, meetings and assessments designed to make them think and behave like lucky people. This was a little different from the usual business motivational training. It was more about looking for opportunities by being relaxed, open and fluid rather than developing drive and focus. The results were impressive, with 54 percent of participants believing that their personal luck had increased, and

75 percent indicating that the company's luck had increased. But perhaps more importantly, this was borne out in hard sales figures – the company's income increased by 20 percent each month.

I: Wow, that is impressive. So Richard, can I ask you, are some people just born unlucky?

R: A survey in the UK showed that 50 percent of the population thought of themselves as lucky, and 14 percent as unlucky. Presumably, these two groups differ, in their behaviour and in their psychology. So I thought we ought to look at that. And our research showed that there were big differences. So, I guess if you say that your genes affect your personality, and your behaviour, which they no doubt do, then, yes, you could be right. Some people are born lucky, or unlucky.

Lucky people are likely to create opportunities for good fortune by being extrovert, sociable, and using open body language that gets people to respond to them. They are relaxed and easy-going, and therefore, more likely to notice chance opportunities that may turn into a lucky break. They also like variety and change. One man, for instance, breaks routine by thinking of a colour when he's on his way to a party. At the party he is supposed to speak only to people wearing that colour. This takes him out of his comfort zone of chatting to those he already knows, and brings him the prospect of new friends and new opportunities. Lucky people also have positive expectations of life and things tend to go their way. A famous experiment illustrates how this can work. Psychologists told American high school teachers that certain children in their class were especially gifted. In fact, there was nothing special about these pupils. The teachers shouldn't have treated them any differently, but they began to shower the 'special children' with extra praise and encouragement. And the children responded by producing better schoolwork, doing better in tests, and generally achieving more than the other children. This study shows the power of positive expectations ...

Track 2.26

1 He's bound to cheer up soon.
2 Aren't we supposed to register at the front desk?
3 You ought to make up your mind.

Track 2.28

1

It must have been amazing to be the first modern person to see Machu Picchu, after it had been covered by jungle for so long. Erm, I think it must have been pretty hard to get there, actually, because nowadays they've built a train, there's a little village nearby, near Cuzco, and it's ... urm, easier to get to. But, the first people that went there had to climb right up the side of the huge mountain without knowing that there was anything there at the top, so they must have been really driven people to ... to make themselves climb up there. But, although they might have felt the same atmosphere when they were arriving, it couldn't have been quite as spectacular as it is today because the ruins now are all there for you to see as soon as you arrive, but it must have had more of a mysterious air when they discovered it

covered in vegetation and all hidden without really knowing what it was.

2

I've often wondered what it was like to have been in the first aeroplane to take off and really fly, not just like the Kitty Hawk going for a 10-second or a 30-second hop, but really climbing into the air. It can't have been easy because you have to realise those aircraft were not very sophisticated. They must have been difficult to fly – physically and even mentally – and you would've had to do lots of calculations that no one else has done before, and then of course it would have been incredibly exhilarating as the freedom increases as you go higher and higher, and then just think of all the doubts: how's this going to work out? Are you going to control it? And then coming in for the landing. How would that have been? In a way, you would know that this is going to be a crash, but a crash that you have to control, and that too couldn't have been easy.

3

I think Yuri Gagarin must have had, I think, missed, mixed emotions about being the first person in space. I think, on the one hand, there's that sort of thrill and excitement of ... of space travel, and the absolute awe of what he's experiencing, seeing Earth from space and being the first person to see that, having never even had any concept of what it might look like from space, and sort of, erm, just the complete vastness of space and just how amazing that must be. But on the other hand, sort of being up there on your own, basically in a tin can, you know, anything could have happened up there, um, he probably didn't know if he would get back home or not. He must have felt alone and also probably quite scared as well.

Track 2.29

1

During my childhood, my parents moved quite a lot, so I was always changing schools, and starting new schools. In fact, in about six years I think we changed school three times, so it was quite often. And that was quite difficult, er, because just when you've met new friends and you've got used to the teachers and the lessons, then you're told you've got to do it all again. It's true that I got quite lonely and I found it quite difficult to relate to other children, especially because they all knew the area, they already had their small groups of friends, and I was slightly out of it. Erm, but this also made me very outgoing, because if I wasn't going to be outgoing and energetic, and entertaining, erm ... it was going to ... I was never going to have those friends. So, er, it was difficult. Sometimes I did feel quite lonely, and I did feel as if it was hard work each time, but I'm lucky that I now have a lot of friends because of it.

2

I think one of my worst memories of childhood is probably a sport-related memory because I'm not really a sporty kind of girl. Erm, I grew up in central Manchester and my school was kind of in the middle of an industrial estate, and lots of shops and ... and things like that. And they used to make us go cross-country running every week, so we'd be out there, in the rain, and the wind, and the snow in the middle of Manchester with the traffic roaring by, running around in our little shorts and T-shirts, looking like complete idiots – I absolutely hated it. I used to dread Mondays, because I knew

Audioscripts

PE lessons were coming up, and it was just going to be absolute torture. I'm still the same now. I still hate sports, and running is just one of the sports I hate the most I think. It's just something that I find so uncomfortable and so unpleasurable, so yeah that's probably my worst memory of childhood.

3

When I was a child, er, when I was a very little girl, we used to go to Majorca nearly every year. It was a real family holiday and my grandparents came as well. Erm, the last time I went we must have been about seven, I suppose. I don't remember the first few times in fact. I don't remember catching a plane. The thing I remember most vividly, um, is arriving in Majorca, and the wall of heat that used to hit us every time we got off the plane. Erm, and the smell of the air, that was so different from England. It was a fantastic smell. And I remember the things that um children remember about holidays, rather than anything too cultural. I remember the pool, I remember how blue the pool was – we used to swim every day, and the breakfasts that went on forever. Just the way the routine was completely different from what we did at home. And er the way we met people from all over the world. We made friends with a Norwegian family one year, and kept in touch with them, which was lovely. So it's just really the colours and smells that er take me back there. I haven't been there since 'cause I don't really want to spoil it. I think the magic of it might go if I was to see it now as an adult.

4

During the summer holidays, I lived in the back of a wood. Er, my parents' garden backed onto this small wood, and I used to climb over the garden fence and my friends and I used to play in the wood, literally all day. We used to climb trees, run in and out of bushes and just have a general laugh and it was just great. It was just a great sense of freedom, that you should really have when you're a child. And it was just essentially a very very good and happy time.

Track 2.30

1

Oh my goodness, I went to the most amazing restaurant last night. You would not believe it, I've never seen anything like it in my life. It was called um, it was called The Bentley and it was in South Kensington, and it was the most fascinating building 'cause it was one of those lovely old Georgian terraces that's been turned into a boutique hotel, so it was all chandeliers and really plush sofas, and incredible service. I mean, they were so polite and charming. The food was kind of French style, but it was very modern haute cuisine, and we had what's called a 'grazing' menu, which was terribly expensive but extremely exciting, because you get little plates of food. Erm, I think we had seven courses in total.

2

I just, I can't stand public transport in this country. I mean, despite the fact that it's expensive and unreliable, it's just so ridiculously complicated. Just look at trains, for example. There must be about twenty different ticket types. And it all depends on when you're travelling, what time of day, how far before you booked your ticket, it's just ridiculous. So for example, you could be sitting on a train and the person sitting opposite you could've paid ten times the amount for their ticket just because they happened to buy it on a different day. I don't understand why we don't have systems like in other countries where you just pay per kilometre and then pay perhaps an upgrade if you get on a faster train. As it is now, it's just so complicated and I, I just, personally I choose not to use it.

3

Well, I really hate smoking and I just think it should be banned completely because it's not ... people who don't smoke ... it's so unfair for us, erm, you know, you're breathing in other people's smoke and you smell of smoke at the end of the day when you've been with a smoker and you know, it's obviously not good for the smoker, but it's not good for the non-smoker either. Erm and it's really quite repulsive that you have to breathe in somebody's second-hand smoke. And, er, smokers will say, well, you know, we'll go to a part of the restaurant where it doesn't affect you or we'll go outside, but it does because even if you're outside and you're walking behind somebody who is smoking then you're breathing in their smoke. Erm, and I think they should just ban it because it's one of the few bad habits that really does affect everybody else. I mean, if you're drinking, it's only doing your body harm, but if you're smoking then you're doing harm to everybody else's body who is around you, and it's not really acceptable.